HOW WE SPEAK TO ONE ANOTHER

AN ESSAY DAILY READER

HOW WE SPEAK TO ONE ANOTHER

AN ESSAY DAILY READER

EDITED BY
ANDER MONSON & CRAIG REINBOLD

COFFEE HOUSE PRESS
Minneapolis
2017

Coffee House Press books are available to the trade through our primary distributor, Consortium Book Sales & Distribution, cbsd.com or (800) 283-3572. For personal orders, catalogs, or other information, write to info@coffeehousepress.org.

Coffee House Press is a nonprofit literary publishing house. Support from private foundations, corporate giving programs, government programs, and generous individuals helps make the publication of our books possible. We gratefully acknowledge their support in detail in the back of this book.

Permissions

Photograph on page 34 is courtesy of V. V. Ganeshananthan.

Photograph on page 148 is from *Don't Let Me Be Lonely: An American Lyric* by Claudia Rankine, © 2004 (published by Graywolf Press). Reprinted by permission of John Lucas.

Photographs on pages 229 and 237 are courtesy of Dave Mondy.

"Wrens" by Eliot Weinberger, found on page 249, is from *An Elemental Thing*, © 2007 by Eliot Weinberger. Reprinted by permission of New Directions Publishing Corp.

LIBRARY OF CONGRESS CATALOGING-IN-PUBLICATION DATA
Names: Monson, Ander, 1975- editor. | Reinbold, Craig, 1982- editor.
Title: How we speak to one another : an essay daily reader / edited by Ander Monson, Craig Reinbold.
Description: Minneapolis : Coffee House Press, 2017.
Identifiers: LCCN 2016027859 | ISBN 9781566894579 (paperback)
Subjects: LCSH: American essays—21st century. |
    BISAC: LITERARY COLLECTIONS / Essays. |
    LANGUAGE ARTS & DISCIPLINES / Composition & Creative Writing. |
    LITERARY CRITICISM / Books & Reading. | EDUCATION / Essays.
Classification: LCC PS689 .H69 2017 | DDC 814/.608—dc23
LC record available at http://lccn.loc.gov/2016027859

Printed in the United States of America
24 23 22 21 20 19 18 17   1 2 3 4 5 6 7 8

To all our *Essay Daily* readers & contributors, past, present, future
(meaning you)

And for
Steven Barthelme, Randy Freisinger, Jack Jobst, and Rebecca Nowacek

Contents

HOW WE SPEAK TO ONE ANOTHER

AN
ESSAY DAILY
READER

ANDER MONSON

Here's How You Use the Lion Mints

An Introduction to *How We Speak to One Another*

Dear Reader,

I want to tell you something about what it felt like to be alive today, November 16, 2015, which means I want to tell you what it felt like to be alive on this date in 1999. I was listening then to the Backstreet Boys, probably, or maybe the bands Codeine or Morphine, living in an un-finished basement a mile away from the Iowa State University campus with a Spice Girls poster in my bedroom there. To get to class, I'd walk over the trestle of a retired railroad bridge that crossed a hundred feet above Squaw Creek, then by a row of power plants. Their steam billowed out in clouds and smelled strongly, strangely, like maple. It clung to me as I passed. Later I'd wonder, catching another whiff of it on my clothes, if I had been sloppy at IHOP or was being haunted by a Canadian ghost. I don't know if anyone else noticed that odd steam or wondered what it was or what was going on in the building ominously labeled Animal Science II and why I dreamed of piggy shrieks and tornados.

That same month *The Best American Essays 1999* debuted. In his introduction to the volume, guest editor Edward Hoagland writes that:

> Essays are how we speak to one another in print—caroming thoughts not merely in order to convey a certain packet of information, but with a special edge or bounce of per-sonal character in a kind of public letter. You multiply

yourself as a writer, gaining height as though jumping on a trampoline, if you can catch the gist of what other people have also been feeling and clarify it for them.

That night, while wandering about the campus, peering into windows for signs of actual human life, as was my habit, I encountered a raccoon peeking up from a sewer grate installed into a curb. I caught its eyes glittering from the streetlight, watching me as I passed, so I paused and turned. We faced each other and did not move for quite some time.

In 1999 I had the custom of carrying around rolls of Lion Mints, promotional peppermints that supported the local Lions Club. I'd buy them for twenty-five cents from a plastic tray that adorned the countertop of the Salvation Army thrift store in Houghton, Michigan, a former mining town that has not had a working mine in fifty years. I was obsessed with these Lion Mints. I bought dozens of rolls of them when I was home and brought as many as I could to carry back with me to Iowa. I still ate candy then, still wasn't as concerned with the damage I would later find out I had done to my teeth, that in fact I'm still fixing, sixteen years later.

Lion Mints were dispensed in red plastic trays that read "Lion Mints: A Fundraiser for Lions Club Projects." Whatever those projects were, they didn't say. In each tray was a slot to slip in coins to pay for what you took. The suggested price was a quarter, but you could just as easily slide a nickel into the slot and hear it chunk down and know that no one would know what kind of coin you paid with and take a roll of mints. Sometimes I took five or six rolls, congratulating myself for beating the system as I headed out the door.

So that night in Iowa, when I faced the sewer grate against the backdrop of the unidentifiable maple mist, I had a roll of Lion Mints with me. I crouched, pulled out a mint, and rolled it to the raccoon. It grabbed the mint with its claws and clutched it to its chest and appraised me for a moment as if it was about to tell me something true before it disappeared into the darkness.

I haven't thought about Lion Mints for at least a decade now, but thinking about that Hoagland quote, somehow they come to mind. It turns out they're made by Sayklly's Candies, an Upper Michigan confectioner, and I'd always thought they were unique to the Upper Midwest, if not my Upper Peninsula, though that appears not to be true. Do you remember them? Do you recognize them? What did they mean to you? I wonder now: What does the Lions Club even do? What exactly was I (under)funding? What cause was I cheating? Why did I love these things so much that I brought rolls of them with me to Iowa, and why did I roll one to a raccoon in the sewer?

Furthermore, what did the raccoon make of this gift? Did it hoard the mint or bring it to its family, break it into pieces, and serve it to its children from its extended paw-claw? Did it present it to its potential mate as proof of its kick-ass scavenging abilities? Did it think to itself about the provenance of its bounty? Or did it selfishly eat the mint itself without thinking, believing that such providence should not be questioned? Or did it taste the mint and spit it out, incredulous, thinking, *This is what you've brought me? This is what your culture's for?* and pad off into the darkness in disgust?

Hoagland says: when we write essays, we're writing to one another. Though I don't think he'd say it this way, exactly, I think he means that essaying is networking, echoing both those with MBAs and those who spend their days connecting machine to machine. In the afterword to the book *Fare Forward: Letters from David Markson,* edited by the recipient of these letters, the poet Laura Sims, Ann Beattie notes that "whether overly or overtly, whether unconsciously, or even as a prank, writers write to other writers. Just because they've died, those writers don't disappear."

That's the thing: we keep speaking to one another, don't we? Even if we don't say it out loud. Even if maybe we don't even know what it is we do.

I wouldn't run across Hoagland's introduction until 2009, when I found *The Best American Essays 1999* in a Tucson, Arizona, Goodwill. If he was speaking to me, he wasn't doing it efficiently.

It's depressing but not surprising that it took me ten years to discover Hoagland. I'm pretty single-minded, obsessive, and slow; like an ai, a maned sloth only found in southeastern Brazil, I don't read much.

I suppose that means I shouldn't have the hubris to be here trying to articulate something about the essay or what brought me to it, but we essayists seem to like to essay about the essay; we don't mind writing about what we don't entirely know. We roll with our Lion Mints metastyle; we wait for our thoughts to metastasize. Sometimes something interesting happens.

*

For a long time I'd thought of my own essaying as mine work, a kind of solo exploration down here in the dark. But then one time I was chipping at a hunk of rock, watching my tool spark, and suddenly it broke through a wall and ran into another tunnel—like the one John D'Agata dug in *Halls of Fame,* for instance—and I realized, oh, hey: this is a cool tunnel. And I saw him there, grinning, and grilling something unidentifiable. "Yo, John, I like what you're doing here," I said, awkwardly. "I thought I was alone. But you shouldn't be grilling down here. Fumes and all." He just looked at me like I was a fool. "This is how you do it, G," he said. And I was. But now I was a fool with a new tunnel to explore.

So I followed that tunnel awhile and saw where it intersected with others, like an Anne Carson tunnel, an Albert Goldbarth tunnel, a Jerald Walker tunnel, or a Jenny Boully tunnel, and farther down it hit a Theodor Adorno tunnel, and then it led to Virginia Woolf, and farther back it all got honeycombed and smelled like fresh animal and glittered wildly, and all of a sudden I saw that this dark underneath that I'd been moving through was both a little less dark and just a bit smaller than I'd thought before. And in the dark down there, I found myself craving a Lion Mint, if just for the little light they make in the mouth when you crunch them up.

That is, when we're speaking essay, we're not just talking to ourselves. We're not just working by ourselves. Or: we don't have to be. Essaying isn't just about the "I": it's about the "we." It takes a community. It takes a nation of millions to hold us back. Is this why essays feel more naturally collaborative than other literary forms? More communicative? Maybe this is in part why working on an essay while online has always felt more natural to me than trying to stay Wi-Fied and yet get a poem right. Maybe this is why Facebook is basically, as David Shields rightly once said (and what a tunnel that dude made), a personal essay machine.

The *New York Times* tells me that we are in the age of the essay. We are, I think, but we've always been. Maybe we just didn't know it before. We're caught in the literary present tense, still being spoken to in whispers by Sei Shōnagon. Good essays essay interminably. They are little simulated minds calculating in the dark, waiting for someone to stumble into their tunnel. They keep listing their hateful things, tallying the pleasures of the contrary. They keep thinking, keep sorting through their stimuli, keep uncovering and echoing meaning. An essay is thinking in action. And interesting thinking doesn't age.

But is it any surprise then that the age of the essay coincides with the age of the internet? I know, I know. The thinking, such as it is, that the internet fosters sometimes seems an anathema to essay. It coasts along the surface, while good essays instead go down. But the *connections* that the internet fosters seem to me quite well suited to making and disseminating essays. That Hoaglandian "speaking to one another" now happens increasingly fast. It's not that essays are going viral, exactly: they're too dense for that, the good ones anyway; they require more work than the six-second Vines that sprout and spread so easily now and creep up the side of my unsold house in Michigan and get inside the siding. But essays online are more accessible, and they get out there more quickly. Thanks to Google, if you're speaking to or with or of others, they might just get an instantaneous notification that their names just showed up and boom, you're connected.

Whether it's good or bad or something else, this availability has become a fact of the modern age. And sure, the numbers mean that we don't read even a fraction of what we come across. But still, when we do, and when I read something that gets me hot, I want to tell someone about it. It's not a shocker that essays, the most rhizomic of literary forms, flourish in the networked—the social—age.

This thought was in part the impetus for *Essay Daily* (essaydaily .org), which came online the first week of 2010 as a website without a big idea but with a hunger for connection. Mainly what I wanted was some kind of place to aggregate our thinking, for us to speak more directly to other practitioners of essays, and to grow the tribe. It quickly became a space for speaking back—explicitly—to those whose words found their way to us. Even if we can't actually contact Virginia Woolf, if we can't rouse her ghost, she still speaks to me and through me, and I want to honor that. Or H. L. Mencken, or Audre Lorde. Or Christopher Smart. Or Robert Burton, here still in my head anatomizing my melancholy.

*

A couple of years after I hatched the site, I read an essay by Craig Reinbold—then one of my students in the MFA program at the University of Arizona—that manifested that exact kind of excitement on making a connection, this time over a translation of a line of Chekhov, how one translator renders a particular post-lake feeling as "delicious," and how that choice bewitched Craig, and how flat-out *stoked* (there is no better word for this) he was to tell us about it. And tell us he did. I could feel a spark, reading it. I told him so. It's a great essay, and these five years later, he's finally published it in the literary magazine *Zone 3*. You should check it out and see if it speaks to you. If I were writing online I'd just link it, but here all I can do is tell you about his work. In a later essay, Craig doubles down on this and writes about how much he loves the music of the band Morphine, and how much he wants to share that with you. I happen also to love Morphine, though I jumped off the train an album or two before Mark Sandman, the singer, died onstage.

In the electric light of his excitement, I understood that I had found a fellow traveler, and I think I told him so (Craig, if I didn't, I am so doing now: welcome to my tunnel; I'm happy to have intersected yours), and so I talked him into joining the site as managing editor and coediting this anthology. He held that post for a few years, until the end of 2015. His tunnel's only gotten bigger since.

Essay Daily doesn't work as a solo effort, its raison d'être being connection and conversation. And we've added many other voices since.

As of this writing (November 16, 2015, quickly approaching midnight, Arizona time, which exists in a kind of unchanged state, whether you want to attribute that to the presence of so much spectacular and unchanging sun or the fact that Arizona doesn't do daylight saving time, on account of we don't feel the need to save daylight, we've got enough already, thank you very much), we have published 483 essays. Included here are forty-six of them, a starter kit, with several that haven't been published anywhere before.

I'd have preferred to include them all, all fellow travelers essaying out there on the site and on the internet and speaking to one another always, but this being a book, and books not being conducive to all-inclusiveness, what you are about to read is only a sliver of what we're about. We offer these essays as overtures to conversation, as prods to communication, as the kind of electric charge you used to get in the boys' bathroom in the old Houghton High School on the very lowest floor when a bunch of us joined hands to make a circuit from one hand drier to the other. What I remember about it is this: as long as you held the circuit you wouldn't feel the shock. But when someone finally released his neighbor's hand, those two would feel the shock, and we all would shout. Then we'd pass around those Lion Mints, put them in our mouths like a communion wafer, and let them dissolve.

*

While editing this introduction a month later—in a Starbucks, as is my habit—I see one of the baristas walking around with sample cups of whatever new Frappuccino concoction they've made for me to try. Or perhaps someone just was training on a macchiato and screwed up, so they made a flaw a feature and spread the failure around? I have my headphones on to isolate and soundtrack myself, but when I see him in my peripheral vision, I take them off to signal my openness to being approached with the prospect of a free caffeinated something. Here, I think, let's make a connection.

I think a lot about balancing two essay practices: that of *openness* (essaying as listening, as paying attention, as aggregation and collage, as a sticky ball sort of thing that can be rolled over the world to pick up whatever it encounters: conversations, auto accidents, the linguistic anomalies of the American Southwest, the play-affections and sparring of a couple reclining on a couch outside) and that of *withdrawal* (essaying as closing, as isolation, as scale move away from, as epic simile, as processing and churning, as analysis, as introspection, as inwardness).

So what if it's a bit of a false binary? One can't ever open entirely or close entirely, I know. These two states aren't sealed from one another. Seepage occurs: we see the self in everything; we see everything in the self. Sometimes you offer a Lion Mint to a sewer raccoon, and sometimes the raccoon brings you treasure from the sewer. It's only in looking and talking back to the world that we allow the self to manifest.

These days, if you're anything like me (and I believe that at heart we are more alike than not), you've got a lot of noisy perspectives you're made to wade through. A lot of voices echo through my days: on social media, television, blogs, websites, newspaper opinion columns, the six or seven magazines I subscribe to, talk radio, satellite radio, podcasts, video game narration, Red Wings hockey color commentary, and so forth. My brother subscribed me to the *National Review* (as a joke? to convert me to his way of thinking? I am not sure). It's jarring, reading it, but I guess I find the jarring bracing. I mean to say I'm trying to be open to it, to not just surround myself with sameness. And every so often I find something surprising and deftly made in there, which makes me reconsider ideas I had accepted without thinking.

Well, the barista runs out of samples just before he makes it to me. I get disappointed, put my headphones back on. Sometimes you wait and it does not come. Still, *Essay Daily* has allowed me to reserve some space in my days for a conscious practice of openness to the world and to the force of others' voices. Though we don't always publish daily, we aspire to that dailiness: we publish essays at least twice weekly, enough to feel constant and persistent, to make these essays— these encounters with other minds—a regular force. During the Advent season each year, we do it daily, offering an essay a day to you as an Advent calendar.

I mean to say that both these modes of essaying—opening and gathering and then withdrawing in contemplation—are practices for me. They're ways of being that feel more and more necessary. I'm sure I've been changed by them. I hope for you that you feel the same. Someday, if not now.

*

At the risk of exposing a wack metaphor: I think these essays are the Lion Mints. I want you to have one. Actually, take a roll. Take all of them and carry them with you. They'll freshen your breath and, if used properly, may abet a random animal encounter that changes the way your day (even your life) is going.

If you want to put a quarter into the slot, great. A nickel's fine, though too, because there are a lot of ways of giving back, of metabolizing shame, of saying *thanks* and maybe *sorry for my ignorance.* I get it now. It took about a decade to get it through my frozen Michigan skin. Perhaps you'll figure it out quicker.

What we'd like best is for you to speak back to us and send us a message back. Now we become raccoons, waiting for you to roll your regional mints into our open arms and ears and mouths where we hang out in the sewer.

Essay us or shout back at us from afar as you see us passing underneath your window, rolling mints into the darkness; though to speak is not necessarily to be heard, it's a start. As are the practices of openness and withdrawal. So come read more. Write a piece for us. Make our practice your practice. Enjoy the mints.

MARCIA ALDRICH

Invisible Engineering

The Fine Art of Revising "The Fine Art of Sighing"

If you don't already, you should know this essay by Bernard Cooper, for its pleasures will make you a connoisseur of the art in question: "Poised at the crest of an exhalation, your body is about to be unburdened, second by second, cell by cell" ("The Fine Art of Sighing," in *Truth Serum: Memoirs*). Its concise and lyrical prose, its brevity and effect of effortlessness, the constructed undertow of its associative method, its inventive demonstration of how a writer's thoughts shape a piece—these qualities make it an exemplar of the contemporary essay.

Behind the ease of "The Fine Art of Sighing" is the writer's art of revision, and that is what launched the inquiry I am about to describe. Can we detect the steps toward its art? How did Cooper shape the breath of its sentences, its elegant respiratory system, the suspended movement of the climax, and the expelled throb of the conclusion? Out of its beginning, how did he craft its final finesse?

*

For me these questions first emerged from pedagogical concerns—specifically a moment when, huddled in my cold office on a winter afternoon, the graduate assistants in an introductory creative writing course turned to the problem of revision.

"How do *you* incorporate revision in your courses?" they asked. "What are your approaches?" In their voices was a yearning for answers.

They had only recently encountered what all experienced teachers of writing know: the difficulty of pushing students forward from their current marks. There could be no writing without revision, we all agreed. However, our students did not necessarily see it that way. Some of them positively bucked revision, as if we were trying to cage their noble and wild words.

One GA in particular, Christine,[1] was perplexed by her failure to communicate to students the importance of revision. She had developed a series of systematic steps they should follow, yet these novices resisted them or implemented them without improving their prose. Students tend to believe that good writing comes out whole. No, we teachers insist, writing has a history. Revision is an essential return, even if only an hour has elapsed between the first version of the words and the second. Students needed to grasp that idea conceptually and experientially. How could we get the point across?

A thought emerged in that frigid room: it might be enlightening to show students the revisions that an admired essay went through to arrive at its final disposition. We had found that students liked "The Fine Art of Sighing," which displays a deceptive ease. It seemed an ideal pedagogical tool, highly wrought, of manageable length, and appealing to the apprentice writers we wanted to help. At the time I did not consider any difficulties that might arise in our inquiry or any counterproductive consequences, and I embarked on one of the longest failed projects of my life.

Christine and I decided to e-mail Bernard Cooper, saying we wanted to document the various stages of "The Fine Art of Sighing," to analyze patterns, methods, specific changes, and authorial choices during revision. We wrote out and sent detailed questions—the mass of which embarrasses me—helpfully categorizing the topics on which we were requesting enlightenment: *General writing practices* (ten questions here), *Conditions of writing* (six questions), *Specific practices in "Fine Art"* (four questions), *Revision of "Fine Art"* (four questions, the second of which had eight parts), *Content of "Fine Art"* (two questions, one of them a two-parter), and *"Fine Art" in the context of your other works* (two questions).

Rather than shake his head at our presumption, rather than politely decline or—more what we deserved—press the Delete key with a stiff middle finger, Bernard Cooper wrote back, answering our questions and betraying not a sliver of irritation. His responses exude personality, generosity, and vividness.

*

When we contacted Cooper, we were operating under certain assumptions—that "The Fine Art of Sighing" went through many drafts and that we could, with his help, map out the revision process. We proposed to look closely at his drafts, analyzing why he chose this word instead of that one, this paragraph ahead of that one. Christine was prepared to undertake a close reading of Cooper's changes and their significance, and to create from them a useful tool for teaching revision. She hoped that "he would create an order within the mystery," that "he would give me a way to teach my students how to revise, a way that I could say, 'Remember that great essay we read the first day of class? Here's how Cooper revises and writes. You should do that too.'" As teachers, we wanted to identify definite steps, from idea to draft to final version, that we could pass on in the classroom.

We were in the grips, that is, of a fetish of the draft. This is not to say that writers don't revise or sometimes hold on to versions of a work as it stood prior to its published form. Obviously, writers often do. But the real process of composition is more fluid, interior, hesitant, oscillating, obsessive, and charged than is represented by black text on white paper or by a file bearing a precise time stamp.

The draft is a pedagogical fiction, a frozen moment when fixed words can conveniently be assessed by an instructor or by peers in a workshop, suitable for classrooms, places where, in the last moments of a session, a teacher raises her voice over the hubbub as students grab their backpacks and pull out their phones, to announce those familiar final words: "Drafts due on Tuesday!"

*

Cooper's essay, it turns out, was inspired by a friend's query: was he aware that he *sighed* all the time, "big melancholy sighs"? No, he was not:

> I was stunned that a routine physiological response as fundamental as sneezing or sweating had escaped my attention. From where, in my body and temperament and history, did all this ponderous heaving arise?[2]

He began to pay attention. The process of writing had begun.

> I started out, simply, by attempting to describe the intake and exhalation of air, the metabolic and emotional release. The rest followed. Note that I do not say, the rest "flowed."
>
> A sigh is invisible, of course, but that never stopped me from turning it over and glancing at its facets as though it were a solid object. I was exploring a simple phenomenon—it is the nature and meaning of the essay to conduct this kind of verbal exploration—instead of setting out to make a point. The point made me, so to speak.

The result was one of his shortest pieces, written in a relatively short period of time.

> The first half of "Fine Art" came fairly quickly (if only every piece of writing would drop off the tree like a ripe fruit!), the rest over the course of two or three more days, then three weeks of small changes.

He also revealed that he had kept none of the working drafts for "Fine Art." He had no paper trail to provide or consult. He might temporarily retain a draft of a longer essay, he said, to keep a record of the narrative.

> With long stretches of prose there's too much to keep track
> of and it's harder to assess in a glance, so to speak, and so
> I like to read long stretches in hard copy.

However, when he finishes an essay, even a long one, and sees it into print, he usually gets rid of the drafts.

This was a blow to our hopes, and there was more disappointment to come. We had pointed out, in one of our bloated questions, that "some writers keep their papers (lying in their treasures) with an eye turned toward posterity and history, perhaps assured of their place therein." Cooper responded,

> I don't mean to sound too humble-pie-ish, but I wince at
> the thought of that kind of close scrutiny being devoted
> to my work; it leads to just the kind of self-consciousness
> I try hard to avoid.

His reluctance to keep his drafts, and hence expose them to scrutiny, arises from a desire to make his writing a "source of pleasure for the reader rather than . . . an academic or analytic labor." Cooper works to immerse himself in the process and to avoid, as much as any writer can, worry about the destiny of his writing. As he put it, "The fate of my work will unfold on its own. I'm happier when I can stand apart from how my work is received, or from how it might be compared to the work of other writers." In short, the *absence* of a paper trail, of the very drafts we were after, was central to Cooper's efforts as a writer. Christine rightly felt the lack of drafts complicated our project. Unpredictably I felt exhilarated and asked myself why. The teacher in me had wanted to scour his drafts to chart his writing process. The writer in me was happy to learn he didn't keep his writing in neat packages to manage for eternity.

Its hull damaged by these rocky shallows, the ship named *Cooper Project* finally ran aground on revision itself. As a teacher, one tends to separate revision from composition. Cooper makes no such distinction.

> Writing, for me, *is* revision. I generate an inchoate blob of language and then try to shape and polish it till the words make sense, though I may not know what sense I was aiming for until revision shows me.

*

It was now clear Cooper was not going to provide us with a methodical approach to revision. Christine bemoaned what seemed a nil payoff: "His answer didn't chart out a practice of revision that I could teach. Where were the steps?"

But there were lessons a teacher could learn nonetheless. A writer in a classroom is different from a writer outside of one. The process I offer my students and the process a writer like Cooper follows are separated by an impassable river. Consider the workshop, that classroom fixture. Before he's finished with a piece, Cooper sometimes shows it to a few friends whom he has cultivated over a lifetime. Although he's participated in a couple of writing groups,

> it is a daunting task to absorb a great deal of commentary about one's work all at once, weighing which suggestions to dismiss and which to implement.

Think of the often-contradictory responses students are bombarded by in workshops, and think of the context: they must, by a fixed deadline, cough up a rough draft for exposure to near strangers whose comments are often untrustworthy.

Many of our students see themselves not as writers but as *students*, with limited time to write outside the classroom. They can't call themselves writers. They do not compose every day for three or four hours in the morning, as Cooper does. They do not go back later in the day, every day, to edit the morning's work. They do not lie awake at night and think about an essay "with a mixture of excitement and apprehension," as Cooper does. They do not beat their heads against "the metaphorical brick wall for quite a while" before they show their work for feedback. Obsession cannot be their method.

We began our project thinking that revealing how Cooper writes and revises would be instructive and encouraging for students. But what emerged was the gap between my own expectations for my students and the actual conditions of their writing. Much of what Cooper models—his philosophy of writing, the intimate relation of an artist to his work, the essay as an aesthetic object brought to vivid realization, his method of revising through obsessive practice, the protection he affords himself until he is ready to release his writing for commentary, his emphasis on the reader's pleasure—does not help bridge the gap between writers and students. Rather, it maps differences. It confirms the distance between a professional, accomplished writer and a novice who dares not even claim the title.

While Cooper's work takes its place in public, his writing process remains a secret I still don't know how to whisper to a listening ear. How can students become so tied to writing that, driving or sleeping, they turn to each facet, over and over, looking hard at image and word until something emerges that pleases?

Far from producing a guide to revision, I think I'm better off going back to where I began—in moments of reading pleasure produced by "The Fine Art of Sighing." Maybe it will inspire the young writer, who will inhale and exhale the sigh of writing: take a deep breath, I will say, release with feeling, attend to its passage, its history, its future. That is the fine art of writing.

Notes

1. At the time that Christine was my coconspirator, she was known as Christine Junker. She has since become Christine Wilson and is an assistant professor in English and the director of faculty development and the Student Success Center at Wright State University–Lake Campus. Her essays and criticism have appeared in *Legacy, Popular Ghosts, The Universal Vampire,* and *Red Cedar Review.*

2. This and subsequent quotations come from Cooper's e-mail correspondence, specifically the answers he graciously provided to questions.

On Chris Marker's *Sans Soleil*

KRISTEN RADTKE

Here

In 1973, a volcano covered half of Heimaey with lava and ash.

No one died.

The lava moved so slowly that the people were ferried to Iceland's mainland before it threatened the harbor.

And when everything was over, most of them went back, rebuilding their homes in a valley between the mountains and the rock that buried the neighborhoods they'd lived in before.

Back at college in Chicago, years before I took a boat from Reykjavik to Heimaey, my friends and I often snuck into classrooms in the middle of the night to watch movies on the projectors.

That was the first time I saw Chris Marker's Sans Soleil, a travel documentary told in letters, which begins on the same island.

"So, it sufficed to wait, and the planet itself staged the working of time."

"I saw what had been my window again. I saw emerge familiar roofs and balconies, the landmarks of the walks I took through town every day, down to the cliff where I had met the children."

It was the "had been my window" that made me wonder.

"Had been" and the way he wandered, or the way I do, or how I looked across the island forty years later and thought:

Majestic Ruins

On the Work of James Agee

My connection to James Agee's work, particularly his nonfiction, feels deeply personal, and nearly impossible to articulate. When I write "particularly his nonfiction," I mean "particularly his entire oeuvre," because I'd say that nearly all of it might be considered nonfiction. His fiction *A Death in the Family* and *The Morning Watch*, both highly autobiographical, would be framed as memoir, most likely, were he to write them today.

Ever since I was sixteen and attended tiny St. Andrew's School, nestled in the mountains of Tennessee, one of the same schools Agee attended (along with Exeter and Harvard), I've seen him as a kind of role model, both for good and ill. My role models have always looked nothing like me and have always tempted me with their wicked ways, both linguistically and temperamentally. In grad school (I first wrote "grand" school), when I was a "gradual student," to quote John Irving, I identified with my teacher and sometime downstairs neighbor, Barry Hannah. In high school, it was James Agee, in whose eponymous library on the campus of St. Andrew's you could find me studying under the not-so-watchful eye of the librarian Mrs. Gooch on most days. Unlike most of my fellow St. Andrewsians, I lived for study hall, and I immersed myself in Southern literature full of madness and disgrace, my PB&J—which accounted for how thin I was back then. As in the children's story in which an alligator is raised by ducks and thinks he's a duck too, I somehow forgot that I was Jewish, born in

New York, and had nothing in common with possessed Southerners like Hannah and Agee.

I had *something* in common with Agee, besides going to St. Andrew's and sitting through Anglican chapel services. Agee and I had both lost our fathers when we were young, his when he was six and mine when I was seven. But that wasn't what forged my connection with him. By the time I graduated from St. Andrew's, I had read almost nothing of James Agee's work. Why is it that a school that half-prided itself in forging at least part of young Jim's character should overlook his writing? The only things that Agee wrote that were pushed on me—I can't speak for other St. Andrewsians of the time—were the letters of James Agee to Father Flye, a former teacher at St. Andrew's who lived past one hundred to Agee's forty-five, dead of a heart attack in Manhattan in the backseat of a cab on his way to see a doctor. Not that Agee's work was discouraged at St. Andrew's—I remember seeing Agee's autobiographical novel *A Death in the Family* on the shelves of the library. I might have even picked it up. I might have even stolen it to read later.

Agee wasn't really Southern literature as defined by St. Andrew's at the time. When I took Mr. Norton's Southern literature class, we read four Faulkner novels. Couldn't one of Agee's books have supplanted one of the Faulkner novels we read? After all, one of Agee's works, *The Morning Watch,* took place at St. Andrew's, for heaven's sake, but Mr. Norton, who didn't seem to care for Flannery O'Connor either, whose great-grandfather had had two horses shot from under him when he was defending against the Northern aggressors, decidedly preferred the old South to the new, even assigning us a book about quadroons and octaroons, *The Grandissimes: A Story of Creole Life,* written by George Washington Cable in 1880. Too late now for me to turn in a negative teacher evaluation for Mr. Norton—not that we were ever asked to fill out such things, but the *Grandissimes* I could have lived without. Agee on the other hand . . . I'm not sure if it would have helped me or hurt me to read *Let Us Now Praise Famous Men* at the age of sixteen. It probably would have confounded and devastated and frustrated and sometimes bored me as it has since I first discovered it years later.

We're all ruins in the making, and that's what I love so much about Agee, that he was a ruin on the page. In 1936 when he ventured with Walker Evans down to Alabama for Henry Luce's *Fortune* magazine, he met three white tenant farm families, forming a kind of ruinous circle of human enterprise and squalor for several weeks. He tried in vain (he thought) to capture these people in his writing:

> If I could do it, I'd do no writing at all here. It would be photographs; the rest would be fragments of cloth, bits of cotton, lumps of earth, records of speech, pieces of wood and iron, phials of odor, plates of food and of excrement. Booksellers would consider it quite a novelty; critics would murmur, yes, but is it art; and I could trust the majority of you to use it as you would a parlor game.

> A piece of the body torn out by the roots might be more to the point.

> As it is, though, I'll do what little I can in writing.

It's what Walker Evans called "night writing," and I think it could only be written by a twenty-seven-year-old who takes himself seriously to the point of pomposity. Still, I love that—I love all the flaws of this great ruin of a book. In it, I see all our failures to capture what we want to capture, yours and mine. I've passed the time when I could conceivably write such a majestic failure. I'm out of grand school though still a gradual student, which means my failures have become increasingly fatal, like a car's slow oil leak.

Had Mr. Norton taught James Agee, I'm not sure how I would have reacted, but I would have reacted. *The Grandissimes* still sits in me, undigested.

I only truly discovered Agee after high school, when I first read his gorgeous evocation of place, "Knoxville, Summer 1915," followed by *A Death in the Family,* the copy I stole when Mrs. Gooch wasn't looking, and *The Morning Watch.* But first, I acted out *The Morning Watch.*

Although I wasn't taught Agee's work, I was taught some good old-fashioned Southern self-destructiveness at St. Andrew's: a little drunkenness, a little pot, a lot of pining for sex, and even more conflict about religion. Jew or not, I had to participate in the high Anglican rituals of the campus along with all the other Agee wannabes. All of the students were required on the eve of Easter Sunday to participate in "Morning Watch," a kind of relay prayer in which we were required to pray alone to Jesus in the chapel for fifteen minutes before being relieved by another student. My watch came at 3:00 a.m., punishment, I'm sure, for being a Jew from New York City, punishment for getting the award from Mr. Norton for best student in his Southern literature class ("It pains me to give you this award, Mr. Hemley," he told me when I went to receive it on the St. Andrew's stage that May). What was I suppose to say to Jesus? Agee suffered spiritual torment during his own stint with Jesus during Morning Watch. For me, there was only burning resentment at having been awakened so early for something I didn't believe in. But there came a reward. One of the girls I had a crush on—none of the girls were crush-exempted, actually—suggested that we do what the main characters in *The Morning Watch* did: ride our bikes out to the lake and go skinny-dipping. She didn't have to ask twice. Half a dozen of us Agee heathen rode our bikes out to the lake and luxuriated in the warmth and freedom of being sixteen and not on the downhill slide. And from that moment, throwing off my clothes, skinny bones and all, when I hit the water, that's the time I mark as when I first understood something about literature.

V. V. GANESHANANTHAN

On Essays, Assays, and Yiyun Li's "Dear Friend, from My Life I Write to You in Your Life"

I am guilty of what many people would consider excessive rereading. The most cherished books of my childhood remain among the most cherished books of my adulthood; if a story resonates with me, I will seek out its best sections over and over again. Those pages will become thumb-worn, and I will intentionally let the binding break there so that, eventually, I will find those preferred places more quickly. But even with all these habits and customs designed to keep my most precious words close at hand, there is an essay I have returned to so frequently that some time ago, even its presence on paper ceased to satisfy me. How to carry it with me, then? An odd solution—I took a picture of one of its passages. Now I keep it on my phone so that I can read it whenever the urge seizes me. There it is in my library of photographs: I can flick my finger to turn from

> a picture of my parents to
> a picture of my brother to
> a picture of friends—to
> a picture of children I know,
> to a picture of a landscape I admired,
> to a picture of a parking space I was trying to remember
> —to pictures of some parts of my past I would rather
>   forget.

Unlike all the other pictures, the one of the essay exists unmarked by time or place. It isn't located *anywhere*, exactly, but on the page and in my head; I don't remember the second that I took it, but every time I turn to that picture to reread, I reenact it anyway. I carry it with me as a talisman not of protection but of uncertainty. Stripped not only of its page numbers but also of the name of the friend who wrote it and its title, it articulates both a question and a terrifying possible answer to that question—an answer that points to my own choices as someone whose two obsessions are the past and guilt over obsessing over the past.

> *19.*
>
> There is this emptiness in me. All the things in the world are not enough to drown out the voice of this emptiness, which says, *You are nothing.*
>
> Perhaps I am only hiding my nothingness from people. I worry that they have been deceived by me: the moment they see my nothingness they will leave me.
>
> This emptiness doesn't claim the past, because it is always here; it doesn't have to claim the future, as it blocks out the future. It's either a dictator or the closest friend I've ever had. Some days I battle it until we both fall down like injured animals. That is when I wonder, what if I become less than nothing when I get rid of this emptiness? What if this emptiness is what keeps me carrying on?

Of course this is the picture from my phone. The essay from which it is taken, Yiyun Li's "Dear Friend, from My Life I Write to You in Your Life," first appeared in *A Public Space* and then later in *Best American Essays 2014.* (Now it appears as the opening chapter of Li's first non-fiction book.) It is impossible to ever finish reading. This year, I assigned the piece to my students. (I should add, by way of disclosure, that I am friends with Li, although I have never spoken to her about the piece.)

I tend to look at the picture in between destinations, appropriately enough; it is about everything and nothing and therefore perfect reading for traveling. Because I have moved so often, it sometimes occurs to me that this is all I have done—traveling: leaving one place and arriving at the next just in time to plan leaving it. (No wonder I find myself at home with, among others, Calvino.) As a writer, and perhaps especially as an essayist, I am simultaneously bound and freed by questions of the past; I am often writing about an experience I wish had gone differently. I am attempting to reconcile myself to what has happened, although really, I would prefer not to; I want *something else*—I am a train for which the engine is regret. I want to honor the past as I destroy it. Is it possible for me to be otherwise? I am always wondering what I could have done differently, or what I am, in the present moment, doing wrong. Is it useful to ask these questions as each second falls away behind me, impossible to unravel? And if not—must I ask only questions that are useful? *What if this emptiness is what keeps me carrying on?* What if, as a writer, I am made of my warring obsessions? The past, and its mirror-hall of endlessly reflected regret?

This particular essay reinforces these ideas, and yet, although it is a talisman of uncertainty, that is comforting rather than disturbing. Unlike most other things I read, which give me the sensation of reading (albeit closely) about someone else, this essay gives me the sensation of reading about myself. This used to be a feeling I could get only from writing, and not from reading; reading was about entering other people's pasts, other stories. I never saw myself on the page. But Yiyun's consciousness opens to me in such a way that I discover something new about myself every time I read this essay; I am able to ask myself another question and also forgive myself for my past a little bit more. What I want is this: to say, the past is not my fault. Yiyun's essay ventures something better: it may be my fault, and that's acceptable.

I can remember a time when I read not to reconcile myself to the past, but to discover the future. I am not quite sure when I crossed the line from one kind of reading to the other.

*

"Dear Friend" is an unusual essay, eliding easy questions of theme and form, and offering among its gifts openness, intensity, and that capacious consciousness. In reading I get the sensation of entering a bare, open, beautiful room—being unable to see the walls—having no desire to leave. This is all the more remarkable considering its spare, decisive structure: twenty-four comparatively short, numbered parts. Of these, it is that nineteenth that makes me feel the most.

At first, I thought that the essay was about being existentially troubled, and then I thought that it was about unhappiness, and then I realized that it had announced itself as being about time: before and after and in between. But for me, existential woe and unhappiness and time are tied up in one another, and of course with writing, and probably with essays themselves. What I want out of an essay is, perhaps, not original: When I teach essay writing, I ask my students to think about the central questions driving each essay. What is the subject? What is it that the writer hopes to learn by writing about this subject? How does the writer arrive at an answer? It isn't interesting for me to begin an essay (at least, a personal one) by asking a question to which I already know the answer; if I knew the answer, I wouldn't have to write it.

But this approach also presumes that knowing will be possible. The modern world, with its urges toward mindfulness, often invites us to *be in the present moment,* and I have to admit that my skepticism of this may have been rooted in one suggestion that sometimes underpins that one: that being engaged in the present moment means that we will know ourselves better and therefore be happier. "Dear Friend," on the other hand, with its unapologetic depiction of ostensibly contradictory feelings and ambitions and thoughts, gives me a strange kind of permission to fail to understand my own inconsistencies, and to be both interested and unhappy in the present. It opens the door to uncertainty. I am grateful for this, engaged as I sometimes am in a flat daily performance of happiness. That performance is often a strange counterpoint to my changeable, contradictory interior. "The present does not surrender so easily to manipulation," Yiyun writes in the third section of this essay. She defines the present as truer, then—but not necessarily happier. I am not sure, and the essay is a space in which that uncertainty is fine. One does not always arrive at knowing.

Yiyun does not write as though she is able to answer the questions she has raised about time. In an interview with *Iron Horse Review,*

Yiyun herself points to the sixteenth section of the essay, in which she writes,

> I had this notion, when I first started it, that this essay would be a way to test—to assay—thoughts about time. There was even a vision of an *after*, when my confusions would be sorted out.
>
> Assays in science are part of an endless exploration: one question leads to another; what follows confirms or disconfirms what comes before. To assay one's ideas about time while time remains unsettled and elusive feels futile: just as one is about to understand one facet of time, it presents another to undermine one's reasoning.
>
> To write about a struggle amidst the struggling: one must hope that this muddling will end someday.

Is there a silent *but* at the beginning of that second paragraph? At any rate, the central question need not be answered; this essay may be a good enough reason for me to stop saying that in my classroom. A question may just lead to another question.

> What a long way it is from one life to another: yet why write if not for that distance; if things can be let go, every before replaced by an after. . . . The train, for reasons unknown to us, always stops between a past and a future, both making this *now* look as though it is nowhere. But it is this nowhere-ness that one has to make use of. . . . One has made it this far; perhaps this is enough of a reason to journey on.

The essay is, among other things, a manifesto for writing—but she does not stop at an after, or an answer; she stops on an *if* without any apology for how nowhere *if* can be. A picture on a phone leads from this passage to a photograph, to another photograph, with no definitive end in sight.

ROBERT ATWAN

The Assault on Prose

John Crowe Ransom, New Criticism, and the Status of the Essay

Prefatory Note

What follows is a little bit of literary history that grew directly out of my curiosity as to why the traditional or familiar essay went into decline for so many decades of the twentieth century. I see the rise of the New Criticism in the 1930s as a major contributor to the essay's diminished literary status. One enduring effect of that critical movement was its relegation of the essay to a minor or even subliterary genre, a relegation that led to the genre's rapid disappearance from serious literary study. This attitude in large part developed out of John Crowe Ransom's assimilation of Paul Valéry's aesthetic principles, which argued for the inherent primacy of poetry over prose. These principles—reinforced by the work of a Chicago semiotician, Charles W. Morris—are central to Ransom's enormously influential criticism that, as I try to set out in a small space here, would shape the study of literature for many years and, in some ways, despite formidable theoretical rivals, still shapes it.

I believe the essay is currently experiencing a revival—at least editors and publishers no longer seem afraid of the E-word, as they were when I first proposed an annual series of essays back in the early 1980s. ("Isn't there *another* word we can use?" my editor asked.) But when it comes to the promotion and marketing of literary works, and book review attention, essays can't compete with fiction. And when it comes to literary status, essays can't compete with poetry. How many essayists do you think are short- (or even long-) listed for the Nobel Prize? And when it comes to literary theory, essays have none that I know of aside from studies that are mainly rhetorical. Yet, as I suggest below, the long association of the essay with rhetoric has prevented the genre from being wholeheartedly classified as literature.

So essayists, though their tribe may be increasing, will still, in my opinion, be denied the awards and attention novelists receive, will be less esteemed creatively as are poets, and will continue to be read without a coherent criticism that would enhance their literary achievements. But perhaps that's what makes essayists essayists.

*

When I decided back in the early 1980s that an annual collection of outstanding essays seemed like a good idea, I was surprised by the negative responses I received from the publishers I approached. Some were put off by the E-word and its marketability, while others doubted essays had serious literary value or, if they did, that enough of them were published in a year to form a collection. Finding a publisher for the series was largely an uphill climb.

I began to wonder about the resistance I encountered. My interest for years had been to advance the essay as a literary genre, but here were many editors afraid to use the word *essay* in a title. One literary magazine editor wrote me to say that no one ever submitted personal essays to his journal. His larger point was that essays were written about literature—they weren't in themselves literature.

At the time I realized that essayists—and by that term I mean writers who regularly compose personal, familiar, or reflective essays— knew they worked in an underappreciated genre. Just a few years before I proposed an annual series, E. B. White (in 1977) famously lamented in a preface to a collection of essays that he was not "fooled about the place of the essay in twentieth-century American letters." "The essayist," White continued, "unlike the novelist, the poet, and the playwright, must be content in his self-imposed role of second-class citizen." I wondered how this situation had come about.

As I studied the twentieth-century essay, I began to think that its marginalized literary status could be connected to its place in the university writing program. E. B. White may never have realized it because he was well known to a reading public, but his work was—and perhaps still is—read and admired at the university level only in composition courses. For at the time, well before the growing popularity of MFA programs, such courses were, with few exceptions, the only places where essays were assigned, studied, discussed, and imitated.

Was the essay tossed out of the literature curriculum as a bone for composition teachers? Was the essay identified as some sort of literary degenerate to be sentenced and exiled to an academic gulag? Did literary studies deliberately and systematically "purify" itself of the essay? What exactly happened in the English curriculum? For let's acknowledge that at one point there was a strong belletristic curriculum in which the essay played a vital role. This was back in the days when *belles lettres* was not a pejorative term, when novels, short stories, and lyric poems didn't sway the syllabus. Years ago, in a *Partisan Review* essay "What Henry James Knew," Cynthia Ozick made an eloquent plea for the essay: "A while ago," she writes, "coming once again on Robert Louis Stevenson's 'Virginibus Puerisque'—an essay, not short, wholly odd, no other like it, custom-made, soliciting the brightness of full attention in order to release its mocking charms—I tried to think of a single periodical today that might be willing to grant print to this sort of construction."

The process that resulted in the death of belles lettres and in the essay's loss of literary status is, of course, a complicated phenomenon. (A valuable recent study is by Ned Stuckey-French, *The American Essay in the American Century*, 2011.) The process involved a spectrum of cultural, social, and economic factors; by the 1930s, for example, the nation's leading magazines were already starting to turn down essays in favor of topical articles. This trend, bemoaned by a number of the leading essayists of the time, was also reflected in a peculiar book that will be the focus of what I have to say about the decline of the literary essay, a decline that began during the Great Depression and lasted into the late 1980s or early 1990s, when the personal essay received a robust boost with the ascent of the confessional memoir.

The book I want to consider was published by Henry Holt & Company in 1935; it was directed to college composition courses. Its catchy title: *Topics for Freshman Writing: Twenty Topics for Writing with Appropriate Materials for Study.* What especially interests me about this collection is that it was compiled and edited by none other than the illustrious poet and critic, John Crowe Ransom, one of the most influential literary figures of his time and a founder, along with Cleanth Brooks and Robert Penn Warren, of a formalist methodology that would come to be called the New Criticism (after the title of Ransom's 1941 book).

Ransom chose the no-nonsense title of his college reader deliberately. The older belletristic essay is conspicuously absent from the collection. Instead of recommending the literary prose of such notable essay stylists as William Hazlitt, Charles Lamb, Walter Pater, or Robert Louis Stevenson, Ransom turned instead to contemporary magazines to find pieces for such elevated essay subjects as "The Planned Society," "Machinery, Overproduction, and Unemployment," and "Nationalism and Foreign Trade." Nearly a fifth of the selections were written by his students, all identified in the table of contents as "Anonymous." Clearly, though compiled by a distinguished poet and one of our major literary aestheticians, this was no guide to the belletristic or familiar essay.

In fact, it was decidedly antibelletristic. A question I want to pose here is this: why was Ransom, a poet-critic whose own literary essays would surely be classified as belletristic, so resistant himself to the older familiar essay? He refuses to expose students to the genre in his reader and rarely refers to it in his criticism. Why would this be?

Actually, Ransom's choice of selections for his college anthology should not be surprising to anyone who closely follows Ransom's literary criticism. The only surprising thing about his textbook venture is that—given his literary disposition—he didn't assemble a volume of poetry instead. Of course, his colleagues Cleanth Brooks and Robert Penn Warren would do just that and make both critical and pedagogical history in 1938 with the first edition of *Understanding Poetry,* a book whose announced literary agenda was not much different from Ransom's—and was, in fact, quite indebted to him. Although he helped promote the poetry textbook, Ransom was never entirely in agreement with the overly "scientific" way his New Criticism colleagues approached the understanding of poetry.

Throughout an illustrious career—in well over one hundred published critical essays—Ransom kept returning to a single literary theme: the primacy of poetry over prose. I say this at the risk of reduction, since his is such an agile and fertile intelligence. Yet—as we read essay after essay—we can see why two literary scholars (Thomas Young and John Hindle) began the introduction to their fine collection of Ransom's criticism as follows: "No other literary critic of this century has devoted so much time and intellectual energy as John Crowe Ransom in attempting to distinguish between scientific prose and poetic discourse."

The differentiation between poetry and prose was consistently valorized—always in favor of poetry—and it often inspired an array of polarities that Ransom would entertain in the course of an essay. I'll cite just one example, an astonishing extended analogy taken from a 1941 essay, "Criticism as Pure Speculation":

> A poem is, so to speak, a democratic state, whereas a prose discourse—mathematical, scientific, ethical, or practical and vernacular—is a totalitarian state. The intention of a democratic state is to perform the work of state as effectively as it can perform it, subject to one reservation of conscience: that it will not despoil its members, the citizens, of the free exercise of their own private and independent characters. But the totalitarian state is interested solely in being effective, and regards the citizens as no citizens at all; that is, regards them as functional members whose existence is totally defined by their allotted contributions to its ends; it has no use for their private characters, and therefore no provision for them.

As we read through Ransom, we can easily construct two columns reminiscent of Norman Mailer's old "Hip vs. Square" or Nancy Mitford's

"U vs. Non-U" types (I realize how these references date me!). At the top of one column put "Poetry," at the other "Prose," and as you read Ransom, the list of opposites begins falling into place nearly at once. If poetry is art, prose is argument; if poetry is iconic, prose is statement. We can keep going: poetry is agrarian, prose industrial; poetry is mythic and traditional, prose scientific and progressive; poetry is religious, prose secular; poetry is concrete, prose abstract; poetry is intuitive, prose logical and rational. This list branches out into all sorts of literary and cultural areas, even to the point that poetry is considered ecologically sensitive and prose environmentally aggressive. Ransom never quite gets around to saying it, but it's also clear that, from his perspective, in the regional scheme of things poetry represents the South, prose the North.

It's not hard to see, then, that in this binary scheme poetry is literature and prose is, well, let's say prose is composition. For if we look closely at Ransom's schematic, we see that the critical dichotomy is not so much between poetry and prose as between poetics and rhetoric, between the aesthetic uses of language and the practical—or, I think it's fair to say—between literature and the essay. Consider again the passage describing poetry as a democracy and prose as a totalitarian regime; Ransom's value-laden analogy makes apparent just what it is about prose that devalues it as an aesthetic experience. Prose discourse is functional, purposeful, and efficient; it surrenders all its elements to expository or persuasive ends. To put it bluntly, prose is rhetorical. And whatever poetry means for Ransom, at its best, it is never rhetorical.

The old conflict between rhetoric and poetics wears many disguises, like the old philosophical debate between the One and the Many. It surfaces in one shape or another just about everywhere we look in modern critical theory and it has had a profound influence on literary and academic politics. As James Berlin once put it: "a number of powerful groups of academic literary critics have divided discourse into two separate and unequal categories: the privileged poetic statement and the impoverished rhetorical statement, the one art and the other 'mere' science." Berlin takes this split even further, discovering behind it an academic conspiracy in which literary critics within English departments seized on the dichotomy as an opportunity to leverage departmental and curricular power. According to Berlin, for these critics to "demonstrate the unique and privileged nature of poetic texts, it has been necessary to insist on a contrasting set of devalorized texts, the kind of texts described in current-traditional rhetoric." What are these discredited texts other than our familiar types of prose discourse—mainly essays?

Although Berlin doesn't reference him, Ransom was one of the early academic critics who consistently fought the older philologists and belletristic instructors—those duffers who gladly taught essays, resisted the New Criticism, and had no stake in carving out imaginative literature as a special domain of discourse. If Berlin is correct, John Crowe Ransom might be seen as part of this literary conspiracy, a very significant part given his enormous academic influence. In his career-long assault on prose he did everything he could to elevate the poetic statement over the rhetorical. "Something," he once wrote, "is continually being killed by prose which the poet wants to preserve."

His college reader, *Topics for Freshman Writing*, it seems to me, was no mere cynical or opportunistic production, but was specifically designed to further Ransom's own critical agenda as well as the pedagogical regimen of the New Criticism. I'm by nature skeptical of conspiracy theories, but by promoting only a serviceable, topical prose, Ransom helped keep the essay in its place for years—that is, inside the first-year composition program and outside of serious literary study. A few years after Ransom's textbook was published, Brooks and Warren would begin theirs with the following words to the instructor: "This book has been conceived on the assumption that if poetry is worth teaching at all it is worth teaching as poetry." Even now it's hard to imagine an introductory textbook on the essay opening with a similar assumption.

On Joan Didion, *Repo Man,* and a '76 Malibu

In "Quiet Days in Malibu," the last essay in Joan Didion's *The White Album* collection, Didion meditates on her family's move to Malibu: the name evokes visions of "the easy life," the kind of clear and hopeful vistas Chevrolet hoped to conjure when they named a car after it in 1964. Coming just after her tumultuous years in Los Angeles during the sixties, the little town north up the PCH promises a redoubt, refuge from everything that man's ruined and failed. But over the seven or so years she lives there, Didion learns, we all learn, that there's no such thing as an easy life. In the present moment, whatever it is, your memories and your lifestyle are always under siege. But at least in Malibu, you've got the hills for defenses.

*

My brother drove a 1976 Chevy Malibu, body colored gold, and most days we traveled with the windows up, the ashtray filling with the Camel Lights he smoked, the car transforming into a smoke-filled bullet. The music was loud and louder. Once my brother drove for two miles on a country road oblivious to the policeman, sirens flailing away, in midspeed pursuit. When my brother noticed the policeman, he pulled over, but he didn't act ashamed or embarrassed, didn't apologize for not pulling over sooner or for the cloud of smoke exhaled by the car like a fog when he rolled down the window; the policeman

47

could fine him or write a ticket. But the state didn't have the power to make a good day bad, to change the power we felt in the music into powerlessness.

*

In Alex Cox's movie *Repo Man,* Emilio Estevez plays a young punker named Otto who runs out of friends when his bestie Duke gets out of prison and steals Otto's girlfriend. Otto wanders dark L.A. streets, a sad sack singing Black Flag songs to himself, till Bud (Harry Dean Stanton) tricks him into repo-ing a car and inducts Otto into the life of the repo man. The A-plot, if a movie as loose as this one has plots, is to hunt down a 1964 Chevy Malibu. The car, we learn, might hold the remains of some aliens crisped in Los Alamos years before, though when we see a photo of the aliens in the trunk, they look a lot like breakfast sausages.

Repo Man was one of the favorites in the Dube household growing up, especially among the boys in the family. It might've been the first VCR tape we owned, and we watched it so many times the picture started to degrade, dust and fuzz creeping in at the edges of the screen, a wobbly line that shook from left to right.

"You like music? . . . Then in that case, you're gonna love this," Lite (Sy Richardson) says to Otto when he pops a tape of nondescript lite R&B into the dashboard tape player of a car they've just repo'd. My brother's car didn't have a working tape deck, but we didn't care. He had a silvered plastic boom box that took a dozen D batteries, and he drove with it on the seat beside him. He had the soundtrack to *Repo Man* on cassette, and that's where I first heard a lot of the famous punk bands: the Circle Jerks, Suicidal Tendencies' "Institutionalized," and others that stay with me now, like the Plugz version of "Secret Agent Man," rerecorded in Spanish as "Hombre Secreto," which maybe made sense in the L.A. setting of the movie but which sounded gloriously otherworldly in Central Massachusetts.

*

The parking lot at the high school my brother drove me to every morning of his senior year, the same year I was a freshman, featured a raised blacktop lip around the perimeter and dipped down into a crater that filled each morning with maybe one hundred cars, my brother's gold '76 Malibu one of them. And because this was in Central Mass, three dozen times that winter the spaces between the cars, the lanes into and out of the lot, the concrete dividers, and small strips of grass filled up with snow. When the Malibu's bald tires couldn't get traction enough to pull us out of the swimming pool of a parking lot, I was the one who had to get out and push, shoulder against the trunk, tires spinning and throwing dirty snow against me, and then, when the car inched forward, scrambling to catch my balance before pushing again.

One snowy day after escaping the parking lot, my brother took us on a detour to the pristine, unplowed parking lot of our church. I was sure the car would get stuck and I'd be the one to push us free, sure that my brother didn't care what he did to me because I was the younger brother, lower in nature than the slave. My brother drove full force into the four inches of wet snow in the lot, then turned the wheel sharp to the left and flooded the engine with gas. The car didn't stall; it spun out with a satisfying slide like the slow motion replay of a high-speed chase on *Starsky and Hutch*. My brother cut the wheel in the other direction, sending the car's lazy backside fishtailing in the other direction. By this point, we were close to the center of the lot, and my brother turned donuts with abandon, spoiling that perfect white field with his corrupting influence. I cranked my window down and whooped along with him.

*

The Chevy Malibu my brother drove, model year 1976, was labeled as gold but the actual body color was less luxurious, whether because it was a decade from the assembly line when he got it or because it was never what was promised, I never knew really. Instead, it was dust colored, a kind of faded gold, a tan with highlights that sparkled in the sun in a way that taunted you for a sucker.

A month ago, I told my brother about writing this essay and I asked him if he had any pictures of that car; he told me he didn't have any pictures from the time before he met Beth, his wife. I asked my mother the same, and she told me she didn't have many pictures from that time, a year when she and my brother yelled at each other daily. It was a deal they made, no pictures to show for it.

*

One of the heroes of Didion's "Quiet Days in Malibu" is a lifeguard with the fishy name Dick Haddock. Haddock's been a lifeguard for twenty-six years, but in Didion's narrative, what happens in the water is more play than work. Water, and what happens in it, is safe and fun; Didion and her lifeguards are tracking fire. Heroic, doomed Haddock is perched on a tower watching the fire advance while Didion watches soot fall into the water, turning it cloudy. Swim all you want, you won't wash off the ash.

Another of Didion's favorites in "Quiet Days in Malibu" is Amado Vazquez, who breeds orchids, mostly for Arthur Freed, who made his money in the movies. Didion admires Vazquez for the recondite quiet of his work, breeding orchids slowly, wasting money at it, holed up in the hills, patient.

*

Being punk rock put you in a weird spot. At least for me, it meant I tried to communicate by my dress and manner that I wasn't like most of the hypocritical assholes and lazy noncombatants I knew. "Ordinary fucking people," Harry Dean Stanton's Bud calls them in *Repo Man,* and I didn't want to be mistaken for one of them. But the people I did admire, the working stiffs at the clothing warehouse, the old black woman on the bus, thought I was too far out to inter-act with at all.

*

"So the salesman says to the farmer, why's that pig got a wooden leg?"

I watched *Repo Man* so many times when I was in high school, I knew every line. I memorized it, even though I couldn't remember the right words to Wordsworth's lonely, cloud-like wander or Lincoln's Gettysburg Address. At my factory job, folding big-and-tall jeans into boxes and putting those boxes away, I found a coworker who knew the movie as well, and we'd spend the afternoon shift going through the movie, line by line. I was sure I'd know that movie forever.

So it's with some regret, some hesitation, that I have to admit I've forgotten most of the movie's dialogue. I watched the movie again to write this essay and surprised myself with scenes I'd forgotten existed (Otto in the grocery store; anything to do with the United Fruitcake Outlet, including Leila and her friend with the metal hand; Otto handed a beating by four strapping brothers who play in a family band), scenes I recited from memory a second after the characters on the screen said the words.

*

There's a car chase in *Repo Man* whose *Mad Max*–style balletics evoke Didion's poetic ruins. Bud and Otto are freestyling in the sluicework viaducts that shadow and capture runoff from L.A.'s ever-present overpasses. It's all paved over, there's no one else around, and you almost feel like the world has ended, until the Rodrigues brothers, driving some amazing drop-top roadster, race alongside them. Both drivers risk death, driving up the steep sides of the viaducts and splashing through rain runoff, and it's all shot in a dusty desert light. It's just the kind of thing Didion imagined would be left after we all burn: concrete, and cars, and water that's not irrigating anything, that's just turned rotten.

At the end of her essay, she tells us that she and the family went back to Malibu for a visit, some months after selling their house. This is always a mistake, a strategy doomed in essay or fiction, fantasy or real life: orchid breeder Vazquez's orchid farm is burned up, a friend of Didion's daughter drowned. Nothing lasts, except concrete, and once you've gone, you'd better not look back. If it doesn't turn you to salt, it'll turn you soft.

*

A car as old as that '76 Malibu, maintained and driven the way my brother did (irregularly and like hell, respectively), was bound to have problems. More than once we waited in a parking lot for my dad to come and jump the dead battery, which seemed incapable of keeping a charge. I learned to change a tire on that car; I don't think my brother ever changed the oil, even though we'd both learned how to from our dad, just a shade less helpless under the hood than either of us. But the most memorable incident involving maintenance was, in the end, the most easily solved.

The road from the high school to home ran along a highway that connected suburb to city. The highway went over a bridge with a water view sufficiently dramatic that several restaurants opened there based on the beauty of the view alone. One spring afternoon, my brother's car died in traffic on the wrong side of that bridge. As other cars honked and threw on blinkers to pass around us, I did what I'd been trained to do: I got out and pushed. I leaned hard into the muddled gold of that trunk. My shadow showed I was there but without even detail to make out anything else: how I felt about it, smiling or resigned, angry or fed-up, puffed up to be strong enough to push a car across a bridge, smiling to be in the middle of another adventure. I leaned into it and pushed. Pushed till we made it to the other side, where my brother steered the car to the shoulder of the road. Then, pocketing the keys with an elegant nonchalance, he ambled out of sight to the nearest gas station, where they'd charge him five bucks as a deposit for a plastic can and a gallon of gas. He left me behind with the car long enough that I got tired of standing beside it and took a seat. Till he got back, he left me there, sitting on the trunk of that car, silhouetted against the sun and just the right color to almost become lost in it.

AISHA SABATINI SLOAN

On Collage, Chris Kraus, and Misremembered Didion

For the last fifteen years, I've misremembered the reason why Joan Didion writes. Mr. Girion had us read her essay "Why I Write" in the eleventh grade, and what resonated most was when she said, "I remember a particular woman in the airport." I always thought that it was the *fact* of the woman at the airport that captivated me. If she had not been there at that time, in that way, in shadow or in a certain kind of light, the book might never have happened.

Earlier in the essay, Didion describes how images fuel her when she works: "When I talk about pictures in my mind I am talking, quite specifically, about images that shimmer around the edges." She says, "You can't think too much about these pictures that shimmer. You just lie low and let them develop. You stay quiet." Because the idea of an image of a woman in the airport reminded me of the moments when I feel compelled to do something artistic—when I'm bored and waiting, idly or actively gazing at people while we wait to board the plane—I latched onto this airport woman as a key to understanding my own way into writing. Over time, this woman took on the air of a creation myth for why I'm attracted to nonfiction in particular. Actual people with actual lives in an actual airport breathing the actual air and perceiving, subconsciously or not, that we share the same space.

Just like the day when my neighbor Kay Parker moved away from our apartment building, and I ran upstairs to a legal pad, flooded with this *thing* that I'd never felt in this particular way, or if I had, that I had not yet connected to the act of writing until that moment. It is the accident of the world as it exists that puzzles and drives me to the page. Like a conversation I had with some writer friends last night about collage. That silk-screened photograph of JFK is on the upper right-hand corner of Rauschenberg's canvas, next to an eagle and above a parachute. The undone feel of the composition, the realness of the image and the roughness of the paint, suggest the ways in which we can't go back. Just like how the house can't be unrobbed. The bike can't be unstruck. And if you want to get political about it, your great-great-grandmother can't be unborn into slavery. Your parents can't uncross the border. Now what.

But in all this time, until rereading the piece today, I forgot this one important detail about Didion's vision of the woman at the airport: the woman wasn't there. The sentence was, in fact, "*I could tell you* that I remember a particular woman in the airport" [emphasis added]. She explains: "I made this woman up, just as I later made up a country to put the airport in, and a family to run the country." After Mr. Girion's class, I went out and bought *A Book of Common Prayer*, the novel Didion wrote while under the influence of this imagined woman in an airport. I navigated the scenes and sentences as one would an interactive exhibition of Didion's brain. For years I was confused about the plot, but I was never confused about the fact that it was fiction. I just had it in my head that there had been a flesh-and-blood moment at the root of that fiction. As it happens, in "On Keeping a Notebook," Didion writes, "I always had trouble distinguishing between what happened and what merely might have happened, but I remain unconvinced that the distinction, for my purposes, matters." And I can't say that the truth or fiction of the woman in the airport matters to me now either, so much as it matters that the idea of "seeing" that woman in a moment of waiting resonated with me, that the image of her shimmered.

On an episode of *Louie*, Louis C.K. gets into a fight with a woman at Ikea when asked if he likes a rug. "It's a rug," he says. "It's *fine*. That's the level of passion that a rug warrants. It's a rug. It doesn't solve all my problems, but it doesn't make me angry. It's a rug. It doesn't smell bad. It's flat, it's blue, it goes on a floor, it's not coated with AIDS, and it's not a portal to another place. It doesn't make me come, but it's fine." This is how the world feels most of the time. In writing, I notice myself trying to pretend that this is not the case. I feel pressure to be consistently fascinated, or to make my thoughts appear this way on the page. But if it were not the case that things are mostly boring, why would it matter that some things, sometimes, shimmer?

Recently, a friend lent me the essay collection *Video Green*. In it, Chris Kraus starts off with a long, segmented piece entitled "Art Collection." There are some very important sections about the L.A. art scene, about the way the art world has been held hostage by MFA programs. These are at once theoretical and critical of what theory can do to art. Then she talks about a very nice real estate lawyer in L.A. and a man who crossed the border from Mexico and opened a gallery. She talks about moving to Hudson Falls, New York, where a poet and art collector named William Bronk lived. His poems are, she writes, "intellectually elegant, annealed and raw . . . tiny arguments for the power of intangibility, mounted with a gravelly kind of pragmatism." Also, she tells us about an S/M affair that she began online with a man named Martin.

Again, I'm brought back to the boredom of Didion's airport. Or the boredom of waiting in the car while running errands with my father, which is how I first discovered magazines like *Granta*, stuffed into a bag with a newspaper or tossed onto the floor of the backseat. Kraus writes for a while about something that bores or bothers her. Then she talks in a slightly less academic voice about something she admires. And then she leads us, with little warning, to a moment of actual, physical excitement. All the while describing a man who, quietly and alone, enjoyed art in his room. This shift in subject matter can't help but make the earlier sections seem dry, and the unceremonious turn is executed with a kind of cockiness that I appreciate. "What?" She seems to be saying. "I'm just telling you a story."

I like how Didion admits to daydreaming when she should have been paying attention. In "Why I Write," she describes how it was difficult for her to finish her degree because she let her mind flit toward random images instead of the lecture on Milton. "In short my attention was always on the periphery, on what I could see and taste and touch, on the butter, and the Greyhound bus." Maybe what I am trying to say is that I like essays that remind me of traveling. They lie low. They don't try quite so hard to prevent me from being bored. They are confident enough to admit that they are nothing more than a rug, and in doing so, have the ability to take it out from under me.

T CLUTCH FLEISCHMANN

Looking for Samuel Delany

The summer of 2015 I go looking for Samuel Delany most evenings with Jackson. He and I have fallen in love and, further, fallen in love a bit with who we are in this moment in New York City and together. I have spent a fair amount of time in the city and have a sense of the queer contours of its architecture. As Jackson has spent less time here, it is up to me to try to guide us a bit, to point us toward the Vale of Cashmere in Prospect Park and the cheap sex shops of the Village. We are looking both for the public places in which men had sex for decades and for the men themselves. When we show up and the men are inevitably not there, it is somewhat like the place is not there, either. Even when we decide to fuck anyway, railing against a fallen tree in the park as joggers catch the cool before the sunrise, the place still seems to not be there, in the place where it is. To perform the *was* of a place does not make that *was* an *is*.

The place we most want to find, and the place that is the least there, is the kind of Manhattan porn theater described so beautifully in Delany's *Times Square Red, Times Square Blue.* The theaters were forced out by the Disneyfication of Manhattan, blow jobs not being tourist friendly although tourists surely love blow jobs. Delany frequented the theaters for years, all well before Jackson or I ever entered New York. Now, our friends tell us no, there are no theaters left. But we keep asking anyway, keep going into Manhattan and looking, because this is not an answer that makes sense to us. We have not yet let that past we didn't have go.

I'm interested in the difference between the thinking of Jackson and I, wandering Manhattan and looking for a place to fuck/be in our trans bodies together, and the thinking of Samuel Delany, eulogizing those theaters he occupied by thinking through their beauty. Thinking as wandering, thinking as failing, thinking as memory, thinking as a new thought that comes out of it all. All of our thinkings, I think, are essays.

Times Square Red, Times Square Blue performs two core functions through its two sections. In the first section, Delany, as a regular in these low-cost establishments, chronicles his countless sexual encounters with other men, most taking place within the establishments, but some transitioning outside, perhaps to a home. In a narrative that is both charming and unsentimental, he focuses on a number of men he recalls in extended detail, while peppering the account with the suggestion of anonymous, perpetual hookups. When this concludes, the remainder of the text draws on that narrative in order to develop a theory of what was gained socially by those theaters (and, likewise, what was lost when forces like sex-phobia, classism, and white supremacy forced them out of Manhattan). In this overtly academically minded section, Delany builds a theory from the ideas of social contact ("a fundamentally urban phenomenon" in which people help one another and rely on one another through their daily interactions in the public sphere) and social networking (a "professional and motive-driven" form of interaction that, by its capitalist nature, cannot provide many of the benefits of contact), praising the porn theaters precisely because of the rare opportunity for cross-class contact they provided, and looking to writing conferences to demonstrate the failings of networking.

There are clear differences between Delany's relation to the theaters and the relation Jackson and I have, or imagine to have, with them. There is the difference of actually having been there. There is the difference of Delany, a cis gay man who is supposed to be there (as are cis straight men), and Jackson and I, two transgender people who are maybe not supposed to be there, or perhaps more accurately, whose existence the place did not realize, although certainly people like us went often. There is the difference of watching the entwined realities of AIDS and gentrification take these sexual-social hubs away and the experience of coming after the fact of their absence, yet with our own identities shaped by stories of thrown ashes and docks. There is the difference of sitting on the carpet-like fabric of a chair in a theater and of having to imagine that the fabric of a chair in a theater might have been carpet-like. There is the difference of Scruff, the difference of every sex act being unique to its moment, the difference of entering a space as one and of failing to find a space as two. These differences matter when thinking of Delany's first, narrative section and of our own searching, which makes me wonder how they carry over into the second part, the philosophy of contact, of bodies meeting, of what is possible.

In the first section of the book, Delany writes

> Furthest down the block from the Capri, the Venus was generally a little too scroungy even for me. The drug activity there was often so high as to obliterate the sex activity. Still, on and off through the years, it provided me with a couple of memorable regulars. Gary was one, a handyman who worked at a Catholic church on Tenth Avenue. A lanky, affable guy with a brown ponytail, he impressed me as someone with very fixed habits who, as long as he was within them, was comfortable. And he always seemed comfortable in the theater. I first met him up at the Hollywood when he was about thirty-seven, but their patrolling and monitoring turned him off, so he moved down to the Venus. Regularly he brought in his two forty-two-ounce bottles of beer, generally to sit in the last three or four rows of the orchestra on the right as you came in, settling back to wait for one of three older guys to service him, me among them. He had a regular girlfriend, he claimed, who'd introduced him to the pleasures of getting things shoved up his behind when he had sex, but her overall sexual appetites simply weren't as

high as his. That's why he came to the movies. He liked two or three fingers thrust deep up his asshole while you sucked his rather thick, cut seven inches, but he was a little reticent about explaining this to new guys. So he pretty much stuck to the three of us.

Jackson and I at one point do find a sex shop back room with individual video booths and believe that here might be the closest analogue to what we are looking for. He grabs my hands and pulls me into a booth. It is too small for two people to sit in comfortably together, and Jackson never wears underwear, so he quickly spreads his legs just that slight bit and I start to work my way up inside his track shorts and into the front of him. "I wonder who all has fucked here before, and if we would have known them," I ask, and then, not even yet started in earnest, an employee pulls open the booth and tells us that we have to leave. "One at a time," he says, and I think of both things at once, the question that I ask and the rules that we did not know we were breaking.

In the more critical, academic conclusion of the book, Delany writes

As are the space of the unconscious and the space of discourse, the space where the class war occurs as such is, in its pure form, imaginary—imaginary *not* in the Lacanian sense but rather in the mathematical sense. (In the Lacanian sense, those spaces are specifically Symbolic.) Imaginary numbers—those involved with *i*, the square root of minus-one—do not exist. But they have measurable and demonstrable effects on the real (i.e. political) materiality of science and technology. Similarly, the structures, conflicts, and displacements that occur in the unconscious, the class war, and the space of discourse are simply too useful to ignore in explaining what goes on in the world we live in, unto two men yelling in the hall, one a landlord and one a tenant, if not mayhem out on the streets themselves, or the visible changes in a neighborhood, like Times Square or, indeed, the Upper West Side, over a decade or so, and the specificities of rhetorical shift.

The same subject, glanced at from multiple angles at once, reveals the dependency of all angles on one another for understanding it at all. Of course, how could it be any other way? Delany went to the porn theaters in Manhattan countless times, and there he gave nameless strangers blow jobs, and there he cared for other humans and was cared for by them, and there social categories existed in modes in which they do not otherwise exist, and to understand how lovely and important that all is, you need to think about it in a few different ways. You need to read more than one essay at once, in the same essay. Which is what Delany is generous enough to let us as readers do, refusing to sensationalize or censor, insisting at once on the winsome details and their broad implications. The porn theaters were there, they allowed a particular, liberatory world to exist, and now that world is gone. How many angles can I glance this from?

With nowhere to go but parks, where we are lone creeps among a crowd, the question of my thinking reveals a new dimension, that *Where is Samuel Delany today?* might be answered by *home*, by *in love*, by *alone*, by *reading*. "I think we both thought we'd have a lot more sex," Jackson says while we are lying in the bed we share.

In her book *Time Binds. Queer Temporalities, Queer Histories,* Elizabeth Freeman talks about the visceral pleasure we can achieve when we engage with history-telling and the past queerly. Queer people, she claims, have "risked experimentation with our bodies and those of others, with affiliation, and with new practices of hoping, demanding, and otherwise making claims on the future, and this has entailed an enormous commitment to the pleasure and power of figuration." Because trans time is complicated: sometimes it seems like the thing we know might be ending, and that we will never get to know what has already been lost, and sometimes that is heartbreaking, and sometimes it might be the only option for renewal, but either way, there's a fast-coming future with so many bits of the past in it. The future comes fast whether we are networking and thinking only of ourselves or seeking contact and caring for others. The future is imaginary like an imaginary number, and essays care as much about what they imagine as about what they think they know.

The last afternoon we go looking, Jackson and I are hand in hand all day and in love. Kicked out of multiple back rooms, poppers in pocket, we are finally given directions by a well-meaning man that lead, through drizzle, only to Broadway's tourism. We're soaking and of course there's no theater here; we always knew there was no theater left. If this is the present we're at, *Times Square Red, Times Square Blue* is the future and past that we need. It avoids accepted modes of analysis, of narrative, and of essaying. Instead, it honors the losses of our past to suggest tools for a better future. It declares the interrelatedness of our intellect and our body, our narratives and our theories, by telling them together. It makes sense that a science fiction writer, invested in the union of fact and fantasy, would pull this off, just as it makes sense that the temporal and routine act of giving some dude a blow job will, in the mind of the right thinker, become an indelible moment of insight, inspiring us to seek renewal once more. What is the new thought born from this thinking, the essay where Jackson and I look for a place to fuck? It is like with all essays, not an answer or an arrival, but rather a question newly informed by an imagined future that has shifted. Samuel Delany today is not where he was yesterday, as none of us are, neither Jackson nor I nor you. We're instead in that place informed by past and future, looking for a theater we know to be gone in hopes that searching might allow us to ask a question again.

RIGOBERTO GONZÁLEZ

Observations about Writing Memoir in My Twenties, Thirties, and Forties

Attending a graduate writing program in California in the early 1990s, there were only two specializations to choose from: fiction or poetry. The third, nonfiction, was looked upon with suspicion. A heated debate was taking place in influential journals like *Poets & Writers* about what this burgeoning field really was—journalism? reportage? essay writing?—and what its proximity to truth should be: only verifiable facts? the truth, the whole truth, and nothing but the truth? Memory, it seemed, was considered such an unreliable resource because it was flawed and subjective. Despite this, the genre did flourish and expanded to include the personal or exploratory essay, autobiography, and memoir; what linked the word *creative* to *nonfiction* was giving writers permission to access the self as a source. Certainly there were many reasons to write about one's past: to recover, to remember, to examine anew, to understand, to revisit, to reconnect. And by sharing those discoveries, the hope was not simply to highlight one's personal journey but to tell a good story, and one that would resonate with the reader because of the immediate intimacy in the storytelling when the writer announces from the get-go: *This is what happened to me.* But in creative nonfiction, the act of reading also triggers the act of empathy, and possibly the act of identification, so that no matter how individual the experience, something is shared and learned about human emotion, human curiosity, human folly, and human growth. What a noble purpose this third genre! However, another prejudice was taking root: who had the right to do this mining of the memory banks to construct a narrative for others to read and consider?

In 1992, I was a twenty-two-year-old. I was specializing in poetry writing at the time, and my autobiographical material was in service to my verse. That year my family decided to return to Mexico, a decision that was announced as temporary but which eventually became permanent. Not returning with them because I was enrolled in graduate school was a difficult choice. And though it was they who were leaving me, and the U.S., it felt as if it were I who was abandoning them, and Mexico. The guilt began to settle, but also the reality of my other losses: the unexpected phone calls, the occasional care package in the mail, the visits home for the holidays, the home-cooked meals, the music, the voices, the crowded little rooms with the big TVs. All of it was irretrievably gone. If I had turned to poetry to write a love letter to my Mexican heritage and homeland, I wanted to turn to prose to write a love letter to my family—one that would capture the multiple dimensions of the stories, the conflicts, and the scars, because that's how I understood them.

In our cohort at the writing program there was a young woman, just a few years older than me, who was writing memoir. Her name was Margaret. She was bubbly and kind, and was writing about her misadventures with a traveling theater group as an undergraduate. I remember how *unkind* many of the other students were, offering unsolicited criticisms that I would hear echoed for many years to come about anyone who dared write memoir at such a young age: how presumptuous, how self-aggrandizing, how vain. Memoir, or autobiography, was considered the territory of the seasoned, the experienced, the industrious, the accomplished: certainly, a graduate student didn't fall into any of these categories.

There were no classes being offered in creative nonfiction, and I would never take one, even though, many years later, I would end up teaching that genre (and giving lectures about it!). So I became a closeted creative nonfiction writer. When I sought out models for learning how to write the personal narrative, the fact that I came across so many veteran writers only confirmed that this was a genre in which the very green writer was not welcomed. I didn't reveal to anyone that I was writing memoir, that I was reconstructing my various journeys: coming to America, coming out, and coming to education. I believe at one time I justified this clandestine writing activity by saying to myself that it was quite possible I might get killed walking across the street one day, so I had to leave a record behind that told people who I was.

By 1997, I had attended another creative writing program in Arizona, this time specializing in fiction. I had written a thesis in prose—a novel about the grape pickers of Southern California titled *Crossing Vines*. Though I had used my firsthand knowledge of the labor, all of the characters were mostly made up. The book might have turned out differently had I not been secretly writing about my family already. Somehow I didn't want these narratives to overlap, not because I ever intended to publish my memoirs, but because the nonfiction was too strange and at times too heavy-handed to pass for fiction. Therefore, I was very public about this novel I had completed, and very private about the ten or so personal essays I had written. But also by 1997, I began to notice that the creative writing bulletin boards that announced fiction and poetry contests and calls for submissions had become aggressive in seeking out nonfiction memoir. This gave me the courage to come out to one of my most trusted older friends. I told her I was writing memoir, a revelation I soon regretted.

Her response: "Memoir? What does a twenty-seven-year-old have to say about the world? You've hardly even lived!"

I might have become paralyzed had I not understood what I had written, and why I knew I was on the right track. I acknowledged that mine was not an unusual experience, but to have someone like me have the capacity and skill to write it down was unusual. I understood that my life journey was important enough to commit to print and that even if my reader wasn't a gay Mexican kid from a farm-working community, he would at the very least learn that such a person existed. And I also knew that writing about my experience as a young man was not prematurely announcing that it was the most important stage in my life but certainly the most formative—wasn't that why the young protagonist was such an important one in literature at large? Weren't we always turning to the adolescent years, not our birth years, to locate our beginnings? I trusted my impulse to keep writing, a choice that was validated by another, better friend who said to me after I had confessed to him how hurt I was by the negative response to my coming out as a memoirist, "Well thank God no one told Anne Frank that. She was only fourteen."

*

In the new millennium, creative nonfiction as a third genre was solidly taking its place between poetry and fiction. Personal essay anthologies and book-length memoirs were becoming increasingly popular, and the field had expanded to include the lyrical essay and microprose or flash nonfiction. University presses were taking notice, establishing series that specialized in creative nonfiction, like Living Out: Gay and Lesbian Autobiographies at the University of Wisconsin Press, which is where I thought my book would eventually find a home. It turns out that the press was on the verge of starting a whole new series, Writing in Latinidad: Autobiographical Voices of u.s. Latinas/os, and the editors wanted mine to be part of that new venture, but they wanted a book-length narrative, not a collection of personal essays.

I wasn't surprised by this criterion because that's what I had been pulling from the bookshelves all this time, so I set out to weave those ten essays into a single book. When I accessed memoirs at this time, I realized that linearity was not a mandate for structuring a book. Linearity seemed to be reserved for biography—a from-the-womb-to-the-tomb time line. Memoir was a journey, a stage in the life of the writer. To give myself parameters, I decided that the book would end just after I became a sophomore in college. I chose that moment because it was a year of reckoning for me—it was the year I was involved in an abusive same-sex relationship, the year I tried to patch things up with my father as a way to seek guidance and solace, the year I realized I would have to continue on my path by myself, making stupid mistakes but, somehow, transcending them. It was also important that there was a decade sitting between the writer I was at the age of thirty and the child I was at the age of nineteen. But most importantly, I wanted the book to be about my relationship to my father.

This last consideration surprised me. Since I had lost my mother when I was twelve, I thought that my memoir was going to be about her—my way of keeping her memory alive. And although she is a key figure in *Butterfly Boy: Memories of a Chicano Mariposa,* the person whom I was still trying to come to terms with was my father. Though my mother was dead, my father was the ghost—it was his absence that still haunted me. This conflict helped me rescue the essays from the sentimentality of nostalgia, from the low emotion in anecdote, and from the frivolousness of crowd-pleasing storytelling. I completed the book in 2005, at the age of thirty-five, and as I traveled across the country in 2006 to promote the book, one of the questions that members of the audience kept asking was: are you going to write a sequel?

I had mixed feelings about writing another memoir: firstly, in my twenties I spent most of the time in college, sitting down at the desk and reading on the couch. Not exactly the stuff of drama. But the more I read from my own book, the more I realized how much I had left out because it didn't fit the main threads, because I hadn't remembered those episodes when I was writing the first book, or because I simply hadn't digested the memory enough to identify its significance. But what really got me thinking I had to write *Red-Inked Retablos,* an antidote to *Butterfly Boy,* was the death of my father, five days before *Butterfly Boy* was released.

A shocking realization: as a writer, thinking about someone who is still alive is a strikingly different experience than thinking about that same person who is now deceased. I was not a writer when my mother was living, so I didn't know that shift in perspective. But now that my father was gone, my artist temperament was coloring memory with another palette altogether. Was it a tinge of guilt, sympathy, grief, regret, emptiness? All of those.

A man once said to me that he knew I had lost one of my parents because there was a light that had gone out in my eyes. I wondered what my eyes betrayed about my double loss, my double sorrow now? Was my stare complete darkness?

Not only did I see my father differently, I saw myself differently, and therefore I wrote about myself differently also, even if I visited that same era I wrote about in *Butterfly Boy*.

*

The thing about loss is that you carry it with you for the rest of your life. It's a strange contradictory image—an emptiness that bears weight. So loss was the theme in *Red-Inked Retablos*, my second book of nonfiction. I not only wrote about my birth parents, I wrote about my literary parents—Truman Capote, the poet Ai, Gloria Anzaldúa, and Michael Nava—writers I had invited to step in as guides when I left home. And surprisingly, I positioned myself as a kind of parent, or rather a mentor, when I encouraged younger writers to take up the cause of autobiographical writing, and when I wrote about two young writers who had passed away before their prime, celebrating their work, keeping its memory sacred.

At about this time, nearing my forties, two interesting developments were taking place. The first was my awareness of long-term memory. I couldn't remember what the devil I was doing the week before, but suddenly I recalled with astonishing clarity the smallest of details about meals, conversations, and encounters that took place when I was a child. One of the challenges about being a writer of nonfiction is the reader's suspicion of embellishment, the distrust in the writer being able to accurately recollect dialogue and to recount events located in the specific hours of the day or night—how do we remember the choreography of bodies and gestures, reconfigure the architecture of a neighborhood so long ago, in a different country even?

The nonfiction writer will answer these doubts with the nonfiction motto: what I write is not how it happened, it's how I remember it. And misremembering is another way of remembering. In any case, the floodgates opened and it all came back to me, including the traumatic part of my childhood that I had deliberately left unexamined because I was not ready to confront it: experiencing hunger, eating disorders, unfulfilled desire.

Secondly, I discovered that the beauty of aging was that I was now able to come face to face with that single demon I could not confront before. Was I stronger? Yes. Was I more confident? Yes. But these traits could not have been fortified without the psychic distance of time. Two decades separated and connected the hungry me and the well-fed me. This allowed me not to forget, even if I had been suppressing the memory, and it allowed the trauma not to consume me because, look, its famished stomachs were so far away from me now.

This didn't make the process of writing about hunger any less painful. I was surprised at how many times the tears and heartache caught me off guard and forced me to stop. I tried to read some excerpts on the phone to friends, and I would break down. But I kept at it, knowing that soon I'd be able to unearth the entirety of the experience without feeling as if I had been purging emotionally. After all, I had gone through this before when I had written about grief and loss.

One of my pet peeves is when memoirists are accused of confusing writing with therapy. I believe that poets are much more sympathetic to this indictment, particularly those whose speaker in a poem is the first person "I." But so too I'd like to plead with memoirists not to deny that there is a level of healing taking place in the shaping of narrative—it is not the only purpose of writing, but it is most definitely one of the outcomes. Writing about trauma doesn't solve, doesn't answer, and sometimes doesn't close—it sifts through the rubble and tries to communicate what happened there. Whatever is put back together is, ideally, outside of the body and the soul, but inside the imagination. It is a map of a place we no longer inhabit, but which still inhabits us.

As a way of confronting my experience with hunger, I expanded the narrative to include other types of hunger—some literal, some metaphorical. I made that narrative reach back to my childhood, but I also asked it to reach forward to my adult years. And most strategically, I contained the episodes in small, bite-sized pieces that were no longer than three hundred words. This limitation was actually freeing because no matter how deeply painful and emotionally draining the writing, I knew there was a finish line to the stumble down memory lane. I called this book *Autobiography of My Hungers.*

*

This summer I turned forty-four years old, and I'm already thinking about the next book of nonfiction, another memoir in which my father is again a central figure. I wrote my first book to argue with him, I wrote the second to honor him, I wrote the third to reveal my most private moments to him, and I believe the next is to forgive—myself. No, I don't think I can say that I forgive him because there's nothing to forgive. My father made mistakes and bad choices, and it took me a lifetime of doing the same to understand that this wasn't deliberate or malicious but human. Yes, this disposition is called maturity. Forgiving myself means revisiting those exchanges and seeing my father, a grown man, through the eyes of a grown man. This ability, however, would not have been possible had I not written about my father through the eyes of a younger, less seasoned, more uncertain man.

I am also, in my forties, seized by an insatiable nostalgia. It's been thirty years since I left Mexico, my family's homeland, though all this time I have been going back through the writing. Doing so at this time of my life is also a way of making peace with the reality that when I decide to return, I will find a very different country there. My memories are my Mexico. And though I have returned to visit over the years, I have explored parts of the country I did not know growing up. What I long for are those places that hold memory for me—the broken sidewalks, the stone fences, the chicken coop in the back where my job was to collect the eggs each morning. I want to go back because these are the places I am most distant from and yet, thanks to long-term memory, I recall with most clarity. Perhaps this is the homecoming I've always heard the old people in my family talk about when they sat in the garden and didn't know I was sitting within earshot. How they collected things when they spoke, how they invoked people and places—a catalog of dates, names, events—all the incredible evidence of a life lived and remembered. How small my world seemed then, and yet how promising that the best was yet to come. Well, now I'm not sitting outside the circle anymore but have earned my place inside of it—not because of my age, but because, sadly, everyone older than me has died. At the ripe age of forty-four, I find myself in the uneasy role of an elder, a storyteller—not of the "I," but of the "us." The task of keeping family, life, and love is now mine. And it's exactly the paradise I imagined.

*

The name of the town at the northeast shore of Lake Pátzcuaro is pure onomatopoeia. Say it—Tzin-tzun-tzán—and hear the hummingbird zip by with each syllable. These elusive little birds are so fast they're invisible and can never be caged. In fact, the only way the people of Tzintzuntzán can attempt to capture a hummingbird is to carve one out of wood or to sculpt one in iron. The only way for visitors to own one is to buy one. I brought two of them with me that hang from the kitchen doorway of my NYC apartment. As soon as I put them up, I realized how ridiculous this illusion was since the wings were frozen midflight and the bodies dangled from fishing lines, because what I "caught" was nothing less than decorated dead weight. These are memorials to the fleeting hummingbird, a wondrous feathered creature whose population has been dwindling over the years. I saw hundreds of memorials in Tzintzuntzán but not a single living example of what all that artistry honors. Still, it is difficult to challenge the town's name—it is the place of the hummingbirds. They are everywhere: on furniture, on pottery, and stitched near the hems of pretty little dresses. And each time I say the town's name—Tzintzuntzán—the hummingbird becomes audible, a ghost sound emanating from the colorful depictions.

Purépecha territory is the land that inspires stubborn memory. "Ya no es como antes," is the phrase that pops out of old and young alike. "It's not like before." And so people try to reconstruct that before in order to pin their good memories there. I often heard my grandparents mourn for the before when they sat in the living room of our California home and reminisced about that state of Michoacán in general, about the towns of Zacapu or Nahuatzen in particular. What they didn't want to admit was that the land had an after without them, that they held on to the before because they now saw those beloved places from afar, like exiles. And when they visited the after, they did so as strangers to the streets they no longer recognized and to the people who no longer remembered them.

*

Do you remember . . . ? my father liked to ask, quite unexpectedly, usually breaking the silence in the room or in the car. *Do you remember your mother? Do you remember Zacapu? Do you remember that time we went to Disneyland?* These were not meant to start a conversation; they were more like musings. Lost in the geographies of his daydream, he would suddenly realize I was nearby, and so I became his temporary anchor to the waking world. I would answer with a simple yes, and then he'd drift into thought again. Except that on this second journey he would take me with him, because indeed I did remember, and so I followed him through the now-lighted corridors of memory.

KATHERINE E. STANDEFER

On the Mysterious Leslie Ryan and the Structure of a Trauma Narrative

You have not heard of Leslie Ryan. Because you have not heard of her, I would like to hand you a book of her razor-sharp prose: maybe a prickly memoir, maybe a collection of essays reeking of creosote and mud.

But you have not heard of her for a reason. It is this: as far as I can tell, there is only one published essay by Leslie Ryan. So you must lean very close. Listen very carefully. The essay is called "The Other Side of Fire." To find it, dig up an anthology published in 2001—*Circle of Women: An Anthology of Contemporary Western Women Writers,* edited by Kim Barnes and Mary Clearman Blew—or perhaps get a photocopy from a friend who read it once years ago, in college. It is the kind of essay people remember from college, but it will mean something else now. After all, the body changes—and so, too, how we draw our power. This essay is about both.

So many essays have been written about terrible things: rape, abuse, teeth-grinding poverty, drugs, abandoned children. These stories climb up the spine, demanding telling; and yet there comes a point when we, as readers, reach saturation. It is possible to become so deadened by a story that one cannot climb back out of the darkness. Here lives Ryan's brilliance: without flinching, she both tells us these stories and spares us. "The Other Side of Fire" includes every one of the experiences listed above, and yet it is structured to offer a ladder back out.

Here is how the essay does not begin: "When I was twelve, my younger brothers and I were abandoned for over a year in an apartment on the southside of Richmond, Virginia."

If the essay were to begin there, we might, as readers, believe that this is the *point:* that this *thing* happened. "The Other Side of Fire," though, is not about the fact of the happening. It is about something bigger—where our power comes from. So Ryan starts big. In her opening, she writes, "For most women the body, like the story, is not a simple thing. It's a battlefield where lies and truths about power go at it." It's such an authoritative opening that we know she will have to back it up—and that's her next move, transitioning us into story.

She takes us into the south Idaho desert, where she once worked as a wilderness therapy guide for troubled youth. "The idea was that direct contact with the natural world could help students gain a more healthy sense of identity and empowerment," she writes. She describes the tattooed teenagers, "[wearing] the tales of their crimes like dogtags," even though "beneath it they seemed to writhe like grubs set down in unfamiliar terrain."

It isn't until page three, then—when we're already thinking about the teens' power and survival—that Ryan descends us into her own experience: "When I was twelve, my younger brothers and I were abandoned for over a year in an apartment on the southside of Richmond, Virginia." By now, the framing lets us know we are dipping into Ryan's own experiences for a specific reason. Though the story is told in such tight, exquisite prose that we might *want* to stay there, we do not. We learn how Ryan used her body to survive—we see her father's *Playboys* beneath the mattress, Ryan examining her curves in the bathroom mirror and whispering *You have one thing,* the drug dealer beating her—and we get out. We go back to the desert. We see Ryan's own process reflected in the experience of one of her students, Dawn.

Each one of these stories says something additive about power and the body, until suddenly—after all this framing—the essay becomes an orchestra, its different levels and themes sputtering with sound and meaning, the prose sharpening under cold and basalt:

> Dawn wasn't moving; she was fenced into one of those partial truths that quickly become lies. The pornographic therapist told her to separate her mind and body and

peddle the body part; her role as a victim told her that power lay as much in being scarred as in scarring. Both lies make battlefields of women's bodies: they require that we keep hurting our bodies somehow, because our power and our identities depend on it. But these lies are based on an incomplete assumption: that strength lies only in our having power *over* ourselves or others.

Thus, the *structure* of the essay builds one of its primary points: while victimhood is a kind of power, it is one to be *moved through.* It is not the end point. The apartment in Richmond is important, but not more important than the desert, where Ryan discovered that

> a mind that wanders far from the body can land a person in strange territories, far from water or cover. If I stopped listening to my body and to my lived experience at any time, I might become lost. I found myself realizing that power does come from my body, after all, but in a very different way.

Whenever I finish reading "The Other Side of Fire," I find myself lit with an understanding about trauma: A thing never happens once. A thing happens all the time, is still happening right this instant—to us or to other people. And the thing turns into other things, transmutes, burns up, reappears. Ryan's life is her students' lives, and in ways it is my life too, all of us complicit, and the structure of an essay can take this into account, widening its considerations through framing and pacing. As a writer, the essay challenges me not to allow the trauma narrative its weak single arc, but to hitch it up to something bigger—to move through it. To go into the darkness, yes, but to build a staircase back out as well.

Now that you have heard of Leslie Ryan, you should read her: the one essay, ropey with calluses, lacy garter belts, pale spiderwebs of scars, bright serviceberries and sage. See what your body says about it. And if you find her, tell her I want a book.

JULIE LAUTERBACH-COLBY

On Arianne Zwartjes's
"This Suturing of Wounds or Words" and
Kisha Lewellyn Schlegel's "Cannulated Screw"

My sister called to say she'd wanted to ask me a question about our childhood but then forgot. When she called back in the morning, it was to tell me she'd remembered and had written the memory down, call her when I could.

The memory turned out to be a recurring dream she has, usually after she encounters a person on the street who resembles our father. Our father, who died when I was thirteen.

In her dream it's as if he's alive again; that whole death thing, it was actually just a cover. He's off somewhere in a new life. The most recent story she'd told herself: he's picking grapes in Napa.

I tell her I have a similar thought, every once in a while. Because I think, to a certain extent, it's easier to deal with grief when that grief has the possibility of temporality. *If I could only see him again, then I'd be able to say my last words and be done with it.*

The trouble with grief (read: pain), I think, is that so often what's aching on the inside manifests itself on the outside. This can be a problem when you're *just trying to deal with it,* and it can make for some awkward transitions in conversation. *So . . . how's it feel to have one dead parent?* (True story there.)

But the trouble with grief is also what draws me to it. When I read works about pain, I relate them to my own. And I'm reminded that if religion and politics are topics we are trained from youth to avoid with others, talking about our pain with company has become second nature. What ails you? How do you suffer in this life? If you are able to get to the heart of the matter, will you know why you are in pain?

I am thinking of my grandparents this summer. Of their aging and, with the years, their increased levels of pain. They suffer, each in their unique way, which only they can explain: the story is theirs to tell; no one else has the right to it. I, and the rest of my family, am held still in their telling. We sit around the campfire, nod our heads, and think of our own discomfort during that moment: the way our sit bones have dug their way into the tree log underneath us; the stiffness in our necks and backs; the itchy, burning heat from the fire against our bare shins.

When my friend Ari's grandfather died, she wrote an essay on how the body physically heals from a wound. How the layers of skin and muscle and fiber stitch themselves back together. But how that *togetherness* comes with a caveat: a scar in the healing's wake. Throughout the essay, Ari takes us into the body's layers. Through the collagen microfibril helices that weave the skin into place. And in the same breath, she points out that as we age, the collagen that has, up until that point, kept our skin soft and elastic, begins to disappear, leaving us hard, brittle, and yes, fragile: more susceptible to pain.

Physical cuts, lacerations

> may be clean and linear if they are caused by a knife, glass shard, or other sharp object. They may be caused by slicing at an angle, separating an entire flap of skin like a peninsula. Crushing injuries, caused by a direct blow or impact, may cause a stellate laceration, irregular in its course. If deep enough, a laceration may reveal underlying tissues: fat, muscle, tendon, or bone.

Different kinds of wounds require different kinds of attention. The pattern/tracing of one's pain creates a varying threshold of meaning, a different narrative for how one might begin to think about the healing process.

Which takes us to Kisha Lewellyn Schlegel's "Cannulated Screw," where we find a different story of pain, a different approach to what gets left behind in the wake of trauma. In the opening lines we read that the author's in bed; she's having two screws removed from her foot. The screws, the nurse tells her, "might break. They could crack and split, cleaving shrapnel to bone. Pieces could get left behind."

In the stories of pain I've read, it is precisely this crack and split that draws me in: I am interested, after having to pick up my own pieces, to learn how others try to rebuild their narrative. (Or seek out a new one entirely.) I'm interested, not so much in the cause of pain itself, but how others choose to live with or beyond it.

Back to Ari's essay, and fracture: "Deep wounds sometimes accompany underlying bone fracture; it's even possible for the broken bone to *cause* the laceration to the skin, sharp, splintered ends jutting through what was intact."

Because the rub is, there's no getting around the physical splintering into the nonphysical. Through what *was* intact, and no longer is: that's where the narratives begin to overlap.

And Kisha: "To remove [the screws], the osteopath cut along the scar of the old suture, made by a careless doctor who cut out a painful tailors bunion and broke the bone of the pinkie toe to straighten its crooked deformity, screwing the healing in place."

What our stories of pain amount to is one big ball of collective hurt. But this individual narrative of pain begins to speak with others'. While our stories of pain are our own, they grant space for this common narrative. They provide an entry point for our day-to-day dealings with others. I've been thinking a lot about these points of entry lately, and it seems to me that if nothing else, pain opens us up, in the very physical sense of the word, but pain also gives us a chance to be open on other levels as well.

In Ari's case, she opens up to a world of hurt all around her, flashes of familial scenes mixed in with those she's experienced in the field as an EMT. In Kisha's essay, the time of healing ("screwing the healing in place") becomes a mathematical equation parallel to the emotional healing of her father dying when she was a child.

Whatever our narrative, be it recurring dreams of isolation, empathy of aging parents/grandparents, real-life loss, our narrative allows us some clarity, a space in which to fight against the compassion fatigue which occurs within such a fragmented world. (To paraphrase Ari's words.)

Today marks the second week of Advent. If we were to consider— which I will—the point of the biblical story in which we now find our- selves, the wise men have left the court of King Herod. Herod, having received word of the mysterious child's birth, has ordered an infanti- cide of male children throughout the land. There is pain everywhere. There are swords passing through women's bellies. And Herod's whole body is wrecked with pain—and fear. That is the common story shared throughout the kingdom. Mothers-to-be are talking in low voices: Did you hear, did you hear what is happening? How I suffer. How we all suffer. And so on, until the narrative swirls and mixes with our own, today: Syria, New York, Libya, North Korea, Nogales, the world over. How we all suffer. Perhaps the hope is in how we are all driven together because of that pain. We notice, and by noticing, we begin to heal.

Living within the Ellipses

On Ilan Stavans's *On Borrowed Words: A Memoir of Language*

*In Mexico, I was, am, and always will be a welcome guest in a
rented house, one I can never fully own.*

—ILAN STAVANS, *ON BORROWED WORDS*

For years, Ilan Stavans has challenged my notion of what defines a
Mexican. When I was an undergraduate studying rhetoric, I stumbled
upon his cultural commentaries. I remember his name to me had nothing to do with someone from Mexico; instead his name simply evoked
a writer, probably of South American descent. He was a Borges or a
Quiroga of whom I had yet to know or encounter. I was young and had
much to learn. I was also a college kid trying to write and make sense
of my own experiences. I looked toward books for answers. In the years
after, as an essayist, I've learned to contemplate the "I," to find ways to
examine the multiple layers of the "self." As a reader, I've also learned to
understand how other writers take on the challenging and often difficult questions that emerge when one examines these layers.

Early in his book *On Borrowed Words: A Memoir of Language*,
Stavans addresses his own inner contradictions while recounting
the lyrics to the classic Jorge Negrete rendition of "México Lindo y
Querido." In the mere action of enjoying the song, Stavans (whose real
name is Ilan Stavchansky) is set to wonder on his own "Mexican-ness."
His memoir poses the question: what makes Stavans a Mexican when

he is fair-skinned, blond, browned-eyed third-generation Mexican of Ashkenazic Jewish ancestry?

Stavans understands the duality in his life: growing up in a country where customs felt foreign and yet familiar; where his upbringing was an insular existence within his middle-class Jewish neighborhood in Mexico City; and where his Yiddish and Hebrew always led eastward—aliyah—to a motherland, a territory that remained intrinsic and nostalgic to the old guard yet was met with such ambivalence by Stavans's generation. He poses another question, which brings him anguish: If he were to die, where would he be buried? Where would his allegiances lie?

What Stavans discovers is that in spite of his own desire to define himself, he can't fully find a satisfying answer—a fact that Mexican Americans are born into.

As a child, language was my way of understanding my identity. Spanish was my first language, despite the fact that I was fully bilingual before the age of four. I am the son of Mexican American migrant farm workers who in the 1980s moved around the United States picking fruit for a living. Spanish was the language I used with my parents, the private one. I also used it in the migrant camps with the rest of the farmworker families, most of whom were undocumented immigrants. I learned very early about these stark divisions. English for me was outward, more open and free to use in schools, in stores, and on television. This understanding of using one language intimately over another is an important aspect of a multilingual child's life. Early in my life, I met Spanish and my culture with the same apathy as Stavans did his Yiddish and much of the diaspora.

My childish thoughts: I knew how to speak Spanish. I grew up in its world. For me, Spanish represented the past—my parents' and my grandparents' own pasts, their world and their struggle—and my present, a waiting station. For me, English was mine (can one own a language?), and it represented a future, a world outside of the one I lived in. For me, Spanish moved with emotion and heart. English moved intellectually, with mind.

These childish thoughts, not so childish. I knew then, as Stavans did, evidenced in the way he approached the notion of language identity in his memoir, that defining ourselves through the language we speak, leads to discovering a space that we (and our families) create. When one approaches the memoir this way, suddenly one's geography, the places one lives, or one's allegiances to our nationalities are not as crucial as how the language influences and moves within these elements.

Stavans's paternal grandmother, Bela Stavchanksy, emigrated from Warsaw, Poland, in the 1920s to Tampico, Mexico. Bobbe Bela was a natural polyglot, a woman who spoke six languages—Polish, Russian, Yiddish, Hebrew, Spanish, and English—giving Polish and Russian up as a way into a new environment. Her past forges into future. Stavans: "Her past needed to be overcome, even erased, if survival was to be achieved."

As Stavans's grandmother willingly let go of the languages of her past, she did what many immigrants do when detached from their homelands. She re-created what she had before as a method of preserving aspects of who she used to be.

Bobbe Bela devoured books with ambition. She even wrote one herself. Her diario described her life in the Warsaw suburb of Nowe Bródno and her setting of roots in Mexico City. Stavans refers to Bobbe Bela's der yishuv (the settlement) in Mexico City as an exact re-creation of the shtetl in Poland, as if to "reghettoize [herself] in enclaves with little but business with the outside world."

These enclaves in Mexico City developed and flourished into Jewish neighborhoods, synagogues, and schools that Stavans's generation grew up in and, as he observes, remain insular and away from the "real" Mexican culture even today. Stavans asks an interesting question: did Bobbe Bela ever fully leave Nowe Bródno? The answer, for me, carries an air of irony and contradiction.

As Bobbe Bela turned away from the languages that identified her past life, she kept one, Yiddish, as her intimate language, the one she spoke to her family, often times, Stavans recalls, fusing it with Spanish.

So, I wonder myself, why did Stavans's grandmother shun her native languages and so willingly adopt the new one? Wouldn't doing so have seemed a betrayal against her past, a sin against her identity?

In Bobbe Bela's case, history shows us the inevitability of the situation for Jews across Europe at that time in the twentieth century.

I'm aware my questioning is informed by what many Mexican Americans who straddle the lines between identity and language across the borderlands go through every day.

Ni de aquí, ni de allá.

Not from here, not from there.

Stavans describes his life this way: "To leave and return." For me, this phrase evokes the journey many migrant farmworkers in the United States, so many undocumented, embark on every season. Like wandering Jews, many do so without choice. Their lives dictated—we leave only to return. A movement: between past and future. And, then again, with only very little to hold on to.

I grew up in migrant camps. Many of these farmworker camps themselves were insular communities shut out from the outside world. I remember as a child asking my parents why we lived there. Our exile from the comforts of our American citizenship was beyond my control; my parents thought it an advantage to not have to worry about finding a place to live in a strange town, a simple room for a family of five was enough for them. Even then I wondered, why did we have to live in such squalor, such poverty? This didn't feel very "American" to me. I grew up wondering about the difference between myself and what I thought an American should be.

A guest in a rented house one can never fully own.

To this day, when I meet new people, many ask me what I am. Once a lady at a dinner party was appalled when I told her I was of Mexican descent. "You certainly don't look Mexican. You have no accent. And your facial features are . . ."

She allows her thought to trail off—Dot. Dot. Dot.

Clearly the woman who questioned my background, diluted and misguided as I take her comment to be, irritates me to the point I begin to ask questions. What truly makes me a Mexican if I am American-born and speak English without a trace of an accent? Can my only connection to owning my "Mexican-ness" be by skin and blood? And although I love and treasure my heritage, I've hardly set foot in my ancestors' country, so I feel no allegiance outside of rooting for Mexico's national soccer team during the World Cup, an allegiance that so many Mexican Americans feel strongly about. I often wonder, how many of these Mexican American soccer fans can recite the Mexican national anthem, let alone "México Lindo y Querido," besides during a drunken stupor? I can't. Recently, I watched Mexican actress Salma Hayek recite both Mexican and American anthems on Letterman—Dot. Dot. Dot.

I begin to understand that I'm just challenged with the same notions and difficult questions Ilan Stavans puts forth in his memoir.

Around the time I finished reading *On Borrowed Words,* comedian Louis C.K. discussed in a *Rolling Stone* interview his "complex racial identity." Louis C.K., a comedian who in his own way essays about the "self" on his television show, refers to himself as an "accidental white person," and explains how his "Mexican-ness" shaped his artistic identity. The *Huffington Post* picked up on the magazine cover story and referred to it as "Louis C.K. Talks 'Mexican Past.'"

I find humor in that phrase, "Mexican past," because in a way, traversing the border north, one is unavoidably forced to also give up one's past. One assumes the future to be the achievement of the "American dream." Then again, it is easier if one is fair-skinned, white, guero, much like Louis C.K. and Ilan Stavans, to do something like that. Louis C.K. acknowledges this privilege as a "leg up in society," while Stavans prefers to meditate on the repercussions of that "leg up."

And what, after all, attaches us to the land where one is born and raised?

I'll say for a Mexican American (and an immigrant), the answer is never an easy one, but perhaps the best answer lies within the tension.

EMILY DEPRANG

On Joan Didion, on the Morning After My Twenties

Being an idealist in Austin in the summer of 2001 was almost perfunctory. Y2K had given everybody the morbid thrill of impending disaster followed by the cocky thrill of still being able to buy gas with a credit card. The WTO riots in Seattle in 1999 had definitely done something, maybe, or at least had given the feeling that something had been done. (The passive voice can be useful.) When I sat in an airplane hangar next to a straight-edge punk girl and watched footage of the riots set to Rage Against the Machine, I felt they meant something, though I couldn't have said what. Bush vs. Gore had given diverse groups something to fight together, and this was before September 11, when we relearned fear and obedience and found out exactly to what degree a small, committed band of citizens can change the world.

Tom Petty supposedly said, "I don't go to Austin. The weather's too nice, the girls are too pretty, and the dope's too cheap. I can't get anything done!" Damn straight. And the nothing that a lot of people got done back then (I moved away in '04) was a kind of spastic activism (spaztivism?) that burns a lot of energy but doesn't get a lot done. You know, the kind of activism that can usually be called a "gesture."

I was an old hand at gestures. I always wanted to be two things: a writer and "good." I didn't know what kind of writer I wanted to be, but I knew how to be good: gestures. One meal a week doesn't keep anybody from starving to death, but getting up early on a Saturday to go serve it makes you "good."

Then, in the summer of 2001, I read Joan Didion's "On the Morning After the Sixties." In the space of ten minutes, it reversed my polarities. Suddenly, I knew exactly what kind of writer I wanted to be, and I had no idea how to be good.

*

"I am talking here about being a child of my time," she begins with enviable confidence. For Didion, contemplating the sixties evokes, foremost, a memory not from the sixties at all—not even close, in fact—but an afternoon in 1953, her sophomore year at Berkeley, when young Joan spent a Saturday afternoon reading Lionel Trilling on a leather couch at a fraternity house and listening to a middle-aged man plunk morosely at an untuned piano. She would recall this afternoon, which she now admits seems "so exotic as to be almost czarist," as a reference point throughout the actual sixties, during which her alma mater would convulse with the political awakening of the children of *its* time.

In their hands, Berkeley would become an ideological and literal battleground, complete with barricades. "And barricades are never personal," Didion claims. "We were all very personal then, sometimes relentlessly so, and, at that point where we either act or do not act, most of us are still." Her generation was defined by having grown up "convinced that the heart of darkness lay not in some error of social organization but in man's own blood. If man was bound to err, then any social organization was bound to be in error."

Didion's so-called Silent Generation, she says, was silent not because they shared the era's optimism or feared its repression but "because the exhilaration of social action seemed to many of us just one more way of escaping the personal, of masking for a while that dread of the meaningless which was man's fate."

When I read this now, the grande dame of New Journalism sounds like Tyler Durden writing for *Vanity Fair.* But that's not how it struck me then. It seemed then so brutal that it had to be true.

Of course, Didion wouldn't have been half as persuasive if she'd been blunt. Instead of grounding her position in the actual issues at Berkeley (racial discrimination and the suppression of student organizing), she offers as evidence scenes from her emerging understanding that adulthood would be "morally ambiguous" and, well, sad. Besides the day-drinking fellow, whose clumsy efforts at the frat piano told Didion "something I had not known before about bad marriages and wasted time and looking backward," there was a woman she spotted picking daffodils in the rain and the teacher who got drunk one night and disclosed to her his bitterness and fear.

Seeing no antidote for disappointment, she elects not to be poisoned by hope. "We would make a separate peace," she declares. "We would do graduate work in Middle English . . . make some money and live on a ranch. We would survive outside history." That'll show 'em.

But that didn't pan out either, exactly. Didion gave it her best shot; she lived alone, read Camus and James, and "watched a flowering plum come in and out of blossom." She swapped coasts, then swapped again. "What I have made for myself is personal, but not exactly peace," she says. Some of her silent confederates killed themselves, but even those who endured live with what she posits as a burden of insight unique to her generation: the futility of working for social change. "If I could believe that going to a barricade would affect man's fate in the slightest I would go to that barricade . . . ," she says, "but it would be less than honest to say that I expect to happen upon such a happy ending."

*

Oh, Joan.

For years, I was sold on this conclusion. And what did it cost me to believe that, really? Didion wrote that barricades are never personal, but as middle-class white women, it's more accurate to say few barricades' successes or failures touch us personally. So it's easy, from a postprandial drowse on a leather couch in the sun, to consider apathy the most existentially valid attitude toward life. And it's also easy, when sentences are beautiful and methodical and frank bordering on shameless, to mistake their content for truth. To a young person manic with good intentions but stalked by the fear that nothing she was capable of would ever do any good, Didion was a bitter relief. "Yes," she told me in her gentle, steady, non-manic voice, "yes. It's O.K. that you're useless because it's all for shit. Isn't it nice to be calmer and more mature than everyone who tries?" She was calling my secret name.

Didion, like lots of writers and like myself, suffered from depression. Not the "depression" that she wrote as characterizing her generation but clinical depression, a disease, one with a cause and treatment and symptoms, like assuming that a stranger fiddling with a piano is trapped in a terrible marriage.

Like I said, "On the Morning After the Sixties" reversed my polarities. Suddenly I knew exactly how I wanted to write: nonfiction, the socio-personal, the essay, the careful cadence, the voice that commands quietly, abstract-concrete-abstract-concrete—all that. And I simultaneously stopped knowing how to be "good." She was right, after all: man is flawed, social institutions are going to be flawed, and if I were honest, it would be awful nice to live "outside history." I underlined it. I felt both called out and excused.

I still made gestures after that, but fewer and fewer. I stopped believing anything I could do would "affect man's fate in the slightest." I stopped looking for my barricade. This didn't exactly help my depression. But medication did, and so did realizing how dumb this beautiful essay is. "Why should the individual make an effort on anyone's behalf unless there's a good chance of, like, fixing the human condition?"

There's no such thing as mankind. There's no such thing as arriving or winning, and there's no scorecard at the end. But we all run out the clock somehow.

How did I idolize someone who could look at an integrated lunch counter and say, "Meh"?

She wrote real purty.

On Writing Young

If you've ever taught or learned in a creative nonfiction workshop, you've probably read the introduction to Phillip Lopate's *The Art of the Personal Essay.* Since the essay club is the only one I belong to, it's hard for me to find an apt comparison, but I imagine it's like getting a white belt on the first day of karate class or a money clip when you join the mafia. You're initiated, welcomed into a new language, and there's preliminary documentation to prove it.

Lopate's is an amazing introduction. It's comprehensive and didactic in just the right way. He sets his parameters and tells us how he wants us to read; no ambiguity, no show. But in every classroom I've ever been in, the conversation has quickly breezed past most of the essay's thorough thirty pages and has centered around one page, one line even: "While young people excel at lyrical poetry and mathematics, it is hard to think of anyone who made a mark on the personal essay form in his or her youth." Invariably, someone reads this out loud. Usually the two or three oldest students in the class sneak glances at each other; some are even bold enough to smile. Then everyone else gets really pissed off. They feel the righteous anger of being young, in a classroom with mostly young peers, fresh off a *The White Album* reading, giddy to start in a genre that in turn says, *Come back in a couple of decades.*

Lopate makes an argument that many others echo: an essay, at its core, is about reflection and learning. "It is difficult to write analytically from the middle of confusion," he advises us. So the essayist needs to have lived (read: earned) a memory worth analyzing and must have had the time to sit back, change, and inspect the event with as much attempted objectivity as possible. It's about trust, I think. We want a reliable nonfiction narrator, and reliability is developed through remove. This basic belief results in a sort of reverse ageism that seems to only afflict the essay genre. After all, precociousness is advertised in fiction writers. We like to quantify it exactly. How many "____ Under ____" lists are there for novelists and story writers? A young narrator—immature, impatient, imperfect—excites us in fiction. But when that narrator bares its author's name, the expectations shift.

I freely admit that I'm oversensitive to the issue. I'm twenty-seven, and I write essays, and that sense of illegitimacy, of narratorial unripeness, is a tension that I've never not felt. As a student in workshops, I remember realizing that all of our critiques started to sound like nervous retreads of the same basic questions—*I mean, not to devalue their experience or anything, but has the author* lived *enough to have a life to write about? Could the author, maybe, perhaps, no disrespect intended, benefit from a little* distance *from their feelings?*

These are, of course, valid questions, but in their onslaught they can become unproductive. They start to push us away from investigation and into poseurism. How many of us spent (or are spending) much of our twenties writing with a narrative voice that is tired and beaten down and *aged* beyond anything we've ever experienced? We attach our names to two-packs-a-day truck-stop troubadours who have already lived and died and lived again, as though if we imply a weight of experience, imply a greater distance between our character and our current narrator, we become unassailable. Instead of writing into the discomfort of a narrator mid-struggle, confused, we create false safety. That's how *last year* becomes a weary "once." How *grad school,* becomes "my years in a run-down apartment at the edge of a small midwestern town where whiskey was cheap and nights were long."

The implication by omission here is that a self-involved, artsy twenty-something isn't the person we want bringing us an essay, even if that's who the writer is. What I want to argue, though, is that many of the essay narrators that grip us in the fiercest ways are ones that do so from a place of hubristic confusion, an uneasy balance of both reflection and discovery that typifies a twenty-something psyche. Often, we find that perspective in works that are not exactly personal essays, but instead blend reportage and memoir. It's a semi-genre that grows out of a young writer's unabashed fear that maybe his or her own experiences aren't yet enough. So part of the personal reflection becomes that quest for information, experience, inspiration. Curiosity begins to coax out memories that are still forming as they're being written down. We've all seen and celebrated this type of narrator, using phrases like *genre-defying* and *groundbreaking*. But I think it's simpler than that. I think we secretly love an essayist who writes *young*.

Let's look at John Jeremiah Sullivan's much-lauded collection, *Pulphead*. The essays in the collection move through his writing life, ending with his musings from a big house, wife and kids by his side. But the book's best essay is the opener, "Upon This Rock," written when Sullivan was twenty-nine years old and carrying the full emotive jumble of that perspective. In it, he sets off to write about a Christian music festival, then lets his own not-too-distant memories push through the story. He is a reporter undetached, transporting us back and forth between his subjects enraptured by their belief and his own experiences as a born-again high-schooler. It's great stuff, funny yet somehow not utterly disrespectful. I think its true power, what makes it transcend to become greater than the sum of its one-liners, is that Sullivan is still not sure how to understand his own belief. His high school memories very consciously don't feel ancient. They feel a part of a conversation still happening within him. He describes leaving evangelism like this:

> My problem is not that that I dream I'm in hell or that Mole is at the window. It isn't that I feel psychologically harmed. It isn't even that I feel like a sucker for having bought it all. It's that I love Jesus Christ.
>
> "The latchet of whose shoes I am not worthy to unloose."
>
> He was the most beautiful dude.

Sullivan is analyzing here, yes, but he is also living with some of the same psyche that he's trying to understand in his former self. And while his narrator is the educated ex-believer, he's also goofy and sincere and maybe a bit stoned. It's a sensibility that allows him to mingle with his young subjects in a role somewhere between observer and participant, skeptic and co-conspirator. He begins to follow around a bunch of rough-and-tumble West Virginian believers. They take him in, he appreciates it, and just that easy proximity signals to the reader that, as much as there's reportage happening here, a personal essay is also being written *in the moment,* memories that will mix with and talk to his high school self are being created as he writes them down. It's a frantic process that leads us to a gorgeous ending, more deeply, personally felt than any reader could have imagined when beginning the essay. Sullivan is among the believers on the last night of the festival, unsure of what to feel. He writes:

> The clouds had moved off—the bright stars were out again. There were fireflies in the trees all over, and spread before me, far below, was a carpet of burning candles, tiny flames, many ten thousands. I was suspended in a black sphere full of flickering light.
>
> Sure I thought about Nuremberg. But mostly I thought of Darius, Jake, Josh, Bub, Ritter, and Pee Wee, whom I doubted I'd ever see again, whom I'd come to love, and who loved God—for it's true, I would have said it even if Darius hadn't asked me to, it may be the truest thing I will have written here: they were crazy, and they loved God—and I thought about the unimpeachable dignity of that, which I was never capable of. Knowing it isn't true doesn't mean you would be strong enough to believe if it were.

Here, Sullivan is caught between reflection, speculation, reality. He is analyzing from the midst of turmoil that may never end. And the excitement that I feel when I read and reread his final paragraphs comes from that particularly twenty-something sense of unknowing. No, that's not quite it. Sullivan knows enough, remembers enough, to support his investment, but also feels no safe remove from the material, complicates it with each new moment, wondering what will, what can, what has to come next. Even when he's looking back, every wound is still raw.

Wound provides a nice transition to Sullivan's heir apparent, Leslie Jamison, and her beautiful collection *The Empathy Exams*. Like Sullivan, Jamison is both chronicler and subject, a personal essayist who looks for stories to bounce her own experiences off or a reporter who can't keep her own memories out of the research, depending on how you look at it. Every essay in the collection is about hurt: hers, others', the personal kind, the global kind. The final essay, and maybe the best, is called, "Grand Unified Theory of Female Pain." It's a hugely ambitious piece, a study of the long, flawed history of how we present and interpret female suffering, yet through all the cultural context we're still left with what is fundamentally a piece of memoir. Jamison is trying to understand her own relationship to pain—what she has felt, what she feels, what she will feel, and what all that feeling means. Early on in the piece she establishes her narrator:

> I was once called a wound-dweller. It was a boyfriend who called me that. I didn't like that. It was a few years ago and I'm still not over it. (It was a wound; I dwell). I wrote to a friend: "I've got this double-edged shame and indignation about my bodily ills and ailments—jaw, punched nose, fast heart, broken foot, etc., etc., etc. On the one hand, I'm like, Why does this shit happen to me? And on the other hand, I'm like, Why the fuck am I talking about this so much?"

Jamison is by no means naive. In fact, she's brilliant. She's well read and unafraid to be so. She careens through references both highbrow and lowbrow, from *Carrie* and *Girls* to Plath and Sontag and Carson. She takes on the critic's "we" and examines our whole society's gendered relationship with pain. But all of that intellect is framed within a perspective that is often confused, sometimes downright maudlin, ashamed of itself and then simultaneously not.

Like Sullivan, Jamison has memories to plumb, but she still feels them as though she's experiencing them over again, and instead of steady reflection we get a writer dancing on the verge of a great unknown. Jamison is not the wise, calm examiner of the female psyche or, rather, she's not *only* that. She's also the subject who shares with us that, not long ago, she wrote a letter that included the phrase, "Why does this shit happen to me?" She is writing about pain in the middle of pain. This perspective leads us to an ending that feels much more like a beginning, or at least a continuation. "Sometimes, I feel like I'm beating a dead wound," she writes. "But I say: keep bleeding . . . I think the charges of cliché and performance offer our closed hearts too many alibis, and I want our hearts to be open. I just wrote that. I want our hearts to be open. I mean it."

I don't mean to use the power of Jamison's writing to suggest that true essayistic greatness happens only somewhere between twenty-three and thirty (though my fingers are resolutely crossed). Nor do I mean to suggest that one can write about memory like these writers do only if they don't wait too long. I'm not after a reverse Lopate dictum here. But I do think that immaturity, or at least the process of maturing, is a potentially riveting, truly essayistic place to write from. After all, what is young adulthood but a hybrid time of life, pushing toward and failing to live up to a set of expectations? The very same can be said about the essay form. When we embrace that tension, instead fleeing from it, real, valuable work is done. We get writers not only analyzing what has ended but also sorting out how to begin.

On Losing Yourself

DANICA NOVGORODOFF

In *A Field Guide to Getting Lost,* Rebecca Solnit says that "Lost really has two disparate meanings."

One: "There are objects and people that disappear from your sight or knowledge or possession."

This is the lost of things lost from you— you lose your wallet, or you lose your dog, or you lose your grandmother.

You are in the computer lab at the Universidad de las Americas, Puebla, when you get the news.

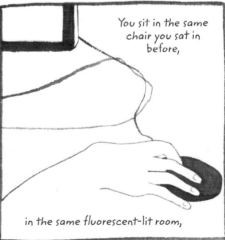

You sit in the same chair you sat in before,

in the same fluorescent-lit room,

the same fabric of the universe,
now punched with one
ragged hole through
which she has
flown. But—

"You still know where you are."

Two: "You get lost, in which case the world has become
larger than your knowledge of it," says Solnit.

You leave the computer lab, walk into the city, and make a wrong turn.

You find yourself on a dirt road, red dust on
rock, last week's confetti ground into tire ruts,

and you follow the
road until it hits a
stone wall scarred by
lover's hieroglyphics,

and you turn again to make
your way back to the room
you've rented, but have
no sense of direction,
never have,

and the sun is overhead at high noon, neither morning east nor evening west.

Quieres que te llevemos?

A van with three young men slows down to offer you a ride.

You are lost, you confess. They look friendly, and anyway you have pepper spray in your backpack just in case, so you feel safe enough,

you know your limits, your power, you know yourself, you accept the ride.

They ask you questions you know how to answer.

"The United States."

"Just here for the summer."

"It's a camera that uses larger-than-normal film."

They ask you questions you're not sure how to answer.

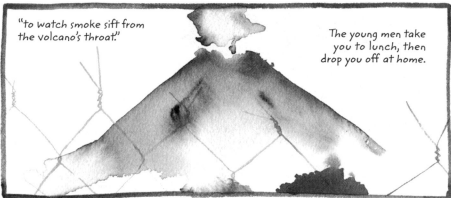

Maybe this is akin to a type of lost that Solnit mentions parenthetically much later in *The Field Guide*, "as in losing a competition, as in the Giants lost the Series"—a **defeat**,

a failure to know yourself, to belong in your own life.

You may be in a familiar place.

You're in your hometown, a city with paved streets that run in a grid.

You have been here before, and your wallet is in your pocket, and your dog is in her doghouse, and grandma's in her grave.

What happens when everything you've learned over the past decades,

the breath within your body,

the fabric of your own intelligence and experience,

goes white and blank?

What about the terror of a *lost* in which you can't find yourself?

KEN CHEN

Is the Essay at the End of Time?

[A white screen]

Q. You! I knew you could procrastinate, but this book is nearly going to press, and you have still not started your essay. In fact, you have procrastinated so much that you now write this essay at the end of time itself!

[Camera opens upon a dystopian tableau (the heat death of the universe, to be precise) and pans toward the author of this essay, who is sitting at a desk garlanded by cyborg wires and extraterrestrial meshes, clearly technology thousands if not millions of years into the future. In the window: Star Trek: The Next Generation–*style starscapes, Dyson spheres, hawkers selling End of the Universe merch.]*

A. *[A wobbling cigar clenched in jowl, the writer bangs his palms against the keyboard—faux-typing as Art Tatum percussionist tantrum.]* I am writing! Can't you see I am writing!

Q. *[The interviewer floats as a disembodied AI consciousness, she (or rather it) materializes a goblet of sherry via the nanotech hospitality services. The sherry levitates in the air and slowly vanishes, so as to mimic imbibing.]* I have to admit that I am surprised—

you are not unfamiliar with secreting out ideas at the behest of
the suspenseful cliff-hanger, but now you have taken your belated-
ness to an absolute level. We scarcely have a few minutes before all
the space-time around us collapses. Will you make your editorial
deadline?

A. *[In a leisurely tone]* To be honest, perhaps I was set back by the
prompt: to write about one essay. I think I felt suspicious about that
directive, a suspicion that when coupled with my aura of cognitive turpitude proved entropic. Though I hold in my hands the very
essay about which I am writing an essay. *[Fans himself with a sealed
envelope in the air, a la the Oscars.]*

Q. Suspicious? Why would it be suspicious to write about essays?

A. Not essays in the abstract, not essays in the multitude, but about
one essay, *the* essay, the definite article. *[Outside, a few of the stars
begin to shut down, the fuses of old bulbs buzzing off. The universe is
leaking its variety like a bad anthology.]*

Q. I see! Might as well write about a food you ate, that one time!

A. Or your favorite breath of air! Your favorite attempt! Your favorite excuse! Your favorite procrastination! *[Flapping the envelope
around, he accidentally flips it into the air, where it wafts and lands
behind him.]*

Q. Aren't you being a little . . . pedantic? You could surely name a singular example of other things with which you possess a similarly
polygamous relationship (say, your favorite book), could you not?

A. Is pedantry the mother of the essay? In addition to the word *no*,
the obvious difference is that the book is an aesthetic object. *[Looks
confused, then gets on all fours to look for the envelope.]* What would
it mean to consider the essay into an aesthetic object?

Q. Is it bad to be an aesthetic object?

A. You should ask a woman.

Q. An essay is not alive.

[Is the essay alive?]

A. *[Stands up, holding the envelope, brushes dust from knees.]* I call it "Casper."

Q. What are you talking about?

A. *[To disembodied intelligence]* Are you Casper?

Q. Who is Casper?

A. The aesthetic, the imaginative, etc.—a cute cartoon of make-believe!

Q. *[Laughs]*

A. *[In Old Testament jeremiad setting]* When the essay believes it has achieved autonomy, what it has gained is not sentience, not a modernism or avant-gardism. Rather, it has become cute. Essay anthologies rarely include, say, lies, prayers, liturgics, scientific treatises, pamphlets, non-stylized journalism, movie reviews, philosophical theory, scholarly encomiums, or my receipts. I need the receipts to get reimbursed for my plane fare to the end of time—

Q. Is a newspaper an aesthetic object? Also, are you going to open the envelope now?

A. That the newspaper would never be aestheticized (except perhaps now as a physical object of nostalgia) is my point. You would never select your favorite issue of a newspaper to anthologize. The

newspaper occurs inside a print culture, a context of news and politics, time and space. *[Holds out the envelope and begins to open it,
but then relents, realizing something with a sigh.]* But I anticipate
what you are saying. You are saying I barter in false analogy.

Q. Is the essay a newspaper?

A. Well, one rarely learns from the contemporary essay because there
is not enough world to go around. The literary essayist is ashamed
of the barbarism of pure content and so turns her own genre into a
pop-up book, for example, through embarrassing formats like out-
lines and lists and faux-interviews.

Q. I see. Or the exception that proves the rule is when the essay (that
most maximalist of genres) becomes assimilated into a nonfiction
wing of the novel through creative nonfiction and memoir. *[Gulp of
sherry.]*

A. See, if our conversation were a literary essay, I would write it as an
essay progressively getting drunker.

Q. Is not the essay different from those other genres in kind? Or do
you see all prose nonfiction as equal?

A. I hope I do not simply palm one gauche purity and substitute an even
less polluted impurity. First, more than any other literary medium,
the essay possesses an unusual function—that is to say, it possesses a
function. Many essays can be right or wrong. And they can possess
means by which to be morally or politically accountable. Can a poem
be right or wrong? Second, the essay possesses a more direct and
unmediated relationship to content. The novel and the poem gaze at
the actual world through a lens that has been greased with auteur-
ship, non-argumentation, and fictiveness. The aesthetic is that which
possesses no function or content—the beautifully useless. When we

aestheticize the essay, we staunch its utility and its reality. The literary essay rarely includes criticism or scholarship, since both possess an object and the literary essay must be its own object. The aestheticized essay is the fossil text—the essay at the end of time.

[Why does science fiction's vision of the future not more often include literary critics?]

Q. Aesthetic as anesthetic! You fear that the genre-fication of the essay represents its gentrification. I can prove you are wrong. I shall do so relying on utterly trivial facts that contradict you in my utterly inventive fabulous forthcoming essay!

A. Do your made-up facts have good or bad politics? Do they come with a cost?

Q. I will make up facts with good or bad politics! I will make up an imaginative cost!

A. *[Cantankerous, shoos away bodiless, noncorporeal entity with the envelope.]* Shoo, the aesthetic, scram you smug mildew, you Casper the friendly ghost!

Q. I suspect something perhaps more and less profound: you are afraid of vulnerability. You do not want to be pinned down. You would invent whole political ideologies and speculative futures before being caught doing something as tacky as loving something—or exposing yourself by naming a single essay you like.

A. While my self-loathing tempts me to agree with you, perhaps the best way to rebut you is by praise. Lately, I have found my favorite prose nonfiction writers to be academics or radical writers like Michael Denning, Katherine McKittrick, Amitava Kumar, David Graeber, Sianne Ngai, Bhanu Kapil, José Rabasa, Benedict Anderson,

Jacqueline Rose, Pankaj Mishra, Cedric Robinson, Timothy Mitchell, Fred Moten, and M. NourbeSe Philip, whose epilogue in *Zong!* is the best essay I have read this year and maybe the best essay I have read on the process of writing.

Q. Hmm . . . I've never heard of them. Do they write short elliptical fascicles? Do they embed actual text messages into an otherwise fictional narrative? Have they ever written a poignant personal reflection in a Choose Your Own Adventure format?

A. No.

Q. Oh, too bad they are not imaginative writers.

A. They are very imaginative writers. They have imaginative politics.

[He sits on the floor in front on a steel-colored pillar constructed from (insert technobabble). Thinks about Nietzsche's comment that Plato's fake plays were the lowest mode of adversarial sock-puppetry.]

Q. *[Awkward disembodied yawn]* When you are bored, do you try to fill it with essay?

A. What is *it,* is the question I guess. *[In a way that is impossible to represent visually, the disembodied voice stares outside the window at gray goo floating through the sky like lazy plankton.]* I am not bored. I am annoyed.

[What would it mean for film to exist at the end of time?]

Q. You have changed, you know, in the ten trillion years that I have known you.

A. Have we really known each other that long?

Q. Yes, I am the computer, the you-computer, you installed in your head to eject you from your head when you feel like your ghost is evaporating out of your skin. Do you think you have changed?

[Ken Chen was born in San Diego, California, in 1979 to two Taiwanese immigrants who had come to the United States on the planet Earth. A resident of New York, he uploaded his consciousness in the sixteenth millennium and became a roaming nebulae when—]

[So you are saying he is a gasbag filled with hot air.]

A. When I think about the eons that the multiverse has expanded and contracted its vast caverns of space, I think about all the people I have known and loved. I think about how these experiences have changed me. One way that I have changed is in my relationship to the essay.

   I used to love the essay for its discursiveness. It is a seismograph of a consciousness trawling through the language. An essay, you see, is a style of thinking. The idea of an exceptional essay insults this idea, curating an exemplary product rather than viewing any given essay as a trace imprint from a larger consciousness. I once found myself comforted by the power of essays to explain—to get a wee bit sentimental, the way they inadvertently act as wisdom literature.

   Lately, I find myself wanting art that knifes away the subtitles.

Q. Is our conversation an essay? *[Pause.]* No response?

A. *[Checking phone.]* Sorry, people I have never met are congratulating me on LinkedIn for an anniversary of which I lacked awareness.

Q. The return of time! Do you believe that prepositions shouldn't be what your sentences end with?

A. If a preposition expresses a relation, what does it mean to end on that relation—on the interval?

[Are stage directions the comment code in the programming language of visual narrative?]

Q. I think you have procrastinated to the end of time, because procrastination is the most essayistic endeavor, and because now that we are at the end of time, we have access to every essay that will ever have been written.

A. I do not like that quantitative and commodifying approach to human noises *[reaches for a spray canister of Borges Repellant]*, but shall I talk about an essay I've been thinking about lately?

Q. You're kidding!

A. *The Communist Manifesto!* You'd never see it in an anthology of literary essays despite it being the most influential essay of the last two centuries.

Q. You don't even like it.

A. The essay I would like to talk about is—

Q. Do you believe that essays are how we speak together? Or more to the point, why are you being so sophomorically antisocial, so unhelpful in this essay?

A. Wait, where did I put that envelope?

Q. That flimsy and renewable source of narrative?

A. Wait, something's coming to me. *[Suddenly the camera shakes, and the two players wobble and grab the furniture melodramatically.]* What was that?

Q. This platform is reversing direction.

A. *[Outside, black holes expand and resurrect into bloated red giants.]* So I've been thinking lately of this poem I once read in elementary school. *[His interlocutor watches the author stare out the window with an autumnal air of wan remembrance and begin to whisper what sounds like the word,* Rosebud.]

I don't remember the name of it. The poem was about this little boy in caveman times. It was about, like, you know, how he'd whip a snake as a lasso or wash himself using a woolly mammoth snout as a showerhead. I once pictured my younger self reading this poem as a young and future poet being struck by the magic of metaphor. Now I realize that what struck me was something more prosaic—

Q. Ha ha.

A. My liking the poem actually betrayed an essayistic tendency. The poem was speculation. I liked the poem because it expressed an idea one could paraphrase, somewhat like an essay, rather than because it made me experience a narrative (fiction) or the materiality of language (poetry).

[Hi, guys!]

Q. You have been quoted in the interstellar transmat media saying that you wish to swallow up poetry and the novel as subgenres of the essay.

A. They have proven rather tough gristle.

[Outside, all matter begins to heat up and swirl. Planets become hot dust.]

Q. What are you doing as you are writing this essay?

A. I am hunched standing at the kitchen table while my daughter Leila plays by herself on the floor.

Q. How old is Leila?

A. She turned fourteen months yesterday.

Q. Through what fourth-dimensional flux can you exist in such separate times at once?

A. The technology of lies, love, and the essay.

Q. What is happening?

A. We have arrived at our end, the beginning of time.

[A white screen]

E-mail from Bonnie J. Rough

O.K., Ander, I just accepted the Blogger invitation to post on *Essay Daily* and then I faced the fact that for a second embarrassing time in a row, I have to let the opportunity go to someone else. I have a rare opportunity to write for the month of September in Amsterdam, and I am going to accept it and focus intensely on my current book project. I realize you probably won't bother with inviting me anymore to contribute to *Essay Daily*, but when I have something, maybe I can just query you. I hope you won't mind my adding that I really am not a big flake, but I am a mom of young children with a delicate balance in my work life. I say no to things I want very much to do. Anyway, perhaps sometime this very predicament itself could lend a fresh thought to *Essay Daily*, although I fear it wouldn't strike quite the right scholarly tone. For example: I'm right now in the Dordogne very close to Montaigne's château and library, and I confess I have found myself thinking of the father of the essay and how decadent it might have been for him to be the father of the essay instead of the caregiver of his daughter, because an essay waits patiently and never interrupts with anything but a gift. Sarah Bakewell's scholarship about Montaigne in *How to Live: Or, A Life of Montaigne in One Question and Twenty Attempts at an Answer* describes his distress at interruptions in the year of his riding accident (1569 or 1570):

> He was about thirty-six at this time, and felt he had a lot
> to escape from. Following his father's death, he had inher-
> ited full responsibility for the family château and estate in

the Dordogne. It was beautiful land, in an area covered, then as now, by vineyards, soft hills, villages, and tracts of forest. But for Montaigne it represented the burden of duty. On the estate, someone was always plucking at his sleeve, wanting something or finding fault with things he had done. He was the seigneur; everything came back to him.

This burden of duty explains why Montaigne's library and writing room stood in a tower separate from the château and also why he loved to escape on horseback to find solitude in the vignobles and walnut groves. *Would that little mouths crying for peaches and saucissons could wait as patiently as the servants,* I thought grumpily after I read this, resenting neither my daughters nor my partner but the idea of Montaigne working—essaying—more or less as he pleased.

Because I was jealous, I plunged into uglier thoughts: Western intellectuals worship too many bright personages who may, in fact, not have been such geniuses but just had extra time to ramble their brains. I even dared to think that the essay, inasmuch as it challenges the essayist to try, to attempt, really doesn't stretch one intellectually or existentially so much as parenthood. Maybe motherhood in particular. And so I had my own backwards little insight, as I looked up from wiping tiny sticky hands to glance out over the green Dordogne just as our seigneur did those 450 years ago: I get more haughty about my status as a mother than about my identity as a writer, perhaps in the same way that a servant might privately disdain of the master of the house. *Such coddling!* I'll think, shaking my head, imagining my essayist self on the other side of the river, perched over bear rugs in a tower, surrounded by books and favored quotations, quill poised. In comparison, domestic work is harder and the pay is less (if you can imagine). And yet, one accomplishes the job rather honorably. It always both surprises and disappoints me to feel a strange frustrated pride in that, a small-minded sour-grapes kind of comfort.

So those are my curmudgeonly thoughts on the essay at the moment, perhaps not in the right spirit for this, but you can decide.

PETER GRANDBOIS

On the Essential Art of Failing

Francia Russell, the director of the school, said to me, "You're perfect for 'Clara,' because you are much more of an actress than a dancer."

It was a condescending compliment. I couldn't handle her honesty, but I did appreciate it. That's why, at sixteen, when Francia Russell told me the most I could hope for as a ballet dancer was as a corps member in some Midwestern third-tier company, I decided to quit. My excuse was that I would act. But really something inside died. An ex-dancer knows what I mean. When I left ballet, I left my identity. None of my dance classmates phoned. I had succumbed to failure.

—RENÉE D'AOUST, *BODY OF A DANCER*

We are the kings of catastrophe, the queens of ineptitude. Princes and princesses of disappointment. We pile the shattered bones of our missteps on the pyre of our imperfections. Our national anthem sings of soot-black air and beaten dogs. We pledge allegiance to distant shores we will never reach and storms that drag us away from any sight of land.

＊

At the club where I fence in Columbus, there is a woman in her early fifties who recently started fencing because two of her three children wanted to fence. She took up sabre, the fastest weapon, a weapon with no room for error. She has been a regular at the club for the past two years, fencing two to three nights a week and going to nearly every tournament. She almost always loses. She is always beautiful.

Beautiful in the way pages fluttering in the breeze are beautiful, in the way snow clinging to the railing outside the window is beautiful, in the way a bird unable to find a branch to land on is beautiful. I watch her and often wonder why she does it, fencing against kids a third her age, all of whom are faster, more agile. I know why I do it, but I, at least, have decades of fencing experience, muscle memory, to rely on, even if those memories are twenty years old. She takes last place in tournament after tournament. And after, she smiles and talks of how next time she'll do better.

A gentleman in his forties at my club also took up fencing because his son wanted to do it. Fencing does not come easy. The movements are unnatural. It takes years of training for them to become normal, much less second nature. The old adage is that fencing takes one life-time to learn the basics, another to master them. I watch this gentle-man struggle through his footwork, his upper body bobbing back and forth like those clown-faced punching bags. When he parries, it looks as if he is swatting at you. His attack appears more of a semi-controlled fall. He's always smiling. He tells me he loves the sport and wants to become as good as he can.

That's it, isn't it? To be as good as we can. That's the best we can hope for as we get older. I fenced my first division 1 national championship in 1988 when I was twenty-four years old. I came in last place. I told myself it would never happen again. I was young. I could afford that luxury. It didn't happen again. Over the next two years, I worked my way from being one hundred and eighty-first to placing somewhere in the fifties and sixties. A year after that, I made the top sixteen for the first time in my life. After that, many top eights or top fours. I had the time and the energy and the drive. When we're older, we're lucky to have one of those. Never all three. So we work hard and hope to be as good as we can.

*

We, none of us, expect to fail. And yet we do. Every day. We fail despite our best efforts. We measure ourselves against that failure. Maybe this time we won't lose quite as badly. Maybe this time we'll make our opponents work at least a little bit for their touches. Maybe this time we won't be quite so sore the next morning. Maybe we won't have the usual aches and pains. Maybe we'll be able to get out of bed. To walk downstairs. To sit. Without pain.

*

A flick attack in fencing involves cranking the arm and throwing the weapon forward with a whip so that the blade bends and the point hits the opponent's back. It used to be my bread and butter. It takes a lot of arm strength. I remember the first time I tried flicking when I came back to fencing at forty-eight. I slapped my opponent across the shoulder. I apologized. I tried again and apologized again. I couldn't generate the torque required to bend the blade enough. No matter. Two years into my return to fencing and I have "tennis elbow." It's difficult enough to attack with a straight arm now, much less attempt a flick. If I did, the pain shooting up my arm would force me to drop my foil. In veteran fencing, practice doesn't always lead to improvement. It often makes you worse. Wisdom is to know your limitations and work within them.

Twenty years ago, I was famous for running my opponents down. My nickname was "the rhino." When I first tried to fence with my old run-and-gun style, I nearly tripped and fell. My hip went out on me. My knees gave way. My body told me its limitations. I didn't listen much the first year, but I've learned to listen since. My game is different than it was twenty years ago. For the first time in my fencing career, I use the clock. I take my time, and instead of attacking, I offer false openings designed to draw my opponent out so I can capitalize on my hand, which thankfully remains quick. My legs are another matter.

*

We drag our wings through dark, cloudless nights, the moon flailing our corpses. We open our mouths to song and hear nothing but dry rasps. We lift our feet in dance but find them tied down by the low sound of distant bells. Time stops, and we fall backwards, teetering on the edge of our regrets. We pull our coats tighter at the throat amidst the ash falling from our hair. We are the fathers of the big flop, the masters of miscarriage. We are the butchers of botchery, and the disciples of disaster. We court failure as if there were nothing else in the world we'd rather be doing.

*

I started and restarted this essay four times before I got it "right." I still don't know if I have it "right." The curse of age is that you know enough to know you are wrong far more often than you are right. The old Japanese proverb: "Fall down seven times. Stand up eight." To know, too, that no matter how much you work at it, no matter how much effort you put in, you may never get it "right." It is also a blessing because at some point you free yourself to be *as good as you can.*

When I wrote my first novel, I was a relatively young thirty-eight and oh so lucky. I didn't know what I was doing. The fool's blessing. I sat down every day at my computer and simply wrote. I completed the first draft in six months, then spent the next six months revising it. I probably put the novel through three drafts total. I sent the novel out to a round of publishers, and the first e-mail response I received was an acceptance. I didn't know enough to know how rare it all was. My second novel took four and a half years to write. I have over forty different drafts saved on my computer. The novel was rejected forty-five times before it found a home. My third novel took five years to write, had a similar amount of drafts, and after forty plus rejections, is still looking for a home. Writing doesn't get easier. When we write, we think we are approaching "truth," but the older you get, the more you realize how elusive that "truth" is. Even if you find it, you understand how difficult it is to express. I remember the summer I began writing that third novel. I wrote to page sixty, then stopped, trashed it, and started again. I repeated this process at least four or five times until I found the voice and the form necessary for the story I wanted—no, needed—to tell. Even when I found the voice and form, writing wasn't necessarily easier. I just knew what I had to do. But knowing and doing are sometimes as different as a boy and his father. Whether it gets published or not, I consider that novel my finest work and my biggest failure.

Several years ago at a library in Sacramento, while sitting on a panel and talking about writing, someone asked how I defined "success" as a writer. I'd never thought about it before and so wasn't ready for the question and was even less prepared for the answer. At the time, I only had two books out. The first had won many awards, had been seriously reviewed, was under contract to be made into a movie, and had sold several thousand copies. The second had sold maybe four hundred copies. I told the audience that the second was a much bigger success to me, though it would probably be deemed a failure by every such metric we use in America. I told them there were two reasons why: The first was that even though many more people had read my first book, I'd received a few personal e-mails regarding my second book, saying how it had changed their lives. In other words, I marked success not by how many readers I had but by how deeply a few readers received it. Finally, I was more pleased with the writing in my second book than in my first. In other words, I'd met my own standards in that book, not the standards of somebody else.

*

Lord deliver us from the ugly hands of "success." Take us, instead, down the road of failure in the trunk of a dying car. We beseech you to protect us from paths with a pot of gold at the end, roads that appear too easy. Let us wake to the blank page each and every day and not be sure how to fill it. Let us enter our daily tournament knowing each and every person there can beat us. We ask that you pluck out our eyes so that our black sockets can roll back into heaven. Grant us scorched earth that our weeds might grow. Only then can we know strength. Only then can we understand character.

*

As in writing and fencing, the longer I live, the less I realize I understand. The more I realize how much of my life is defined by failure, how failure defines me. You can't go through life without making mistakes, and I've made more than my share. A ruined first marriage. A nearly ruined second. I have failed to keep up with so many friends. Failed to listen to myself at key points in my life. And yet I would argue that these failures are not even the important ones. The ones we see clearly, the ones we remember right away, those shape us, but less so than we think. It's the thousand little failures we ignore each day that really make us who we are, and nowhere is that more clear than in parenting.

As a father with two teenage girls and a headstrong ten-year-old boy, I've almost completely given up. Children have no lack of compunction in letting you know when you've fallen short of the mark. The teen who reminds you of the promise you failed to keep or the conversation you failed to hear or the fact that you failed to understand her need for a break from piano practice or homework. The child who reminds you that you failed to see when he needed help or when he didn't need help, when he wanted your love and when he didn't. To give your teen a kiss or a hug when they don't want it can sting worse than a bad book review.

But parenting is only one part of a very long day. I fail to play with my dogs enough. I fail to pay the bills on time, to keep the house clean, to maintain the yard and clean the garage, to keep up the deck and the exterior paint. I fail to prepare enough for the classes I teach and spend enough time on the papers I grade. I fail to get the cars in for a tune-up or an oil change or a tire rotation or to check the battery. I fail to love my wife enough. I fail to sleep at night so I can be rested for my failure the next day. Failure to be *as good as I can be.*

And yet, I wouldn't have it any other way. That's not quite true. Rather, I know there is no other way. In fencing, I will always lose more bouts than I will win, at least if I'm pushing myself. In parenting, I know if my kids love me all the time, something is wrong. I haven't done my job. I've tried too hard to be their friend. In writing, if my book is reviewed in the *New York Times* (don't worry, my books will never be reviewed in the *New York Times*), I know I've failed to express the deepest part of who I am, my vision of the world. For good or ill, our lives are measured by our mistakes.

∗

We are the rulers of ruin. We are the tyrants of tragedy. We court calamity at every turn. We wake to upheaval and work through confusion. Mayhem, havoc, pandemonium are our middle names. We live for discouragement. We pray to be washed up, washed out, let down, and defeated. We settle for setback and know in our bones that we'll spend far more time in the anticlimax than the climax. We are born thinking we are conquerors but we die knowing life is a rout.

∗

So why do I fence? Why return to a sport in which I have no hope of being as good as I once was, a sport where I'll be reminded of my failures, my shortcomings, every day? It is the great lesson of getting old: to accept that we are 90 percent failure in blood and bone, that we take last place more often than not, that we are all desperately trying to be as good as we can be. The body is the first to remind us, when at thirty our backs start to go out from time to time and our arms aren't quite as strong as they used to be. At forty, our legs don't quite carry us with the same grace. By the time you reach fifty, if you don't understand that you've failed at nearly everything, you've either got your head in the sand or you never set your bar high enough in the first place. Failure is necessary for growth.

That lesson can be the hardest of our lives: to know that we live on a receding shoreline and that soon everything will abandon us. Grace lies in looking out from that shore, knowing no one will come, but standing there anyway. We live in an age of instant gratification. In all my years of coaching, I've seen hundreds of young students come to fencing thinking they want to be Aragorn or Luke Skywalker, then quit a month later when they realize they can't be instantly good at it. They lack the necessary character. As a professor, I get e-mail after e-mail from students trying to convince me I should let them into my classes: "I have a passion for the short story." "I have a passion for poetry." "A passion for words." "A passion for writing." They love the word *passion*, mistaking it for character. And yet, when I tell them to come on the first day and see if a spot opens up, none of them show. How quickly their passion fades when things are not certain, when life is not handed to them. Much of the fault lies in youth. Character is born from pain and sacrifice. Discipline and time. Above all, time. Age understands the way in which character is tindered in work, ignited by failure.

Our culture celebrates winning above all else. We call our sports figures "heroes," as if somehow they've sacrificed for us. Maybe they have. Maybe the ten thousand hours they sacrificed practicing, trying to get better, wasn't really for them, but for us, so that we would have a model of perfection and grace. Maybe. But I'll take the people who don't make the six and seven figure salaries, the people who don't make the news. I'll take the woman who doesn't win a bout but keeps getting up and donning her mask anyway. I'll take the old man I used to fence with in Denver, who was always the first to arrive at the club and the last to leave. He was dying of cancer, and though his legs could barely move, he was the only one to never take a break. "Do you want to fence?" he would say with a smile. And how could you refuse. His hand was still quick. He knew what it meant to fence *as good as you can.* He lived it. And for a moment, when you fenced with him, you lived it too. Despite youth. Despite the false promise of what lay ahead. You hoped that someday you would understand enough to make a parry riposte the way he could. Simple. Without thought to the past or the future. Without a worry about who you were or who you would become.

*

We are the memory of winter. We are dying birds sputtering over the ground. We are open mouths without sound, abandoned cars at the bottom of a ravine. We are the last drops of rain to fill the muddy tracks. We are the long nights when the rain doesn't stop. We understand our lot. Still, we return again and again. And we won't stop. Not ever.

Leaping

He was a rake, a tavern jackanapes, a diddler and tippler and easy smiler, this John Donne. His love poems hit all of the lusty notes from fully invested passion to a charmingly sly persuasion: they wink, they sigh, they caper, they hector, they play with logic as if it were juggler's balls, if required they'll use two compass points that might circumscribe a map of the world, they'll use the pinpoint figure of a flea whatever it takes.

And yet I should have, in that first sentence above, accentuated one word by way of italics: "*this* John Donne." There's the *other* John Donne as well, the author of "Holy Sonnets" (of which, "Death, Be Not Proud" is still alive nearly five hundred years from the poet's own death) and, writing as a clergyman—he was by then dean of St. Paul's Cathedral the author of sermons with such majestically oceanic rolling of language, full of undertow and overflow and heaved-up glittering treasure-gems of phrases, that I believe they'll live for so long as there are sensitive human ears to tryst in the brain with the human heart.

These sermons ("devotions," as he termed them) are essays on Spirit and World (a love affair, although not the fleshier kind we find in the poetry, but a love affair none the less, with all of its yokings and separations). They move me in spite of my happy atheism—they move me by their acumen and wit, their brilliant metaphor-making, their born-in-the-marrow sincerity, and their cadences so assured and so capacious that they dwarf our lesser daily speech to snails on a beach while out in the limitless waters the whales breach.

Perhaps the most well known of these is the sermon that serves up the title of Hemingway's novel *For Whom the Bell Tolls*. It is, of course, a funeral bell and, when you hear it, no matter whose is the corpse-of-the-moment, "it tolls for thee"—our mortality is one great sign of our human commonality, a sign that (as the sermon also famously says) "no man is an island."

This idea is taken up in Izaak Walton's biography of Donne, in an anecdote I've always found eerily stirring. In fact I quote from it in an essay of my own, in my book *A Sympathy of Souls* (Coffee House Press, 1990, and probably written in 1988 or 1989). And in fact that book title is a quotation *from* the Walton piece on Donne. Walton tells us that later on in Donne's life, when he was contentedly and passionately married, and his wife was pregnant and weak from the strain, he was still talked into accompanying his friend and patron Sir Robert on a two-month-long ambassadorial mission to France:

> Two days after their arrival there, Mr. Donne was left alone in that room in which Sir Robert, he, and some other friends had dined together. To this place Sir Robert returned within half an hour; and as he left, so he found, Mr. Donne alone; but in such an ecstasy, and so altered as to his looks, as amazed Sir Robert to behold him; insomuch that he earnestly desired Mr. Donne to declare what had befallen him in the short time of his absence. To which Mr. Donne did at last say "I have seen a dreadful vision since I saw you: I have seen my dear wife pass twice by me through this room, with her hair hanging about her shoulders, and a dead child in her arms: this I have seen since I saw you."
>
> To which Sir Robert replied, "Sure, sir, you have slept since I saw you; and this is the result of some melancholy dream, which I desire you to forget, for you are now awake." To which Mr. Donne's reply was: "I cannot be surer that I now live that I have not slept since I saw you:

and am as sure that at her second appearing she stopped and looked me in the face, and vanished."

It is truly said that desire and doubt have no rest; and it proved so with Sir Robert, for he immediately sent a servant to Drewry House, with a charge to hasten back and bring his word. The twelfth day the messenger returned with this account—That he found and left Mrs. Donne very sad and sick in her bed; and that, after a long and dangerous labor, she had been delivered of a dead child. And, upon examination, this circumstance proved to be the same day, and about the very hour, that Mr. Donne affirmed he saw her pass by in his chamber.

It's this phenomenon (what our twenty-first-century physics would call "entanglement") that Walton calls "a sympathy of souls":

It is most certain that two lutes, being both strung and tuned to an equal pitch, and then one played upon, the other that is not touched, being laid upon a table at a fit distance, will . . . warble a faint audible harmony in answer to the same tune.

It isn't surprising that core ideas might remain stable in a writer's life, even if over the years they appear in different guises A "sympathy" of "equal pitch" exists between the clergyman's sacred think hellfire sermons and the young rake's lust-think poems. Each explores its version of the invisible (but very real) bridges connecting island-states. (And of course this essay I'm writing in 2014 has allowed me to leap the distance of twenty-five years, in sympathy with an essay a younger me created in 1988 or 1989.)

In his wonderful poem from 1633, "The Flea," Donne addresses a woman: the eponymous insect "sucked me first, and now sucks thee," so that "in this flea, our two bloods mingled be"—in its teeny body they "more than married are." It's a crazy-ass fantasia, but no less winning for its fancifulness, as the little leaping consanguinovore, in its feeding, bridges body to body, pleasure to pleasure, self to self, I-land to I-land.

ALISON HAWTHORNE DEMING

Julian Barnes Brings Light to a Thanatophobe's Conundrum

I admit I've been obsessed with death since 2011 when my brother and mother died within six months of each other. I shepherded each of them through that backcountry and, while they are gone to whatever version of nothing exists beyond biology's terminal station, I remain here at the desk with death as a closer companion. It seems to sit on my shoulder demanding my attention. If I get through a day without thinking about death (*my* death, to be specific), I feel exhilarated. As soon as I notice this joy, death carps at me as if I have been unfaithful. I'm not sure that I fear death more after their departures. I just have a more familiar, more intimate relationship with it.

So the thanatophobe's conundrum: is it better to fear death or not fear it? As if one could choose. I'll be more honest. I've been obsessed with death since I was seven and it first slipped into my childhood bedroom to make my heart race like a runaway horse. It could happen now. Or now. Or now. Unlikely. Maybe now. With my genetic legacy, I have a good shot at getting past one hundred. And I plan to be in love with life all the way. So how can I be so attached to death while being so committed to life? I am a bigamist.

Enter Julian Barnes with a wry grin on his seasoned face, holding a copy of his two-hundred-and-fifty-page essay on death, *Nothing to Be Frightened Of.* Emphasis on "nothing." While the deaths of his parents may have triggered the writing, the book is not a memoir, not an attempt to tell their stories or his. Barnes does not trust memory. That is why he is first a novelist. Much safer to make things up than pur-port to know or divine what has happened. No. The book is decidedly an essay, a long ramble of a beast without a single chapter break—O.K., there are space breaks—in which Barnes is bent not on re-creating his parents but "trying to figure out how dead they are." This is an essay-ist's intent. Those who dismiss the work because it does not contain enough self-revelation miss the point. It is how death reverberates in the artist's mind that matters here. What does death have to do with the faithless artistic sensibility?

After all, Barnes is a man who never visits the graves of his fam-ily members but frequently seeks out those of writers and artists. Artists are his ancestors. He tracks his inclinations to Montaigne in whom he sees that "modern thinking about death begins." The family member who plays the most prevalent role in the book is his brother, who teaches ancient philosophy and proves to be an admirable con-versational partner in the book, allowing for Plato and Aristotle and Cicero to pop up as elements of a chat with his bro, rather than as pedantic asides. What have the philosophers and writers had to teach about death in all the years of their sense making?

Of asides, something must be said, because Barnes is a sentence maker par excellence, juxtaposing a deliciously subordinated beauty next to a clipped fragment. And his conversational asides are among the quirky cadences that I find very seductive in this work—an essay-ist essaying his own method as he goes:

> Platonists believed that, after death, things started look-ing up. Epicureans, on the other hand, believed that, after death, there was nothing. Cicero, apparently (I use "apparently" in the sense of "my brother also told me"), combined the two traditions into a cheery Antique either/ or: "After death, either we feel better or we feel nothing."

But I have gotten ahead of myself. Barnes became an atheist as a teenager and an agnostic at sixty. His inquiry has to do with what the faithless are to do with their thanatophobia or lack thereof. He opens the book: "I don't believe in God, but I miss Him." And there you have the man: assertive and vulnerable, heady and witty. And such good company in his essaying that I end up feeling, yes, sure, life is dire, but it is also funny, which is a good cure for self-pity. I learn that Sibelius had the routine of joining friends at table where they were required to talk about death. Rachmaninoff, who suffered dreadful death terrors, was cured apparently by a sack of pistachio nuts. Flaubert wrote of aspiration for "gazing down at the black pit at one's feet, and remaining calm." Daudet died at the dinner table after a spoonful of soup and chatter about his latest play—then poof. Stravinsky went to see Ravel's body before it was placed in the coffin. What music did he hear, I wonder, in those moments, composer to composer in the great silence? And so the trivia that is far from trivial mounts up in this book, carrying its learning lightly and yet earnestly.

Humor, I've read, is a defense mechanism, and probably one of our more mature ones. It beats denial. Perhaps both life and death are funnier without religion. In any case, as Barnes says, art and religion shadow each other, though I am in the Barnes camp in feeling that art sheds the light and sometimes the lightheartedness that make death-awareness bearable. *Nothing to Be Frightened Of* does not resolve any of the thanatophobe's conundrums. Is it better to be conscious of your dying or not conscious of your dying? Who cares. You don't get to choose. But this grand essay brings the twin lights of mindfulness and playfulness to bear on the matter and that seems to me an apt gift for Advent.

On Tom Junod's "The Falling Man"

Tom Junod's essay "The Falling Man," originally published in *Esquire* (September 2003), is at once an essaying of an iconic photograph, an interrogation of the role of journalists and newspapers, a journalistic investigation of the central question (who is the Falling Man?), a confrontation of cultural taboo, and a meditation on the ways we witness and memorialize the dead in this country, specifically the way we deal with the tragedy of 9/11.

The essay begins with a detailed description of the image itself, a photograph that appeared briefly and then was censored, removed from the public consciousness and deemed taboo, almost pornographic. This act of writing alone is fraught with peril, as there are still a great many people who believe that anyone who cares to meditate on this image, or on the story of the hundreds of other jumpers that day, is sick and twisted, or worse, actively trying to exploit the deaths of this man and of others who chose to jump. Junod's initial salvo is a shot at those who choose to look away. Whether you've seen the picture or not, Junod gives it to you in the first paragraph, one that ends with this statement of his dilemma when trying to "solve" the mystery of the Falling Man: "In the picture, he is frozen; in his life outside the frame, he drops and keeps dropping until he disappears."

In the essay we meet the photographer Richard Drew and hear the story of how Drew captured the infamous image of a man leaping to his death from the North Tower, an image that is—though it may be hard for some people to admit—sublimely beautiful and arresting and, as such, also profoundly disturbing. Junod seems to be simultaneously trying to redeem Drew in the eyes of a public that saw him, or others like him, as some kind of monster feeding off the suffering of others, while also shoring up his own tenuous role as a journalist.

He says of Drew, "He is a journalist. It is not up to him to reject the images that fill his frame, because one never knows when history is made until one makes it." This one image, so striking in part because of its artistry and composition—and because as Junod says of the Falling Man, "Though oblivious to the geometric balance he has achieved, he is the essential element in the creation of a new flag"—is also just one image in a series that Drew captured of the man's final descent, and just one amongst hundreds of images of other jumpers that were captured on film and likewise censored or ignored. We learn that the balance and apparent harmony the Falling Man seems to achieve in this one moment isn't necessarily present in the other photos in the series and is, at least in part, manufactured by the camera lens. The photo itself is then a kind of pretty lie, a selected slice of history, one sublime moment amidst a slew of horrific images. Junod says,

> Photographs lie. Especially great photographs. The Falling Man in Richard Drew's picture fell in the manner suggested by the photograph for only a fraction of a second, and then kept falling. The photograph functioned as a study of doomed verticality, a fantasia of straight lines, with a human being slivered at the center, like a spike.

In one section, Junod repeats, "They jumped," or some variation of it ("they began jumping," "they streamed"), about nine times, and we are staggered by the weight of repetition, hit repeatedly with the sound of their falling. And we learn that other artistic interpretations of the Falling Man elicited such strong feelings that bomb threats were called in demanding censorship.

We learn about Norberto Hernandez, the man originally and erroneously identified as the Falling Man in an earlier article by a different author, and we meet his family, a family torn apart by this identification. His wife and children refused to believe the man in the photograph was their father. In a very real sense, Junod saves this family from their grief by showing them the sequence of photographs that Drew took, allowing them to see the Falling Man really for the first time and confirm that he wasn't their father; but Junod doesn't present himself as a savior, doesn't put himself in the foreground and instead mostly just lets the people talk and interact with one another. And when Junod takes his own risk at identifying the Falling Man, it's not without struggle, not easy for him. Junod performs like a journalist but struggles like an essayist. He talks to family members, interviews artists, and administrators, numerous people who'd lost a loved one in the tragedy, and he ultimately "solves" the mystery and identifies the Falling Man; but interestingly this doesn't come off as the authoritative definitive answer on the question, much less a closure to the open questions that run through the whole essay. Nor does this identification, his solving of the mystery, really seem to be ultimately what the essay is about in the end, but rather just the terminus of one minor thread that Junod weaves throughout.

My favorite sorts of essays are often those that advertise themselves as one thing while performing several different, often contradictory, functions, essays where the stakes shift between the first paragraph and the last. "The Falling Man" does this. It was a feature piece in *Esquire,* and I think at least part of why I like it is because it seems like the sort of piece that the *Esquire* editors would have normally sanitized and polished into something much smoother and less interesting, something less intimate and confrontational, less risky, digressive, and essayistic. Consider, for example, the odd section where Junod narrates a phone call with the mother of a possible jumper through an artificially distant third person point of view, referring to himself as "a man" talking to "a woman." Perhaps this creation of an implied first person is a trained journalist's way of removing the "I" from the page, or perhaps it is tangible evidence of Junod's struggle on the page with his own definition of a journalist as little more than a lens. As often happens, the implied first person really only amplifies the "I," drawing more attention to Junod's efforts to distance himself from the events, drawing attention to his deliberate use of craft. There's an odd tension in this that I find compelling, if only because of its oddity and vulnerability. We might also take a look at the ending, where Junod risks all-out sentimentality and essentially argues for keeping the Falling Man in the realm of myth, symbol, and metaphor. He compares him to the Unknown Soldier at Arlington Cemetery and suggests that the Falling Man must on some level remain an abstraction, an unknown, because in that role he has more power, more meaning. He can be named, but he cannot be reduced or ignored or easily dismissed; and on some level, he lives forever only in the tomb of Richard Drew's photograph.

We Sought but Couldn't Find

Coming Up Empty in David Shields's "Death Is the Mother of Beauty"

When my father was five, his heart stopped beating. My grandmother had taken him to the doctor because he had sparked a high fever, something he'd experienced sporadically and inexplicably since birth. From nowhere, he'd break a heavy sweat, his skin would turn red, his eyes would roll back. Totally unresponsive, sometimes he'd convulse. That day, the fever didn't come down, and finally, with his heart stopped and stopped and stopped, the doctor pronounced him dead.

*

Eight months ago I gave birth to a healthy girl her father and I named Harriet. When she was about three months old, I set her down for a diaper change and a sharp wheeze escaped her throat and her chest stopped moving. And then it stayed stopped. Her body went stiff, and her eyes locked into mine. I went hot with panic. I scooped her up and she gulped an enormous breath of air and then screamed a terrific, terrified scream.

About 1 percent of babies will stop breathing for any number of reasons. Although it isn't common, it isn't always reason for enormous concern. But still. My baby was breathing, and then she wasn't; and then she did, but I was scared. I rushed her to the doctor, who ordered a few tests but assured me it was most likely just reflux. We'd been treating the issue with bi-daily doses of Baby Zantac since she was born, but she grows quickly and it's hard to keep the dosage growing with her.

"The acid will back up and close off the throat so that the airway is constricted," the doctor told me. This explains why she breathed again when I lifted her. This explains why I struggle to let her out of my arms.

Now, months later, Harriet and I go about our day—nursing, reading, playing—but in the midst of all this ordinariness, I am never far from that moment: her eyes fixed on me, her chest raised and stuck. So I give her more solid foods, more meds. I keep her upright for thirty minutes after she eats. With Harriet full-bellied and swaying against my shoulder, my mind often lands on my father, fifty-odd years ago, how he lay in that hospital bed, a doctor sliding a stethoscope around, listening for a heartbeat and hearing nothing. How my grandmother watched idly—what could she do?—as the doctor declared a time of death. How I am sure that moment lasted and lasted and she felt like there would never be any other moment to occupy ever again until, from nowhere, he breathed a deep, full breath.

Like so many family narratives—especially the mysterious, hard ones—no one has told me the story of my father's death top to bottom (for example, I am not actually sure how he came back to life: if he was resuscitated, if he spontaneously breathed again; if the details of this story inch toward myth; I don't know). It's only told in bits and pieces. I can't even remember the first time I heard it. But after I returned from the pediatrician, I phoned my family to assure them Harriet was O.K., and my grandmother told me she knows how scary it is. She remembers how his fevers would spike, and she'd hold him in bed, soaking him with cool cloths, and he'd convulse until the whole bed shimmied against the floor. Once, she was home alone and his fever boiled and then he went limp and turned blue; she bolted down the street calling for help until a neighbor gave him to mouth-to-mouth and there, in the middle of the street, his eyes shot open and he gasped.

*

As a new mom, I think of the life/death dichotomy a lot. I worry—like we all do, I'm sure—and these worries are always fixed squarely on my daughter. In the first trimester of my pregnancy, I worried about miscarrying. Closer to her due date, I worried about lungs pumping and her heart closing without holes. In labor, she was twisted in the umbilical cord, as many babies are, and at each contraction her heart stopped, and after the contraction ended her heart stayed stopped, and stayed and stayed. A doctor did a small procedure that worked, but for the rest of the labor I thought of that flatline, a sluggish dash ticking across the screen, not rising or falling, just staying stopped. Now that she's here I worry about food allergies. About fevers. About SIDS. About oncoming cars swerving into our lane. About tripping down the stairs with her in my arms. About icy sidewalks and fractured skulls. About reflux squeezing her airway shut. All this to say, I worry about death.

And so, maybe unsurprisingly, I've gravitated to David Shields's *The Thing about Life Is That One Day You'll Be Dead*.

Like me, Shields looks at his daughter and realizes how peculiar it is that the act of giving life makes the reality of our death all the more pressing and inescapable. Early in the book he relays a story about his father landing on the third rail in a New York subway and how, improbably, he lived. We are both obsessed with the girls who will outlast us and the fathers who have cheated death—a skill, we know, they haven't passed down.

It's a fine book, pastiching family stories with startling data on the body's inevitable decline. But the lyric essay, "Death Is the Mother of Beauty," is the book's heartbeat. Here is Shields's showstopper. While much of the book seems to demand that we think about death (as though this reader isn't already doing that all day every day, as though Didion's line "Life changes in the instant" doesn't circle in my head each time I put my daughter in the car, feed her a new food, let her out of my arms), this little essay does something different, something quiet and powerful. It's a list essay, flipping through ninety-nine television channels at two in the morning, cataloging their contents, from ads for Retin-A to exercise videos and news reports of tragedies.

The essay is a real ass-kicker. First, it's the only section of the book that has this kind of punchy, pop-culture vibe: "On channel 87, Hair Color for Men got the gray out." And while much of the book is built of lists, those lists are nearly all strings of statistics about the body's failings, or quotes from great thinkers about the body's failings. So "Death Is the Mother of Beauty" is a content shift. It resists staring squarely at the subject of death (which after 172 pages of death-gazing is a nice switch-up). At first, I'm lulled by the fluffiness. I am in that room, my face reflecting the TV's neon glow, bored and interested all at once. For a second, my mind wanders away from all those worries—the constricted airways and failing hearts; for a second I forget.

What's more, this averted attention is particularly powerful because by the time we get to the last line, "On channels 2 through 99, we sought but couldn't find a cure for the fact that one day we would die," I'm not only reminded of our imminent death, I'm stunned by it. I'm stunned that I was so easy to distract—if only temporarily. And this temporary relief only underscores how insufficient the distraction was.

I'm stunned, too, by that final line's candor. Instead of telling me to think about my own death (and hasn't this been the charge of so much art for so long? From Shakespeare to Tolstoy to Shields; Picasso and van Gogh; shoot, even *Six Feet Under*), which, as confessed above, isn't something I need to be asked to do, this essay says something else. It says, "Well, shit. Try as we might to forget the fact that we're all dust, nothing cuts it . . . not for long, anyway." *We couldn't find a cure.* It acknowledges the downright stickiness of the issue. It calls it out for being the big, hairy mess that it is. It doesn't offer a quick solution. I appreciate this.

This is a particularly stellar move because in the discussion of death, everyone (including Shields, sometimes) offers (faulty) solutions. Earlier in the book, he quotes Zola: "As I grow older, I feel everything departing, and I love everything with more passion." It's a familiar sentiment; understanding that life is short, death imminent, we appreciate everything more fiercely. I remember holding Harriet just after she'd arrived. The sun fell in long swaths into the hospital room, and I watched her sleep. I remember telling myself that giving birth is totally pedestrian. Literally nothing is more common. Don't think yourself too special. But still, this little person grew all the right pieces and was here now, healthy. It felt improbable. Impossible, even. And so I cherish each second with her because her existence is a wonder, and it (and I) won't last forever. So, yeah, Zola. I am loving passionately.

But I'm not 100 percent sated (or as Shields might say, cured) because loving passionately doesn't save us from death. It doesn't keep me from thinking about how much of Harriet's life I will miss after I'm gone (best-case scenario) or how fragile her life is (worst-case scenario).

Shields offers other equally inadequate solutions, too. Much of his writing suggests that immersion therapy is the ticket. If we just focus on death enough, maybe we'll become fast friends, thus the onslaught of death data in the earlier pages. But in "Death Is the Mother of Beauty," he calls himself out. He knows the jig is up. Here he concedes that we can focus on death as much as we want; all that obsessing won't fix a thing. Channels 2, 24, 41, 49, 72, and 85 prove this.

In the same vein, religion won't cure us: channels 38 and 89. Resistance won't cure us: channels 42, 59, 64, 80, and 87. Sex won't cure us: channels 7, 11, 36, 55, and 77. If these are fixes, Shields isn't buying 'em.

So I'm spurred to look deeper. For all the piece's candor—how it resists the quick-and-easy solutions—it doesn't merely throw up its hands in dissatisfaction. Shields tells us he's found no cure, but quietly, beneath the layers of all that TV chatter, he offers us something else.

"On channels 2 through 99, we sought but couldn't find a cure for the fact that one day we would die." Here, the heart of the essay that's the heart of the book. Here, a distinct and audible beat; here, a gasp of air. For all the moments we can't seem to escape—the second when our baby stops breathing, when the doctor's stethoscope picks up nothing, when the chest stays stuck—here's one moment Shields will always occupy, I hope. Because here, faced with the sobering hard truth that the cure we so desperately long for doesn't exist, he is not alone. *We sought . . . we couldn't . . . we would die.* There's power in that slim two-letter word, power in its repetition.

I imagine the scene at 1:45 a.m. The whole house is silent. Shields turns in bed, readjusts his pillow, rolls onto his back. He stares at the ceiling. He woke from a dream, something about his daughter, and though the details are hazy, there's a boulder in his stomach, some vague worry he can't place. Or he woke because his back, which nettles him more and more each year, is tightening up. Or he woke because he heard his father fill a glass with water, heard him sink into his armchair, heard him futz with the remote control.

Realizing that sleep is hopeless, he kicks off his blanket and wanders to the living room. His father leans forward in his chair, jamming buttons on the clicker. Outside, moths flit around a patio light. They land on the screen door and flex their dust-colored wings. They lift and vanish. Shields holds out his hand and his father gives up the remote. He points it at the TV. Nothing. He shakes it. Points it lower, higher, re-inserts the batteries, points again, and the TV flicks on. His father takes it back and turns up the volume. He offers his son a swig of his water; the son accepts. They flip and flip. Then a highlight reel flashes on ESPN. A Yankee rounds third base, then home, and the scoreboard rolls over. Cut to a girl in the stands catching a pop fly. Cut to the Celtics and the Nets in double overtime. Cut to a game-winning three-pointer from way downtown. Cut to Boston's bench flooding the floor. Cut to a commercial for Red Bull; it gives you wings. Cut to a parent and child finding solace if not a cure.

DAVID LEGAULT

Movie Quotes as Misery

On Claudia Rankine's *Don't Let Me Be Lonely*

I am not one for quotations. I'm not sure if it's because I don't have the memory for it, or if I'm an inattentive reader (not absorbing the words well enough to recall them later), or if I'm simply not interested in repeating others' words verbatim. I am in the early stages of applying for a number of teaching jobs and fellowships, and as I've been reading through countless craft discussions, cover letters, and teaching philosophies, I am amazed (and slightly overwhelmed) by the callbacks people make. I have heard memorized quotations from Stegner, Didion, Weil, Mann, and Montaigne, and these quotations seem to evoke a sense of writerly influence, a sense of historical or cultural weight that I do not connect with.

And, yes, most of these quotations are probably not recalled from memory—any number of these lines can easily be found with a quick Google search—but still I am astounded at how so many of my friends and colleagues can draw so directly from literature, can draw the lines so clearly between their own ideas and their inspiration, while I often find myself describing books in such vague phrases as "during that one scene on the boat" or "when the main character said that thing about his sister to the judge."

And maybe I'm just so troubled by it because, like many of us, I have no problem quoting movies or television. I can rattle off entire episodes of *Seinfeld* or *The Simpsons* from memory, and yet I cannot begin to do the same with books, even ones that have so significantly shaped me as a writer and (I would argue) a person. Perhaps it's because television is so passive, or because it's easier to encounter repetition (I can watch a rerun while eating dinner, and a half-hour sitcom is much easier to repeat a dozen times than a book). But still, I am somewhat bothered that my cultural language comes more directly from TV than it does from the books that mean so much to me.

I mention this because there is an exception to the rule. There is one phrase, one image, that I have not been able to shake in the six years since I first encountered it.

"This is the most miserable in my life." "This is the most miserable in my life." It has become something of a mantra.

It comes from Claudia Rankine's wonderful book-length essay *Don't Let Me Be Lonely*. To give some context: Rankine is referencing a friend who is suffering from Alzheimer's disease, and in the span between diagnosis and being moved to a live-in facility, he writes this on his chalkboard, seen above. And perhaps it is the visual—the extra layer of authenticity, the sharp, shaky letters that seem sick in and of themselves—that keeps these words echoing in my mind. Perhaps it is because these words are so mimetic of the condition, the missing article (the most miserable *what*?), or that the phrase is pure declaration. It is as if language is breaking down, unable to capture the grief: that it is impossible for us to completely reach that headspace until we, too, are the most miserable of our lives.

Most likely, it's the fact that the words are *scratched into the surface* when chalk would have been so much easier, and more easily erased. And because of that extra dedication to the words, we are paradoxically met with permanence in the transitional space of the board, capturing the extent of that misery, the loss of language so directly tied with the loss of self.

Is it dropping my daughter off at day care for the first time? Getting on a bus to go to my shitty job at 5:30 in the morning? When I'm drinking Mountain Dew and skipping out on my evening run? This is the most miserable of my life.

Or perhaps it's because of the movement, the cognitive leaps of the essay. We get a mother's miscarriage and movie deaths and 1-800-SUICIDE and a picture of breast cancer cells and television commercials and DO NOT RESUSCITATE and *Boogie Nights* and Gertrude Stein and we are only on page 6. We get *Murder, She Wrote* reruns that I can only describe as haunting. Sections are interrupted with photos, artwork, the repeating image of a television screen, the ghost of a profile creeping out of the static.

And this essay is television. It is a flipping of channels, a deluxe cable package. It is a series of commercials reminding us that we are alone, depressed. Our medications will save us but have potentially serious side effects. We are told by the voices that the world is broken, dangerous. We are told that the television is the voice that we can trust.

So what can we do when that voice is speaking to white middle class men ages eighteen to thirty-four? What voice do we trust if we are not a part of a target demographic?

Abner Louima is sodomized while in police custody. Anyone of Middle Eastern descent is treated like al-Qaeda in a post-9/11 world. Rankine tells us, "There was a time I could say no one I knew well had died." This is the most miserable of my life.

And so the essay gives voice to a lot of voiceless situations, adding subtlety to the black-and-white, right-and-wrong representations "as seen on TV." We can see where the loneliness comes from: the disconnect between TV and reality, between the way the world is represented and the true world. Laugh tracks are added to sitcoms so we never laugh alone, but are we really part of a group when we are separated by glass and light?

Rankine gives me a new understanding of quotation, one I think I can live with: By placing the words in a new context, by juxtaposing quotation with image and personal experience, each element takes on new meaning, becomes communal. To quote another is to share knowledge, to connect, to never be alone.

A Paperback Cabinet of Wonder

Unlocking the Long Lyric Essay

I'm thinking today about the challenges of the long lyric essay, which I'm defining as anything from about forty pages to book-length. For me, a lyric essay works like a poem can, with pressurized language and associative leaps, and although it may contain narrative, story is not the main engine pulling the reader through the material. And like a poem, the lyric essay can take a turn at the end—sometimes a sharp, surprising turn.

Let's face it. no matter its length, the lyric essay presents challenges to the reader as well as to the writer. Narrative is a powerful tool to discard. And the language in a lyric essay can be dense, concerned with sound as well as with meaning. The pleasures of the lyric essay— the unhurried delight it takes in surprise and thought—can turn too easily into its downfall. Syntax can tangle; lines of thought can turn self-indulgent. This is prose of the kind that Robert Coover called "disruptive, eccentric, even inaccessible," but I believe that despite its challenges, the long lyric essay can provide a space for the reader and the writer to delight in each other.

In thinking about this question, I've been reading critic Tom LeClair's book *The Art of Excess*, in which he discusses prose that makes a "quantitative deformation of conventions," something I believe the lyric essayist sets out to do, consciously or not. Even more important for the terms of my argument, LeClair cites key points from Roland Barthes's *The Pleasure of the Text*. Barthes defines the "text of pleasure" as "the text that contents, fills, grants euphoria; the text that comes from culture and does not break with it, is linked to a comfortable practice of reading." But the text of pleasure differs from the "text of bliss," which "imposes a state of loss . . . discomforts (perhaps to the state of a certain boredom), unsettles the reader's historical, cultural, psychological assumptions, the consistency of his tastes, values, memories, brings to a crisis his relation with language." How can bliss coexist with a state of loss, discomfort, and boredom? How can bliss bring to a crisis one's relation to language? Barthes says we want to be shaken, challenged when we read. If that's right, then the long lyric essay must strive to be a text of bliss.

In order for this text of bliss to succeed, I believe that the long lyric essay demands a strong narratorial presence to draw readers' attention to, and guide them to make meaning from, what would seem like bare facts. More: the lyric essay's images must startle; its juxtapositions, surprise—while feeling inevitable.

Briefly, here are three models for the kind of long-lyric exploration I want to do in my own work. Two are nonfiction, and one is poetry. Each example, longer than the last, depends on something other than narrative to bind it together, and each one reaches some kind of resolution.

My first example—Joan Didion's essay "The White Album"—clocks in at about 12,500 words. It depends on shape, but even more, on an intensely hermetic sense of time—the late 1960s. The air is close, the entrances sealed shut. In fifteen sections, the narrator leads us through the Manson murders, campus riots, and music culture. When the end comes, there's no easy conclusion, but there is a sense of resolution, with callbacks to previous images.

What holds the piece together? The narrative arc of the Manson case is part of it; the narrator's grip on herself is part of it. The persona of the narrator herself is part of it, but that's too easy. The narrator resists the notion that any simple answer could come of all this: as the last line says, "writing has not yet helped me to see what it means." The essay might resist easy meaning, but it still satisfies. Why? Of course, Didion's sentences are lovely, and I find her steely narrator very sympathetic. But there is something more at work here. Could it be the physicality of her details—a lit match and Jim Morrison's black vinyl pants; the smell of jasmine and a crumbling tennis court—juxtaposed with the unanswerable questions of her time, a time that more and more, with its violence and dread, reminds me of ours? When the narrator first hears of the Manson killings, she says, "I also remember this, and wish I did not: *I remember that no one was surprised.*"

Didion's essay demonstrates one of what I believe to be the lyric essay's natural strengths: while clearly art, it feels more realistic than a strictly plotted narrative would. And with that strength, a question follows: is this a peculiarly postmodern form fixated on fragments? Not for me. I appreciate its affinity for fragments, because oftentimes, that's what we find—shards of pottery or a few words of chalked graffiti. But I want the reader to have an intellectual and emotional payoff at the end. If not a conclusion, then a resolution, and Didion's essay provides that.

My second example is Anne Carson's "Just for the Thrill," which runs at about 15,000 words. Here, two shapes corset the material. The first shape, told via travel diary, is that of a cross-country drive and camping trip the narrator takes with her soon to be former lover, a scholar of Chinese wisdom. The second shape is a list of places, with names such as Cross-Fire Zone, Ten-Heart Hermitage, and Flesh and Blood Bridge, mentioned on a historical map made by a royal courtesan in 1553. There are sixty-seven items on the map list; there are sixty-seven sections in the travel diary. Matching each item from the map with its corresponding entry in the travel diary provides sparks of meaning. Like a terrific last line in a poetry collection, the map slingshots you back to the beginning so that you reread the piece with that new revelation in mind.

As an example, I'd like to read section 58 in the travel diary. By this point, the relationship is deteriorating between the narrator and her lover; they are also passing through Las Vegas, which surely isn't helping.

Las Vegas, Nevada

On the radio someone is interviewing Ray Charles. *When I do a song I like to make it stink in my own way,* Ray Charles is saying. With eyes closed I can smell the fickle Tao of

Las Vegas heating up in layers. We seem to be driving through the center of town, to judge from the frequency of stops. Traffic intersections smell like underfur of dogs. Raw liver as the humans wash past hot, cold, hot. Neon smells like shock treatment and makes that same ice-pick nick on your mind. I remember on the eve of my thirteenth birthday, I overheard my aunts talking to Father about young girls and the dangerous age. "But she isn't going to be one of them," I heard Father say firmly. I was filled with pride, which smells like rubies. *I got seven nights to rock*, Ray Charles is singing, *got seven nights to roll.* His voice smells like wooden rain. Who will I be instead? is a question I never got around to asking Father. *Every night goin show my face with a different chick in a different place.* Well I suppose I can be anyone I like or rather, with eyes closed, nobody at all. *A dream dreamt in a dreaming world is not really a dream,* says classical Chinese wisdom, *but a dream not dreamt is.*

The corresponding map item from courtesan Lady Cheng's list reads "Bridge of Just Tears," which is preceded by number 57, "Straight Road," and followed by 59, "Stations of Refreshment for Travelers on the Straight Road." I'm struck by the ways in which the polyvocality within the essay—as here, with the Ray Charles quotes, lines from blues singers are spread through the piece—is underscored by the map list at the essay's end, a kind of phantom doubling or recasting of the events that take place within the essay's sixty-seven sections.

Carson's essay demonstrates a second natural strength of the lyric essay: it allows the writer a space in which to make meaning out of events and sensations and thoughts it would be easy to overlook. This, too, matters, says non-narrative nonfiction, which creates meaning through accretion. I think of the marine worms who live in the shallow waters off the Gulf Coast, collecting bits of broken shell and seaweed and cast-off crab claws and barnacle flakes; with these, they knit long socks in which they encase their soft bodies. Every piece is a necessary part of the disguise and the armor; the chips are no good on their own, but only as assembled.

My last example is A. R. Ammons's book-length poem *Garbage.* Part of what ties this book together is the act of writing itself, as in lines where the narrator calls our attention to the process:

> . . . how to write this
> poem, should it be short, a small popping of
>
> duplexes, or long, hunting wide, coming home
> late, losing the trail and recovering it

The narrative voice is pleasingly unsure of itself, and this self-questioning feels right for the non-narrative, non-mastering modus operandi of this piece. But more than that, the narrator himself ties the poem together. He's clearly present from the beginning, with his musings on soybeans, departmental meetings, and trips to the farmer's market.

And here I see a third natural strength of the long lyric: the particular pleasure it takes in rigorous language. Each word and its placement count. It comes to its conclusion in its own good time, and its realizations bubble along, almost subterranean, until they break upon the reader, who seems to get it at the same time the narrator does.

An odd thing happens when I read the poem's last lines, with their gesture toward the superlative:

> the gentlest, the most
> refined language, so little engaged it is hardly
>
> engaging, deserves to tell the deepest wishes,
> roundabout fears: loud boys, the declaimers,
>
> the deaf listen to them: to the whisperers,
> even the silent, their moody abundance: the
>
> poem that goes dumb holds tears.

The gentlest, the most refined—I'm struck, here, by our longing to define the outer limits of something, an urge that comes on us early in life and sticks with us.

As evidence of this, let me present the book fair of my memory, Concrete Elementary School in Anderson County, South Carolina. We lined up with dollar bills our mothers had paper-clipped to the order forms, to buy the *Guinness Book of World Records.* Even though it was chunky as a dictionary, you could read the *Guinness Book* straight through. At lunchtime, we read it aloud, savoring the things people thought up to do, and the fame their odd successes brought them.

Even now, staring at the Guinness World Records home page, I'm hooked. Here's a man towing an airplane; here's the world's largest collection of sick bags. Here's the statistic for the fastest mile covered on spring-loaded stilts. Says Ammons: "anything, / anything, anything is poetry"; O.K., here's the most toilet seats broken by the head in one minute—forty-six, he was from Indianapolis.

We want to push the limits. Here's proof, a long list poem doubling as the book most stolen from bookstores (unless that's the Bible). It's a book of wonders, a paperback cabinet of curiosity. Writes Ammons,

> we're trash, plenty wondrous: should I want
> to say in what wonder consists: it is a tiny
>
> wriggle of light in the mind that says, 'go on':
> that's what it says: that's all it says.

Reading *Guinness,* alongside Ammons, I'm attracted again to the prose Coover calls "disruptive, eccentric, even inaccessible." Disruptive, yes. Eccentric, yes. But these two qualities need not lead to inaccessibility. Isn't that life; isn't it the text of bliss? What challenges the reader, upends her expectations, forces her to recast her assumptions in a new frame.

Walk with me through the art of excess. Past the house in the desert made of old green bottles, chinked with mud and glowing in the sun. Past the fabulous show costumes Liberace wore, glittering and glistering with several oceans' worth of factory-made shine. Right on up to the big sphere that lives in its own glassed-in house, audacious and disruptive and strange: The Biggest Ball of Twine Made by One Man, of Darwin, Minnesota.

The Biggest Ball, they say, weighs nine tons, is forty feet around, and took twenty-nine years to make. I have seen it, and I can tell you this: it's tall as corn in August of a good year. It pulls dust to itself, smells like mice, and started with a yard or so of leftover baling twine. He twisted it around two fingers and tied it into a knot to save. By and by, the saving of it became more important than anything else.

This, too, is a text, a memorial. I think of Barthes again: to examine it brings "discomfort (perhaps to the state of a certain boredom)." It "unsettles . . . the consistency of [the reader's] tastes, values, memories." It "brings to a crisis [one's] relation with language." I stood before it, and knew not what to say. Says Ammons, "We mean to go on and go on till we unwind / the winding of our longest road." No matter how closely you look, you can't find the place where he stopped. The end is like the beginning, and there's a long, long line between.

JOHN D'AGATA

The Essays of Ansel Adams

An Allegory

Until 1927, the photographs that Ansel Adams had taken were not very good: documentary records of an afternoon with friends, a tree that he admired, a sunset worth remembering. They were placeholders for meaning, but not particularly meaningful themselves.

Of course, it isn't that Adams didn't consider photography art. Rather, he hadn't figured out yet how to make photography work, how to render with light and luck and dark the deep and powerful truths that he felt when in the mountains. As Adams will write toward the end of his life, "When I am ready to make a photograph, I think what I see in my mind's eye is something that is not literally there. What I am interested in expressing is something that is built up from within, rather than something extracted from without."

When I am ready to make *a photograph.*

Not just "take" one. Not just capture through hope and a lens whatever it is that the world might provide. As one critic has written about Adams's work, it is this acknowledgment of the difference between receiving information and actively making art that allows Adams eventually "to voice the moods of light, to use textures like different instruments, to make clouds float, waterfalls flash, snow reveal its hidden life, and grasses bend in infinite delicacy under dew."

It is April. And once again Adams is in Yosemite National Park, halfway up the granite face of a structure called Half Dome. He's on his way to a popular spot among hikers called the Diving Board, a long and narrow projection of rock from which you can look up and see the sharp sheer face of the Half Dome's cliff rising up before you. Along the way, Adams stops to take some shots—his girlfriend, his buddies, a bird, his shoes—until he realizes upon reaching the Diving Board that he has only two pictures left. He positions the camera to face Half Dome, that great and monstrous cliff face that looks as if it has punctured the earth from the inside out.

Wow, Adams thinks, then clicks.

Immediately, however, he knows that the picture he has taken is not going to work, will not relay to viewers the true experience of the Half Dome. So with only one picture left, Adams takes a risk. He allows himself to "revisualize" the scene. (His word.) He places over his lens a heavy red filter that immediately darkens the sky, transforms it even darker than the cliff face itself, so that an abyss opens up on the left side of the cliff, as if the brooding shelf of Half Dome has torn straight through it like a cleaver made of light, terrifying and bright.

As he himself later put it, this is the first time in Adams's career that he has managed to make a mountain look like how it feels. To do this however, he has deeply manipulated the mountain he loves, he has wrangled the reality of the world around him into what he has needed it to be. "Photography is really perception," he wrote. "As with all art, the objective of photography is not the duplication of visual reality, but an investigation of the outer world and its influence on the inner world. . . . All of my photographs are photographs of myself."

10 Thoughts on Elision

1. The act of writing nonfiction has always been an act of elision. Only when a writer knows what to leave out, does she know what to leave in.
2. You see this so clearly in the work of Joan Didion and James Baldwin and Janet Malcolm and, more recently, writers like Sarah Manguso. This is not matter of style—a baroque sentence can still be as pointed as an ice pick. This is a matter of choice.
3. Elision is not the same thing as distortion, though it can result in distortions, some of which may be more truthful than anyone's unabridged whole.
4. Abridged is not the same thing as incomplete, which implies unfinished—a house without a roof, a winter without snow. An aborted thought is not the same thing as looking at snowdrifts with one eye closed.
5. This is not news, but for some reason we keep needing to hear this report from the front, as if the frontline has ever been anywhere else.
6. *Elision* comes from *elidere,* "to crush out." This violence is generative, resulting in "omission" but also "join together, merge, esp. abstract ideas."
7. Any patient in an Oliver Sacks essay may be a composite character, an amalgamation of many patients merged into one, more useful, person. This is not a secret. It does not put Sacks's insights in danger. He has still seen what he has seen.
8. "You can't do that." Yes, you can.
9. "You shouldn't do that." Another matter, entirely. And utterly dependent on circumstance. Rules are only useful if everyone is playing the same game.
10. Choose your game. Then elide.

THOMAS MIRA Y LOPEZ

On Donald Hall's "Out the Window"

I first read Donald Hall's "Out the Window" in the *New Yorker* a year ago at 5:30 a.m. I was a barista at a French Moroccan restaurant in the West Village, and the morning shift began at 6. Two or three times a week, I would wake up before dawn and take the L train from Brooklyn to Manhattan in the gloomiest of moods if I did not have something to read.

Subway reading is tricky business. You want to choose something that can withstand and accompany the bumps and jostles of the ride. Light and engaging is good, yet at the same time you are conscious that fellow passengers notice what you read, that they can either approve or disapprove, even read over your shoulder. I like to read magazines because they are pliable and compact and the *New Yorker* in particular because I want to look like a serious, well-informed young man. Magazines are also ideal for prolonged visits to temporary spaces (the subway, the bathroom, jury duty, doctors' waiting rooms). They serve as buffers and distractions to whatever waits on the other side of that space—the news the doctor will deliver or the fact that once again I will put on a striped, coffee-stained American Apparel shirt and cap in order to look like a French sailor as I work a job that has no foreseeable future but also no end.

But Hall's essay does not distract. It confronts, ever so quietly, ever so memorably. And so while the L at 5:30 a.m.—reggaeton muffled on headphones, passengers bundled up like pigeons, the car locked into its tracks—might not be the most suitable space to read an essay about a poet gazing out his New Hampshire window, it is an intuitive one in which to read an eighty-three-year-old's acknowledgment of his own mortality and fatigue.

What first drew me to "Out the Window," what made me resist the urge to flip through the cartoons, is that it's about nothing. I like essays about nothing—or essays that don't feel as if they have to be about something—because they usually then become something only after they've spent a long time thinking and reflecting about how they're in a sense about nothing. Or, rather, "Out the Window" is about the everyday, which can be everything and nothing. The essay opens with Hall sitting at his window, a place he often occupies now that he is eighty-three. He is looking out at the birds in his feeder and at his family's barn that must withstand another winter. He begins: "Today it is January, midmonth, midday, and mid–New Hampshire." We are trapped alongside Hall in his armchair, yet still we move, homing in, both in time (from month to midmonth to a time of day) and place. The ease with which Hall directs our focus underscores the dexterity of the language: today, a day, is not exactly January, just as the movement from time to a place both catches us by surprise and yet maintains a fluidity in the repeated prefix *mid-*.

Sentences such as the above strike me as admirable. Hall's tone is quiet, sober, considered. Most of all, it's considerate: as Hall documents his losses at eighty-three (one of which he says is language), he retains a control over the very language that his admissions claim to contradict. These losses—that of his wife, Jane Kenyon the poet, who died of leukemia at forty-seven, or his father, who died at fifty-two— cause Hall to reevaluate his own physical and mental regressions. In doing so, he makes a small, quiet observation, one I did not expect him to make and one that lets you glimpse the full weight of his life's sadness as well as its blessedness: "I feel the circles grow smaller, and old age is a ceremony of losses, which is on the whole preferable to dying at forty-seven or fifty-two." Hall does not set these up as juxtapositions but as coexisting, even harmonious. More than that, in writing that "circles grow smaller," he rephrases a metaphor his wife used to describe his mother's death and is thus enacting his own words, "a ceremony of losses," by repeating and honoring hers. Hall goes on to write: "When I lament and darken over my diminishments, I accomplish nothing. It's better to sit at the window all day, pleased to watch birds, barns, and flowers. It is a pleasure to write about what I do." He darkens over diminishments (a verb to match its object) and then sits, in the light, during the day, to watch birds and his barn. He is doing nothing, yet now we know the reason why: because if he were to do something (i.e., "lament and darken"), that would truly be doing nothing. We return to the essay's beginning and feel the circles of Hall's prose growing tighter.

And then there's his use of adjectives. Here is how he describes his grandmother's death: "Three years later, in the Peabody Home, I sat beside her listening to Cheyne-Stokes breathing. I was holding her hand when she died." It is difficult, I have found, to write death. Even more difficult to write it concisely. Yet here Hall nails it with one adjective that does not necessarily encapsulate death, but death in this specific case: not everybody has Cheyne-Stokes breathing when they die; not everyone who displays Cheyne-Stokes breathing is dying (they could be sleeping), but it is appropriate here. It's a proper adjective, capitalized, a medical term in a poet's lexicon, yet it does not feel out of place, nor like a difficult adjective just thrown in for the sake of opening our dictionaries. Earlier in the passage Hall has discussed his mother's smoking habits: "two packs a day—unfiltered Chesterfields first, then filtered Kents." Not only is this language rhythmic (from unfiltered to filtered, from first to then, from the *Ch* of Chesterfield to the *K* in Kent, unfil to field to first to fil to Kents, ter to ter to ter), but it surfaces very subtly, very coyly in the Cheyne-Stokes line: Cheyne-Stokes looks a bit like the word Chesterfield and, even though we are reading of Hall's grandmother here and not his mother, I'm left scratching my head as to why this all sounds so familiar until I realize, ahh, that Cheyne-Stokes rhymes with *chain smokes.*

Hall writes about difficult subjects—death and aging—with seeming ease. Not just all ages ("thirty was terrifying, forty I never noticed because I was drunk") but old age. Not just old age, but his old age.

As with the essay's opening ("January, midmonth, midday, mid-New Hampshire"), Hall approaches his situation from all angles: how he sees himself, how he sees others, and how others of all ages see him. Here's one such passage:

> Over the years I travelled to another universe. However alert we are, however much we think we know what will happen, antiquity remains an unknown, unanticipated galaxy. It is alien, and old people are a separate form of life. They have green skin, with two heads that sprout antennae. They can be pleasant, they can be annoying—in the supermarket, these old ladies won't get out of my way— but most important they are permanently other. When we turn eighty, we understand that we are extraterrestrial.

How sly is this sentiment: we don't become extraterrestrial, but we understand ourselves as such, which implies that others might have been understanding or seeing us like this long before we came around to such a viewpoint. This works because it's true and not true (the elderly are not aliens but they can have greenish skin, extra [sort of] heads, and most definitely strange protuberances) and because it both extends distance (by speaking of extraterrestrials and outer space) and collapses it in Hall's honesty about his own condition, his own old age, his own body.

This capacity for subtle surprise pervades the essay. "Cornflowers bloom," Hall writes near the end, describing his landscape. Here is another great word choice—cornflowers are blue, and so how much more important does that verb become, how much more connotation and suggestion does he get by pairing it with a cornflower instead of, say, a daffodil. He claims, "New poems no longer come to me, with their prodigies of metaphor and assonance. Prose endures." New poems might no longer arrive, but that assonance is surely there—even in the sentence where he doubts its place ("poems" and "no," "me" and "prodigies"). And then there is metaphor. For the duration of the essay, Hall sits and looks out at his barn. As he traces its history, I do not realize till the essay's end that this barn, its age, its past, runs con-current with him. That it is, in fact, him: "Over eighty years, it has changed from a working barn to a barn for looking at." That's the thing about Hall's metaphor, his prose in general: it is so quiet yet so in com-mand that, like a hushed train trip at dawn, you do not realize you have reached your destination until you are already there. And while that destination—an essay's end, a life's end—may be both necessary and undesired, it at least leaves you with nowhere to go but walking up, through a turnstile and into daylight.

DANIELLE CADENA DEULEN

On the Virtues of Drowning

Lidia Yuknavitch's *The Chronology of Water*

There's a heat advisory in Cincinnati today, so I'm out on my porch. I'm writing in the heat because I want to sweat while I write this. Because I'm trying to reenact the first time I read *The Chronology of Water* by Lidia Yuknavitch, or because the book demands that kind of attention to physicality. I don't know which. I remember sweating when I first read it, though it was February, the most bereft of months—a soul sweat, maybe. I was too hot and then too cold. I kept saying yes, and then no, and then yes again as I read, damp with water and salt. What I mean is, it did to me what I want literature to do to me; it took me to an edge. Sure, sometimes Yuknavitch's ever-exclamatory, frenetic aesthetics pushed me a little too deep into the River of the Grandiose, but I'd rather drown in luxurious water than stay forever on the shore of overly prim prose. Yes, I know my metaphors are getting out of hand. Let me start over.

Yuknavitch works in a distinctly maximalist style. It's not ironic. It's not thin. It's not coy. This book-length essay is sinewy and savage. And you may take umbrage with me calling *The Chronology of Water* an essay. Go ahead, take umbrage. It's pushed as a memoir, after all, and has all the trappings of a mainstream story of loss and survival: Olympic hopeful swimmer escapes abusive family, loses it all when she becomes mired in her own self-destructive tendencies, ultimately finding transcendence in love and literature. There's trauma, drugs, lots of sex—everything a voyeur could want. That's not what excites me about this book.

Most everyone I know has a sad story to tell, but none of them thought to write it like this. Although marketed as a memoir, it moves like a collection of linked essays. The larger numbered sections, and especially the shorter named works within those sections, are essays. They begin in impulse and end where you don't expect; they assay and contradict; they deviate and are deviant. Earlier, I said the book demands a kind of attention to physicality, and I'm coming back to that now. I don't necessarily subscribe to the notion that our current literature represents puritanical notions of sexuality. Certainly, the hegemonic standards have been set, but there are plenty of writers who've thwarted them powerfully. Yet, I find Yuknavitch's frankness about the emotional and physical experience of being a woman (in sex, in athletic competition, in childbirth) surprising. Not because it offends my sensibilities but because it affirms them. Consider the first paragraph of the book:

> The day my daughter was stillborn, after I held the future pink and rose-lipped in my shivering arms, lifeless tender, covering her face in tears and kisses, after they handed my dead girl to my sister who kissed her, then to my first husband who kissed her, then to my mother who could not bear to hold her, then out of the hospital room door, tiny lifeless swaddled thing, the nurse gave me tranquilizers and a soap and sponge. She guided me to a special shower. The shower had a chair and the spray came down lightly, warm. She said, That feels good, doesn't it. The water. She said, you are still bleeding quite a bit. Just let it. Ripped from vagina to rectum, sewn closed. Falling water on a body.

Yuknavitch writes about her emotional-physical self in a manner that is both lyric and direct, and later in the book, in more sexually explicit passages, with a frankness that might be called pornographic. It's a quality that I admire and reminds me vaguely of Irigaray's *This Sex Which Is Not One*, meant to call into question and make uncomfortable phallic-based Freudian theories by writing with intense anatomical focus about the autoerotic attributes of female genitalia. Completely different genre and aim, of course, but both are refreshingly unflinching in their representations of femaleness. They both write about being a woman as if no one ever told them not to—or, more accurately, they were told not to a lot and did so anyway, with great verve. So, O.K., I like the exhibitive aspects of the work too. You caught me: I'm as voyeuristic as anyone. But in this case there is a marriage of exhibition and voice that makes the interested voyeur feel not so bad about it. This writing is outrageous and nervy, yet finely calibrated, and amidst the candid heartbreak there is enough style and humor to place her firmly in the position of narrator, and so, the voyeur of herself. In part, she does this by drawing our attention to the way she writes. She tells us early on that she remembers things in "retinal flashes," that she won't be giving us the conventional narrative structure: "It's all a series of fragments and repetitions and pattern formations. Language and water have this in common." I love this book because it's made of water. And because a book made of water seems more honest to me.

I'm not talking about "honesty" as part of the long-suffering debate over the ethics of creative nonfiction, so rooted in what I see as an essentialist's naive faith in the possibility of incontestable knowledge—which is not to say there's no such thing as fact, or that our lives aren't structured by traditional narrative (they absolutely are), just that so little of human experience can be verified. And when the creative impulse is to capture nonfiction of the internal—nonfiction about imagination, dreams, lies, mistakes, betrayal, and superstition, and about the messiness of being a subjective and contradictory self—I want the structure to also be at least a little bit messy. I want associative leaps, repetition, backtracking, fragments, red herrings, a different kind of sense-making than traditional narrative. I want a way of writing that feels closer to perception and memory. Or probably I just want a literature that's closer to *my way* of perceiving and remembering. Since this is all interpretation, and interpretation is always symbolic of one's own mind, let me be more direct:

I used to love to swim. When I was a girl and it was summer, my father often took us (my sisters, my brother, and I) to the Columbia River, which is a wide, deep body of water always opaque with mud and oil (a beautiful rainbow covering, the way I saw it then) from the city runoff and its strong churning currents. It's a river banked with gray, gritty sand—not the smooth, white seashell erosion of ocean shorelines, but a sand more like ground peppercorn. I liked to dig in it. When I got tired of digging, I'd swim out in the river as far as I could go, out past the buoys because it was forbidden, and the danger of an undertow, still just a word in my mind, excited me.

There was a spot in the river where the buoys separating the swimming area from the wilder water, and there was a row of floating logs loosely chained in place, soft, splintery, warm as bodies in the sun, and one day I swam out to them. Believing myself otter-like, I made a game of spinning them and clutching on while they spun to let them roll me into the water, then out, then in again, keeping my eyes shut tight. The faster I could spin them, the better momentum for throwing me into the water, so I worked hard on that last spin, really revved it up, and when I belly-flopped onto the water, I hit it hard. Disoriented and blind, instead of swimming up, I went down, down, down, until the cold made me open my eyes in the mud-dark infinite. My breath was running out, and I didn't know which way my head was pointing. I panicked and swam harder, but still not far enough, or in the wrong direction, I didn't know which—all I knew was that I was completely out of air, trying to breath in and out the only stale breath I still had in my lungs, which seemed to push around inside me like a trapped ghost. It was the first time in my life that I realized I had a real shot at dying. Not the stories of heaven, but the actual corporeal manifestation of death: my body, a corpse. I thought of the first water pose my father taught me: the Dead Man's Float.

Then I thought of my father on the shore with his eyes closed beneath the sun, burning his skin darker with coconut oil, working up a beer sweat. Some nights I still dream my father is driving us toward the river, my sisters and I grown but weary like children in the heat, our thighs sticking to the vinyl of our metallic-blue Chevy, windows down, the breath of sand-dust and green-water lost in traffic when he turns at a light, parks in front of a theater, sends us in single file before him, buys us tickets and popcorn, but stands in the aisle smoking, a silhouette of refusal and ash. Where he was then (wherever he is now), he couldn't help me. Underwater, I became very still, thinking on that Dead Man, and let my buoyancy turn me around, lead me up, until I could perceive a faint, refracted light above me. Since I'm not writing this posthumously, you can guess what happened next: I surfaced, choked on air, grasped at anything, found myself on the wild side drifting toward wherever the river lead, then kicked furiously until I reached the logs to catch my breath, then continued until I pulled myself whimpering and exhausted to the gritty shore. Dizzy, my eyes not quite able to adjust to the sunlight—everything blurred in overexposure—I lay there breathing, too afraid to cry, until the sun dried the water. Until I began to sweat.

Catharsis. Aristotle understood artistic power as medicinal, generating a kind of innocent emotional purgation in one who allows herself to be affected. It presupposes a natural tendency, an innate desire for aesthetic reenactment of experience, even, and perhaps especially, experience that is terrible—for viewing the wreck from a safe distance. So as voyeurs of artistic expression, we are always voyeurs of ourselves. Lidia Yuknavitch's *The Chronology of Water* does not, ultimately, tell us what we didn't already know; it's just more conscious and gorgeous in the way it tells us: our memories are fragmented, our lives are broken. Lying there on the shore that day, I couldn't remember exactly what I knew about baptism, but I thought I understood more clearly what it meant. It meant there was a darkness in everyone, and you had to delve down into it, where the sun looks broken and a ghost knocks inside your chest. That you have to emerge from the darkness to know the sun. That you have to lie beneath it, let it fill you with fever. Because fever is the dark water pouring out of you. You sweat it out to feel whole again.

JOHN T. PRICE

On Hoagland, Animal Obsession, and the Courage of Simile

Early in my training as a nature essayist, I was taught to avoid certain kinds of simile like the plague. I was told that to imply, either directly or indirectly, that members of another species are like something or someone else, or that they think or feel as humans do (otherwise known as anthropomorphizing), invited a dangerous disrespect for the needs of that species as distinct from our own. That was true, as well, for entire ecosystems such as the prairie wilderness of my home region, which was described by early white explorers as being "like" a desert or "like" an ocean, anything but itself, and thus was ultimately destroyed to be "like" yet another something—an Eastern forest, a cornfield, a suburb, a wind farm, a vein of ethanol. Now most of that prairie wilderness is like, well, nothing at all.

Despite this, I have repeatedly violated the simile rule, especially when it comes to animals. I blame Edward Hoagland's "The Courage of Turtles." From the first time I read that essay in my early twenties, it disarmed me, broke down boundaries, decimated the nature-writing rulebook, and set me off on wild tangents that at first invited, but ultimately defied, easy understanding—just as, according to Hoagland, good essays should. "Essays don't usually boil down to a summary, as articles do," he wrote in "What I Think, What I Am." They are, instead, "a combination of personality and originality and energetic loose ends that stand up like the nap on a piece of wool and can't be brushed flat."

"The Courage of Turtles" has this kind of nap, and no matter how many times I read it or teach it, which is a lot, I can never quite comb it flat, though I continue to try.

It was first published on December 12, 1968, in the *Village Voice*, but that meant nothing to me when I first discovered it as a graduate student in the late 1980s. What mattered to me then was that it was about turtles. At the time, my future wife and I shared custody of an eastern box turtle named Methuselah, so I was moved right away by Hoagland's description of how turtles and other wildlife were displaced (or killed) when a pond near his boyhood home was bulldozed to make it flow "like an English brook." I had been feeling a little guilty about purchasing a turtle at a pet store but felt momentarily vindicated by this sad story and by Hoagland's claim that turtles "manage to contain the rest of the animal world." Saving them, as he suggested, could thus become a major "case of virtue rewarded," and he used a ton of similes to compare turtles to, among other vulnerable creatures, giraffes, warhorses, hippos, penguins, puppies, elephants, turkeys, and cow moose. I would have only added that turtles are also like hermit crabs, full of surprises, such as the day when Methuselah appeared to be excreting all of his internal organs out his backside—a huge, wet tube of purple, pink, and amber. Panicked, I called the vet who, after conducting additional research, informed me that Methuselah was simply experiencing "arousal." Prior to that, I had not considered turtle sexuality as anything more interesting than two rocks knocking together. Now I thought of it as being like the colors of a sunset or a tropical flower or a clown hat.

This is the kind of wild tangent I'm talking about when I talk about reading "The Courage of Turtles"—I mean, who needs it? I did, apparently. As a midwestern nature writer, living in a state where there is less than one-tenth of one percent of native habitats remaining, I was just beginning to understand that I would have to do a lot with a little, and Hoagland's essay was a good model. The list of my own animal obsessions was fairly short at the time, and decidedly non-native, but his piece encouraged me to take stock. The earliest was tigers—a fascination shared, as it happens, by Hoagland. "We have wiped tigers off the earth," he wrote in "The Problem of the Golden Rule," "and yet our children hear as much about the symbolism of tigers as children did in the old days." I was one of those children. My maternal grandparents called me "Tiger" and gave me all kinds of tiger stuff, such as a tiger sleeping bag and tiger slippers and tiger pajamas and tiger posters that I used to paper my bedroom walls. I was a small, physically awkward kid who mostly hung out alone in his room, so I suppose tigers symbolized everything I wasn't: power, confidence, beauty, grace. During that same period, my grandparents regularly took me to the now defunct restaurant chain Sambo's, where wall murals depicting the Lil' Sambo story taught me that tigers could also be a little like racism.

I often wonder if that early obsession with tigers led to my more recent obsession with mountain lions, which are returning to their home territory here in the Loess Hills of western Iowa and facing a tough time of it. Hoagland wrote about his own obsession with the species in "Hailing the Elusory Mountain Lion," and why I don't teach that essay more often, I can't say. Perhaps it's because my experiences with animals here in the Midwest have, for most of my life, been less about respecting their wild freedom than the ethical conundrums associated with creatures over which we have complete control. Cows and pigs, for instance. Also, domestic pets—that kind of power relationship with animals (as Hoagland's essay testifies) offers up its own distinct set of responsibilities, personal associations, and similes. In kindergarten, for instance, I owned a couple of painted turtles, Jack and Jill, but was forced to "set them free" in a nearby stream, on the verge of winter, because my mother had heard on the radio that turtles can be like *Salmonella*. Most of the hamsters I owned escaped and ended up dead in the old coal room in our basement, which, I guess, was like some kind of elephant graveyard for hamsters. In first grade, I fell in love with a calico guinea pig named Peppermint Patty, but then my teacher convinced my parents that it would be fun and informative to mate Patty with her own monstrous white guinea pig, which she kept in the classroom. Patty and her pups died during birth not long before my only brother died during birth, which became its own unfortunate simile. Perhaps because of this, I temporarily moved away from relationships with flesh-and-blood animals and, in the fourth grade, became infatuated with a rubber spider monkey purchased at a dime store. I named him Chico, safety-pinned him to my shoulder, and wore him to school for a couple of days. There I learned that spider monkeys were a lot like public humiliation, which felt like just another kind of death.

As a grown-up nature writer, I have, like Hoagland, explored obsessive relationships with numerous wild and domestic creatures in my published work. These include bison, mice, pheasants, squirrels, praying mantids, falcons, Triops, daddy longlegs, woodchucks, moles, elk, brown recluse spiders, prairie dogs, monarch butterflies, roaches, hummingbirds, robins, frogs, and children. I am currently obsessed with peacocks. In writing about these creatures, I have rationalized that my anthropomorphizing and liberal use of simile are less about arrogant assumptions and more about trying to create in the reader what Hoagland refers to in "What I Think, What I Am" as a "grand and golden empathy"—though he claims such empathy is primarily the stuff of fiction, not the essay. Or maybe what Buddhists call sunyata, the interconnection of all things, which implies not only complete dependence on other life-forms, but also the necessity of humility, even in the wake of what we think at first is knowledge. While arguing that "our loneliness" makes us avid essay readers, Hoagland claims that essays themselves "belong to the animal kingdom." As such, they often elude easy capture or containment, which is how it should be when a nature essay—or an ecosystem—is working well. Inside such a place, on the page or on the earth, people think they are chasing down one kind of animal, one kind of knowledge, but then an almost-connection leads them to another and another, until the meaning and responsibility for that meaning lands back in the collective lap of our own species, in our own historical ways with one another.

This is part of the brilliance of "The Courage of Turtles," as I've experienced it, but I didn't fully appreciate that until I was preparing to teach it in one of my first writing classes as a TA. I was once again puzzling over the ending, where Hoagland describes an aquatic terrapin he rescued but ultimately found "exasperating" because it exhibited "none of the hearty, accepting qualities of wood turtles." In a well-meaning, but botched "born free" moment, Hoagland tosses the terrapin off a New York pier, only to realize that the water was too deep, the currents too strong, and that the turtle would likely die. The essay concludes: "But since, short of diving in after him, there was nothing I could do, I walked away."

This scene, when I initially read it, seemed a powerful statement about the human relationship to the natural world. Here was an example of the dangerous limits of our knowledge, and the even more dangerous limits of our ability to risk true identification with other living beings, because of what it might require of us. The danger of simile, perhaps. But then, probably because I was about to teach the piece and felt some additional pressure to be thorough, I reconsidered the publication date, 1968, and an entirely new set of associations presented themselves. I went back through and took note of Hoagland's description of a captive turtle as having a "swollen face like a napalm victim's" and also this description of the turtles fleeing Mud Pond: "Creeping up the brooks to sad, constricted marshes, burdened as they are with that box on their back, they're walking into a setup where all their enemies move thirty times faster than they. It's like the nightmare most of us have whimpered through, where we are weighted down disastrously while trying to flee; fleeing our home ground, we try to run." Later, when I shared these observations with my students, I had the luxury of watching them conclude on their own and fairly quickly that this essay was not just about turtles but maybe also about the Vietnam War and empathy for its victims, civilian and military. This was 1989 or so, and some of their family members were veterans of that war, or, like me, had heard people talk about those they knew, even loved, who'd been emotionally or physically injured or left mentally ill or killed. After further discussion, some of the students concluded that the final scene might also be suggesting that the American government would, in the interests of protecting itself, walk away from Vietnam and those it was supposedly going to "free." Those it had, at the very least, promised to protect. Including our returning soldiers.

In this way, we discovered that an essay—on top of all its other admirable qualities—could be a lot like prophecy.

But time, like nature, cannot be contained, and my teaching experiences with "The Courage of Turtles" have roamed dramatically in that last twenty-five years. Nowadays, when I mention 1968 and napalm and ask my students for their associations, far fewer of them volunteer anything specific about Vietnam. This inevitably disappoints me, but this disappointment, because I invite and expect it, is likely nothing more than cheap compensation for growing older. The history lesson I now feel compelled to deliver, though important in its own way, too often allows me the delusion that the large-scale, murderous forms of hubris I knew in my youth, during that wartime, are in some essential way different from those known by my young students in this wartime. Setting up such a generational hierarchy becomes, for their aging professor, yet another case of virtue rewarded, a chance to "free" them from their own ignorance. That supposedly heroic effort leaves less time to examine the still urgent, uncompromising fact that we remain at our most dangerous when we think we know what's best for another being, when we make assumptions or create expectations about how they should best live or feel or mate or believe or know. Whether that being is another species or another person sitting across a classroom or halfway across the globe.

Still, I can't help myself. Case in point, my current obsession with writing about peacocks. Or rather, a particular male peacock that has been seen running around our heavily wooded neighborhood with a gang of wild turkeys. He was first spotted a couple of years ago by my then nine-year-old son, Spencer, crossing the road in front of our minivan—a strutting riot of blue and green amid the dull colors of his adopted tribe. The peacock and turkeys have been spotted many times together since then, by many people, and on certain spring mornings, his high-pitched screech has shattered the otherwise trickling, Zen-like music of the songbirds leaking in our bedroom windows. His call sometimes sounds like a child screaming for help, and in the stunned silence that usually follows, I often wonder if he is, in fact, in need of help. Should I do something? Call someone? I can't resist wondering

if that bird feels vulnerable or lonely, or perhaps rebellious or coura-
geous. Does it take courage for a peacock to run with a gang of turkeys,
to attempt to be like a turkey? Is he a living example of the courage of
simile, the grammatical expression of the desires and actions of a creature who needs, for whatever reason, to overcome his isolation and
connect with another species, another being—to be like another, and
therefore, in some way, become another? To make their needs his own?
Or if those needs are beyond understanding, to at least make their fate
his own? To finally, and without hesitation, dive in?

The questions and challenges presented by this kind of "golden
empathy" seem as relevant today as they were in 1968 or, say, the day
Jesus was born. But will future readers of my peacock story see it that
way? I'm a bit worried about that, about future readers, because I'm
not sure I'll have any. If I do, I kind of both love and hate to think
about somebody teaching my essay and saying something like, "Yes, it
may seem to be a vapid piece about a peacock, but look at the publication date—2013! What does that year in America mean to you, class?
It was, of course, the year of the government shutdown, the closing of
our national parks, the botched Obamacare website, and the death of
Andy Griffith—but also the Boston Marathon bombings and the devastating tornadoes in Oklahoma and our endless wars in the Middle
East! It's all there in Price's essay, if you look closely."

Will anyone care enough to look that closely and see all of these
things? If so, will they also see through the camouflage of historical
relevancy to what Hoagland has designated as the true subject of all
essays: "the fascination of the mind"? Will they see—do I want them
to see—that the real reason the author first became fascinated with
that singular peacock is that it seemed funny and out of place and in
its pathetic self-deception, almost, but not quite, graceful? And that
the year 2013 was, among other things, the year when the author, moving toward fifty, was especially appreciative of all things funny, out of
place, pathetic, and almost-but-not-quite graceful.

Sort of like him.

MAYA L. KAPOOR

On David Quammen and Writing Trout

Lately, I have appreciated David Quammen's trout thoughts. Quammen, whose career took off with the popularity of his Natural Acts column in *Outside* magazine, moved to Montana for the trout. He has a lot to say on the topic of trout, such as in "Synecdoche and the Trout," an essay included in *Wild Thoughts from Wild Places*. When he was fresh out of graduate school, Quammen writes, "Trout were the indicator species for a place and a life I was seeking." These days, I am trying to write about trout, to write my way into a story about trout in the Southwest, about native trout species in Arizona and New Mexico specifically. I have no idea how to fish, mind you, and am not entirely confident I could pick a trout out of a game fish lineup, although I am working on it. This glimpse through the eyes of a man who loves trout—who loves them as synecdoche, part and symbol of a place and way of being—has been immeasurably helpful as I study the strange connections between human and fish.

But what especially catch my eye these days are Quammen's asides, the places where trout swim to the surface of his thoughts unbidden—in an essay about mountain lion hunting, say, or a chapter on komodo dragons. In such moments, the trout are Quammen's way in. Quammen translates lion-speak and komodo-speak into trout-speak, not his mother tongue perhaps but a language in which he is fluent. In "So Huge a Bignes," a chapter of *The Song of the Dodo*, Quammen compares the egregious overestimation of komodo dragon length by researchers—in one case, biologists guessed a komodo to be *four feet* longer than it actually was—to what happens when an angler tries to recall the size of a fish.

> Trout fishermen are familiar with that phenomenon. When an animal is vividly impressive—struggling and leaping at the end of a fly line, say, or ripping apart a water buffalo with its teeth—it assumes a certain enhanced bigness, which mysteriously dissipates as soon as the contextual terms change and a tape measure is brought into play. The twenty-three-foot komodo is the one that got away.

Yes, I think. Quammen is right in his approach. And then—what is my way into the story of trout? It is not, obviously, trout. What are the metaphors with which I make sense of things stirred up in men and women by the thought of these cold-water fish? I remember the passage from "Eat of This Flesh," where Quammen is trying to bridge an ethical distance between lion hunters and himself. One doctor from a small town in Montana recalls to Quammen the moment when he first saw a lion, before ever trying to hunt one, and how the moment moved him to somehow *interact,* as he put it, with the cats.

> His interactions took the form of hunting, and though that leap of logic may seem perverse and paradoxical, I can't dismiss it as nonsense, because I remember a similar weird logic in my own feelings about trout. When I first became familiar with wild trout in mountain rivers, they seemed so exquisitely gorgeous, so thrilling, so magically animate, that I wanted to interact—yes, exactly the right word, vague but candid—with them somehow. I wanted to participate in the darting, lambent dynamics of their lives within their environment.

I remember what I said to a bemused writer friend when I first started researching trout. I was interested in Gila trout specifically. "I want to see a live Gila—I want to see one, to try fishing, to catch one, to eat one!" To appreciate the synecdoche as part and whole. Never mind that wild Gilas are nowhere to be found in a bikeable distance of my university neighborhood home in Tucson. I have mentioned already that I do not know how to fish; now might also be a good time to mention I became vegetarian twenty-one years ago. But this is how I learn the names of plants when I botanize in the desert, a much more familiar activity to me: I never feel I *know* a plant until I've touched its surface, observed its colors, and sometimes, chewed and swallowed one or two specimens. How I know plants is how my mind wants to know trout.

But Quammen's essayistic asides about trout do more for me than provide examples of using prior knowledge to bridge distances in understanding. Quammen's use of such trouty musings reminds me of how he defines research. "The researching and writing of a piece is always an experience of discovery, challenging what you think you know and what you feel you believe," Quammen said in a 2008 interview with Simmons Buntin, founding editor of *Terrain.org: A Journal of the Built + Natural Environments,* "If it isn't, you're in a rut, working too formulaically on subjects that are too comfy and safe." In other words, if no trout (or plant, or other familiarity) swirls into the imagery of an essay, if there is no need for it, perhaps the essay isn't doing enough.

Quammen wrote "Eat of This Flesh" after a mountain lion hunter (the Montana doctor mentioned above) objected to what Quammen recalls as "some shoot-from-the-hip sarcasm on the subject of mountain lion hunting" in an essay for *Outside* that was reprinted by the Montana Wilderness Association. Quammen took the reader's angry response as an opportunity to explore the topic of mountain lion hunting from an angle that made him uncomfortable. In "Eat of This Flesh," Quammen invokes trout to connect with someone whose worldview seems, on the surface at least, completely at odds with his own. The trout are a symbol of Quammen's willingness—desire, even—to find his way into the story of Man Who Hunts Mountain Lions. "This is not a retraction," Quammen writes, ". . . but it is an admission of incompleteness." He pushes the research and himself. He meets up with the hunter; he accompanies him on a lion-tracking trip; he tries, at least, to hear him out.

So when I write about fish, it will be with Quammen's trout in mind. Is there something about how I came to understand and connect with plants as a botanist that will guide how I now investigate fish, the way that Quammen's trout fishing informs so much of his writing? The urge to start in a place of familiarity—a fish, a lure, water slapping boat—then write a way into a new and disconcerting reality—that is what I'm learning from Quammen's trout moves these days. As for making a meal of this endeavor: I don't know if I will get my trout, but Quammen? He goes there. He does the work. He casts his line; he eats some mountain lion.

On Long Winters, Short Essays, and a Sky That Stretches Forever

We suffer from snow blindness, selecting what we see and feel
while our pain whites itself out. But where there is suffocation
and self-imposed ignorance, there is also refreshment—snow on
flushed cheeks and a pristine kind of thinking. All winter we
skate the small ponds—places that in summer are water holes
for cattle and sheep—and here a reflection of mind appears,
sharp, vigilant, precise.

—GRETEL EHRLICH, *THE SOLACE OF OPEN SPACES*

As I write this, April is in sight and the long Wyoming winter is only now showing signs of breaking. I spent the last few months far from any town center, surrounded by cows and mule deer and only a small handful of neighbors, thinking incorrectly that the isolation would be conducive to writing. It was something else entirely: in the great expanse that surrounded me, I found myself longing for smallness. In a harsh winter climate, one way to survive the elements, if you find yourself at their mercy, is to carve out a space in the snow and ice, just big enough for yourself. This is how you stay warm.

Gretel Ehrlich, in her novella-length collection of essays on Wyoming, *The Solace of Open Spaces,* writes, "Winter is smooth-skulled, and all our skids on black ice are cerebral." She's right; this stuck of mine is all in my mind. I like to say it's something about the snow, the shut-in-ness, the screaming wind, that has inhibited rather than encouraged my writing, but I've been the one fighting myself, not the fields that stretch forever or the boundless ice-blue sky.

In "Wind," from his collection *Where Rivers Change Direction*, Mark Spragg asserts,

> This place is violent, and it is raw. Wyoming is not a land that lends itself to nakedness, or leniency. There is an edge here; living is accomplished on that edge. Most birds migrate. Hibernation is viewed as necessary, not stolid. The crippled, old, the inattentive perish.

When I'm being honest, I have to admit that I'm afraid of that edge. All winter I've been hanging back, playing it too safe to get any real work done. I've been lenient with myself—staying warm instead of sharp—afraid of the despair that I sense out there in my own cerebral snowfields.

*

Judith Kitchen in *Short Takes* defines an essay as "the building of a process of thought through a singular contemplative voice—to show how we see the same world differently."

If that's an essay, then my Facebook feed has been an essay about winter ever since November. All over the country, everyone has spoken in a singular, if choir-like, voice of Instagram filters and weather.com screenshots. Sometimes the voice is awed, "It's actually sunny today!" And sometimes the voice can't believe it is snowing *again*. Today, in Ucross, Wyoming, it's over fifty degrees but another snowstorm is predicted to hit this weekend. Winter has been too long over me, an endless avalanche of words: *cold, snow, ice, more, still.*

*

Ehrlich's book is not long. Weighing in between feather- and light-weight, she has nonetheless crafted as notable a "Wyoming" book as heavyweights John McPhee's *Rising from the Plains* and Owen Wister's *The Virginian.* Even in a compressed collection though, "The Smooth Skull of Winter" stands out as the shortest essay in the book. In my paperback edition, it's just over three pages long.

Buried in the exact middle of six months of winter, I was angry the first time I read it. Or tripped across it, as I may have described it at the time. Would anyone write a book about California, or Florida, and give only three and a half pages to the ocean? This is not a book for residents (at less than half a million people in the state, that would be a very targeted and limiting demographic)—so how can anyone else understand the gravity of this thing I'm in, I thought, if it can be shrunk down into the same space as a preface?

But Ehrlich, in three pages, gets the better of winter. She turns the January wind into an opportunity. Ehrlich is not trapped by her three small pages, but distilled to clear purpose. She carves her shape into winter, not to hide, but to be carried forward, like a standard. This is easier to see in winter's wake.

I was recently on a panel discussing some finer points of short form nonfiction. One of the panel members, the managing editor of a respected journal, said (and I'm paraphrasing), "Please, no more funerals and hospital rooms."

She said between 10 and 15 percent of the submissions she receives take place in either a hospital room or at someone's funeral. I began to wonder what it is about the form that lends itself so well to pain, loss, and melancholy.

Bret Lott, seems to speak to this drive in "Writing in Place" from the *Rose Metal Press Field Guide to Writing Flash Nonfiction,* when he says "every time I put a word down . . . I am inside a moment in which I had better be attempting to wrestle with a matter of life and death."

Too often, the editor in the above example might say, the problem is that submitters confuse a *matter* of life and death with the *moment* between them. The real loss might come later, trying to match all the saucers to the teacups for the estate sale, or worrying about what hieroglyphic notations in an old field guide meant, the intrepid explorer, now gone.

In "Winter," an essay collected in Kitchen's *Short Takes*, Larry Woiwode recounts his struggle to refire an outdoor furnace that had gone out on a night when the temperature, including wind chill, was negative eighty-five degrees. He fights the snow and wind to the furnace and then struggles with a blowtorch to melt thick ice that is preventing the damper from opening. As he starts to fade from clear thinking into hypothermia, he lists loved ones, and thinks to them,

> It may be by a row of words you remember me, or maybe not. Or images, once my body is gone. You'll have to resolve the distinctions between the two for yourselves, if I can't keep the torch on target, get us heat, undo the miscues that brought us to this, so you'll know it wasn't my interior and its revolving search for words that held me here, but you.

It's a startling moment, and comes one sentence before the dénouement (this is nonfiction, so I don't think I'm spoiling it when I reveal that he lives). He manages, by keeping the moment singular (torch, heat, the day's miscues) and the language neutral (body, distinctions, interior), to avoid what could have been an easy slip into oversentimentality. He literally stops short of the happy ending and lets the reader float in the interstitial white space at the end of the essay, assuming the best or worst of his narrator-self's struggle back to the house from the restarted furnace.

Woiwode takes us to the exact minute when he thought his life might end, but the feeling that resonates is not sadness—it helps that he lives, I'll grant—it's something warm, even in all that snow. In less-skilled hands, this essay may have read like a *Chicken Soup for the Soul:* all lesson, no learning. Instead the reader is on the same edge as the narrator, all along, until this last moment of exhale, out of nowhere comes this idea—we are the sum of our love.

In a short essay (unlike a long winter), there is no time to get maudlin. The form itself asserts stolidity in the shape of brevity. There won't be room for gnashing teeth, rending garments, Fourth of July fried chicken, and all of Grandma's teacups—something will have to go. The craftsperson can see beyond the glissando of the stalling EKG—to the moment when her deeply personal sorrow breaks away from the "self-imposed ignorance" of the solo voice to join a whole choir of humanity.

*

In Wyoming, the sky is very big (at least as big as Montana's, but not on record as such). This can create a sense of freedom—and Ehrlich, along with many a cowboy poet, found her song in its open spaces.

But it can be a discomfort, too, all this unbound landscape.

I remember lying in summer grass at the Brooklyn botanical garden, listening in disbelief as a friend tried to explain her childhood fear of stars. It was after she learned in science class that the universe was endless, she said, that the night sky became terrifying. Vastness is like ecstasy in this way (the state of consciousness, not the drug).

Smallness, then—as distillate rather than cage—can be its own solace: a way to refine some of the more difficult feelings for the writer, while opening the ideas up for the reader.

I suspect this is why some stories seem ripe for condensation: any more than five hundred words and they might swallow you whole. But it isn't the word count or formal considerations of an essay that protect (the reader, the writer); it's what the constraint requires you to discard.

It is fair to say that what I am still stuck in is the moment of winter—and I may not grasp the matter of it for some time.

Ehrlich's and Spragg's Wyoming has laid down lenient cowboys, lazy ranchers, and lesser writers. It's the edge they are talking about, not the space stretching away from it. And it is their focus on that icy line, their characterization of the line as a threat and a comfort, that allows them to reach past state boundaries, past definitions of rancher or pioneer to the place where the elements bend a person. There, you are changed or you are broken.

*

Mary Cappello, in her *Bending Genre* essay, "Propositions; Provocations: Inventions," attempts to define creative nonfiction:

> The operative distinctions are "transform" rather than "transcribe," and "apposite" rather than "opposite." Creative nonfiction remakes rather than reports. Like poetry, it relies on novel appositions that make exquisite demands: opposition cancels, apposition makes appar-ent. . . . Why not call it poetry then? Because of the way it enjoins and calls upon a *witness,* but also an interloper, and eavesdropper: placing oneself where one is not sup-posed to be.

Spragg knows too well the transformative power of a Wyoming winter. If you grow upright, the wind will cant you; if you sprawl like a rangeland, the weight of the snow will press into you, until you remem-ber it all year: a thawed and muddy water hole after years of winters becomes a summer pond.

Ehrlich, too, is concerned in "Smooth Skull," not with winter's length—though it is acknowledged—but in its oppositions. A snow wall threatens but also protects. "The deep ache of this audacious Arctic air is also the ache in our lives made physical." But this ache makes personal connections all the more urgent, as friends and lovers check in, help out, warm one another up with words or food or a fire.

The right short essay offers a view of where-we-shouldn't-be as a single day, one storm, or a small lake we can skate. The beauty of concision is that all you need is the hint of the grinding squeal that signals cracking ice, and the reader will fill in the dark, cold water, the struggling for purchase and air, for long moments after you, the writer, have left the page.

*

A recent study by researchers from the University of California, San Diego, found that social media posts about crummy weather in one part of the country were more likely to put people in other parts of the country in bad moods.

And yet, a 2008 neurological study used functional magnetic resonance imaging to prove that sad music tends to make listeners happy.

I recently asked my own social media circle for recommendations of good "divorce songs" to inspire an essay I'm writing—and within a couple of hours, I had over one hundred suggestions. Did thinking about divorce make my friends sad, or did listening to their favorite sad songs cheer them up?

If I had to read 130 pages about the torture that half the year inflicts upon the landscape between the Big Horn and Snowy Range mountains—if I had to write each moment as it had happened, status update by status update—would I pack right up for some proverbial summer beach, instead of learning anything from these last few months?

*

Yet if I were to try to write five hundred words about the life and death matters that this winter has asked me to consider, I might still fail before I even begin, because I could not make the sky smaller, or the staggering weight of the snow on the fields lighter. It is useful as an exercise to begin with the fence in sight, but not as a practice.

Instead, I must write and write and write until I have wrung all the ache of this damn unending winter from me. Only then can I start to prune—and in pruning, learn the shape of the thing. One makes a mistake in thinking that the antidote for fear of edges is a fence. The antidote is to learn the exact shape and degree of the edge. You can only do that right up next to it.

Spragg says that in Wyoming "there is the wind." Because here, the wind is a constant. It is vast, and it demands attention. The wind is huge. But he also says, "The winds wail a hymn of transience." Because even this, the wind, the cold, even winter, passes.

When talking about the value of writing in place, Lott says first to find a sacred place "in which the world seems to present itself in its mystery and beauty, its sorrow and grief, its vast breadth and its ulti-mate intimacy." It's here, he argues, that you are most yourself. Where else "are you more you—are you more a partaker in the whole of man's estate—than in that place where you are alone, and you are simply and complexly and utterly you?"

This is the place—this middle of nowhere—and the season—the sharpest, longest—where we can get past the moment to the matter. This is where to fire up the blowtorch, where to carve a figure eight in the ice.

On Wendell Berry and Why I'm Not Going to Buy a Smartphone

Hey, Wendell—Can you hear me now?

Late last year, when my 2008 Nokia "Twist" finally up and twisted itself into two parts, when a Verizon Wireless salesperson bantered with me in a textbook sort of way—as if his employee manual had suggested engaging in such a tactic to close a sale—I was forced to explain, once again, Why I'm Not Going to Buy a Smartphone.

There is no word, anymore, for a phone that is not smart. I want a normal phone, I'd said. A not-internet phone—I want just a phone.

Why? he had asked, concerned.

Keeping the overhead costs low on the writing life, I said. Too many screens in my life already. One more gadget to maintain, one more piece of plastic in my life, one more tie between me and Apple's belching factories in China.

But wouldn't it be nice to have one? he asked.

Yes, yes, of course. It would be nice. Sometimes I get lost driving around or between strange cities and I think, well shit. It sure would be nice to have a smartphone to tell me which way is which.

Slowly but surely the tide turns against me, against the list of reasons Why I'm Not Going to Buy a Smartphone. But there is always Berry to back me up—Wendell Berry, who said it first and said it best.

Why I'm Not Going to Buy a Computer was originally published in the *New England Review* and *Bread Loaf Quarterly*. Berry, writing from his farm in rural Kentucky, begins the essay with the stridently articulate rhetoric that makes him so eminently quotable—and occasionally intolerable.

"Like almost everybody else, I am hooked to the energy corporations, which I do not admire," he writes. "I hope to become less hooked to them." For this reason, Berry farms by the work of horses and writes with the tools of pencil and paper. "My wife types my work on a Royal standard typewriter," writes Berry. "As she types, she sees things that are wrong and marks them with small checks in the margins."

He goes on: "I would hate to think that my work as a writer could not be done without a direct dependence on striped-mined coal. How could I write consciously against the rape of nature if I were, in the act of writing, implicated in the rape?" (Where, dear Berry, do you think wood pencils and their rubber erasers come from?) He goes on: "For the same reason, it matters to me that my writing is done in the daytime, without electric light."

This is—it almost goes without saying—a rather annoying statement to those of us living in cities and liking our Facebook pages.

But we don't read Berry for his stridence—to compare ourselves against such unachievable measures. Rather, we read Berry for his in-the-world complexities, and when Berry got bombasted by readers, *Harper's Review,* where the essay was subsequently published, gave him a chance to respond.

"Wendell Berry provides writers enslaved by the computer with a handy alternative," wrote one reader. "Wife—a low-tech energy-saving device. Drop a pile of handwritten notes on Wife and you get back a finished manuscript, edited while it was typed. What computer can do that? Wife meets all of Berry's uncompromising standards for technological innovation: she's cheap, repairable, near home, and good for the family structure."

Berry replies: "I am surprised by the meanness by which these writers refer to my wife. Maybe she likes doing this work, finds it meaningful." But reader wrath didn't cease, so Berry wrote another response and called it "Feminism, the Body, and the Machine," and this is where Berry shines. Where he goes out into the world, pokes around it, and wonders about what makes for good work and, by proxy, good lives.

"If I had written in my essay that my wife worked as a typist and editor for a publisher, doing the same work that she does for me. . . . It would have been assumed as a matter of course that if she had a job away from home she was a 'liberated woman,' possessed of a dignity that no home could confer upon her," Berry writes.

It's a provocative argument. As we know it today, work takes place outside the home. Work is something we do out there; chores are something we do in here. But what makes for good work? If a wife edits her husband's manuscript because it contributes to the economic well-being of a shared household—and because she enjoys it—is this better work than what she might do for someone else, somewhere else, to earn a paycheck for that same household? The better question might actually be—is it more pleasurable? "More and more, we take for granted that work must be destitute of pleasure. More and more, we assume that if we want to be pleased we must wait until evening, or the weekend, or vacation, or retirement," wrote Berry in a later essay, "Economy and Pleasure." "We are defeated at work because our work gives us no pleasure. We are defeated at home because we have no pleasant work there."

But back to the computer. Wendell Berry himself admits that the Wendell Berry Who Won't Buy a Computer does "no real, practical public good." The materials and energy he saves are not significant, just as "no individual's restraint in the use of technology or energy will be 'significant.'"

But here's the crux. Here's the reason that Berry is Berry, the reason we suffer through his black-and-white proclamations. Why does his computer-less-ness matter? Because "each one of us, by 'insignificant' individual abuse of the world, contributes to a general abuse that is devastating."

Wendell Berry still drives, still flies on airplanes, heats his house. What is permissible abuse? Where do we draw the line? Berry says, "It is plain to me that the line ought to be drawn without fail wherever it can be drawn easily. And it ought to be easy . . . to refuse to buy what one does not need."

And so it is, for me, easy not to own a smartphone—and cheaper too. The shorthand I use when explaining myself to a Verizon Wireless salesperson—keeping my overhead costs low—is actually the heart of the reason Why I'm Not Going to Buy a Smartphone. The higher the cost of doing business, the more that business must earn, and the same is true for an economy of one. Rather than working to earn money to pay for my smartphone, I am—slightly, thirty dollars a month—more free to work/write however seems most meaningful to me—at home *or* in the world.

But we all have our wife at the typewriter, assisting our endeavors— no one is an economy of one—and so it is that I must call *my* boyfriend when I am lost in a new place, helpless at the hands of my dumb phone.

It Is a Shaggy World, Studded with Gardens

No man ever yearned more for a "hard and active life out-of-doors" than the great Scottish writer Robert Louis Stevenson (1850–94), and few men ever faced such an endless litany of ills, keeping him, generally, from the wild world he loved so. ("My body which my dungeon is," as he wrote.) Yet the frail Stevenson, the most popular writer of his time, was able to catch and celebrate the vigorous natural world in work that ranged freely in genre (novels, essays, letters, stories, poems, fables, tracts, and prayers) and in setting—capturing the flavor variously of the Scottish Highlands, French countryside and mountains, Swiss Alpine valleys, dense North American wilderness and plains, and lush islands of the South Seas, where he spent the last six years of his brief and exuberant life.

Despite his spotty health, he spent much time in his adolescent years among the Scottish mountains and islands—hiking, sailing boats with friends, and working outdoors, and one memorably strenuous summer, with his engineer father Thomas, the most talented in a family of engineers still famous for building lighthouses along the Scottish coast. After college he began to write, and his first books were Thoreauvian accounts of his travels through wild country—a canoe trip through rural France, which became *An Inland Voyage,* and then a long hike in the French mountains, which became *Travels with a Donkey in the Cévennes.* The wild Scottish Highlands and coast he loved starred in his novels *Kidnapped* and *The Merry Men,* and the deep forests of New

York's Adirondack Mountains, where he spent one bitterly cold winter, are the setting for much of *The Master of Ballantrae.*

Everywhere he went he clapped his sharp eye on the land and wrote of its temper and creatures with respect and affection. He wrote of the Scottish coast,

> The earthy savour of the bog-plants, the rude disorder of the boulders, the inimitable seaside brightness of the air, the brine and the iodine, the lap of the billows among the weedy reefs, the sudden springing up of a great run of dashing surf along the sea-front of the isle, all that I saw and felt my predecessors must have seen and felt with scarce a difference.

And of his native land as a whole,

> It is a shaggy world, and yet studded with gardens; where the salt and tumbling sea receives clear rivers running from among reeds and lilies; fruitful and austere; a rustic world; sunshiny, lewd, and cruel

Of the great plains of Nebraska, which he crossed by train, he wrote with amazement,

> We were at sea—there is no other adequate expression. . . . It was a world almost without a feature; an empty sky, an empty earth; front and back, the line of railway stretched from horizon to horizon, like a cue across a billiard-board; on either hand, the green plain ran till it touched the skirts of heaven. Along the track innumerable wild sunflowers, no bigger than a crown-piece, bloomed in a continuous flower-bed; grazing beasts were seen upon the prairie at all degrees of distance and diminution. . . . Day and night, above the roar of the train, our ears were kept busy with the incessant chirp of grasshoppers—a noise

like the winding up of countless clocks and watches, which began after a while to seem proper to that land. To one hurrying through by steam there was a certain exhilaration in this spacious vacancy, this greatness of the air, this discovery of the whole arch of heaven, this straight, unbroken, prison-line of the horizon.

Of the Marquesas:

The land heaved up in peaks and rising vales; it fell in cliffs and buttresses; its colour ran through fifty modulations in a scale of pearl and rose and olive; and it was crowned above by opalescent clouds. The suffusion of vague hues deceived the eye; the shadows of clouds were confounded with the articulations of the mountains; and the isle and its unsubstantial canopy rose and shimmered before us like a single mass . . . The cocoa-palm, that giraffe of vegetables, so graceful, so ungainly, to the European eye so foreign, was to be seen crowding on the beach, and climbing and fringing the steep sides of mountains. . . . In every crevice of that barrier the forest harboured, roosting and nestling there like birds about a ruin; and far above, it greened and roughened the razor edges of the summit.

He was a student of the linguistics of the natural world:

The Scotch dialect is singularly rich in terms of reproach against the winter wind. *Snell, blae, nirly,* and *scowthering* are four of these significant vocables; they are all words that carry a shiver with them. . . . The inclemency of heaven, which has thus endowed the language of Scotland with words.

And he was eerily prescient of the future of the wild too. He wrote this while living in Monterey:

> California has been a land of promise in its time, like
> Palestine; but if the woods continue so swiftly to perish,
> it may become, like Palestine, a land of desolation. . . . We
> may look forward to a time when there will not be [a tree]
> left standing in that land . . . man in his short-sighted
> greed robs the country of the noble redwood. Yet a little
> while and perhaps all the hills of seaboard California
> may be as bald as Tamalpais.

For nearly three years Stevenson wandered the Pacific, visiting
the Marquesas, the Paumotus, the Hawaiian Islands, the Gilberts,
the Marshalls, the Society Islands, New Zealand, Australia, and the
Navigator Islands, better known collectively as Samoa. At each landfall he would wander briskly and joyfully into the forest and along the
beaches and spend many hours with residents; he was by all accounts an
indefatigable walker and talker, no respecter of position or privilege,
and so a man who explored nature and natives to a degree unusual
among writers of his time. He and his wife finally settled in Samoa,
on the main island of Upolu, where the Stevensons bought three hundred acres of land, built a house in the hills three miles from the harbor, and settled in.

Their land was so veined with creeks and rivers, or "burns," as
Stevenson called them, that he named the property Vailima, Samoan
for "five waters." It was the first wild land he'd ever owned, and he rev-
eled in it, partly for the stunning variety of its flora and fauna, but
partly too because finally he had enough health and strength to work
his land. "It is like a fairy story that I should have recovered health and
strength, and should go round again among my fellow-men, boating,
riding, bathing, toiling hard with a wood-knife in the forest," he wrote.
And in a letter to a friend:

> Went crazy over outdoor work, and had at last to con-
> fine myself to the house, or literature must have gone by
> the board. Nothing is so interesting as weeding, clear-
> ing, and path-making . . . it does make you feel so well. To

come down covered with mud and drenched with sweat
and rain after some hours in the bush, change, rub down,
and take a chair in the verandah, is to taste a quiet conscience. And the strange thing that I mark is this: If I go
out and make sixpence, bossing my labours, plying the
cutlass or the spade, idiot conscience applauds me; if I sit
in the house and make twenty pounds, idiot conscience
wails over my neglect and the day wasted.

For three years he worked his woods and farmed the soil, hosted an
endless stream of visitors (among them Henry Adams, who was peeved
that Stevenson didn't know who he was), became deeply involved in
the chaotic political life of Samoa, and wrote furiously—most notably
half of a Highlands novel called *Weir of Hermiston* that, had it been
finished, might have been among his very best books.

On December 3, 1894, he "wrote hard all morning" on *Weir*, spent
the afternoon writing letters to friends, and came down from his study
at sunset. He opened an old bottle of burgundy, set to making a salad
for dinner, and was cheerfully chaffing his wife when he suddenly
clapped his hands to his head, cried out in pain, and fell to his knees.
Within minutes the massive stroke sent him into a coma; and at ten
minutes past eight o'clock he died.

At dawn, forty local men cut a path through the woods to the flat
summit of Mount Vaea, "no bigger than a room," where they dug a
grave for the man they called Tusitala, the teller of tales. In the afternoon his hand-carved coffin was carried to the summit and laid to
rest. Among the prayers said over his body was one he had written
himself:

Lord, Thou sendest down rain upon the uncounted millions of the forest, and givest the trees to drink exceed-
ingly. . . . Teach us the lesson of the trees. The sea around
us, which this rain recruits, teems with the race of fish;
teach us, Lord, the meaning of the fishes. Let us see ourselves for what we are, one out of the countless number

of the clans of Thy handiwork. When we would despair,
let us remember that these also please and serve Thee.

The next day the chiefs of Samoa forbade the use of firearms on
Mount Vaea so that the birds and animals "might live undisturbed,
and raise about his grave the songs he knew so well." Some years later
a large tomb was raised over his grave. On the tomb there are bronze
plates with bas-reliefs of a thistle and a hibiscus flower, the character-
istic plants of Scotland and Samoa, and Stevenson's poem, "Requiem":

Under the wide and starry sky
Dig the grave and let me lie.
Glad did I live and gladly die
And I laid me down with a will.

This be the verse you grave for me:
Here he lies where he longed to be;
Home is the sailor, home from sea,
And the hunter home from the hill.

Nonfiction Like a Brick

Sometimes, when you're writing, you feel you're beating your head against a wall. That's not only an appropriate metaphor—it's part of the point and part of the fun. This is not to say writing is exclusively a masochistic endeavor. Why do it if it's only painful? But the "wall" in this metaphor is an important element to writing and one that helps to make creative nonfiction a literary endeavor.

I teach and write both poetry and nonfiction. This last semester, I taught a poetic forms class to my graduate students. Sonnets, sestinas, villanelles. I wanted my students to know the forms to help them understand in their work, which tends toward free verse, why they break lines, why the poem turns when and where it does, and the possibilities of rhyme and repetition. But I also wanted to make them suffer a little. Not because I'm a sadist (at least not in this class), but because when there are bounds, chains, rules, laws, something inside the mind breaks free. The language becomes sharper. Images become richer. The meaning intensifies. You only have so many iambs to get your point across. These chains and laws are the wall. Your head, beating against that wall, shakes free newly creative ideas.

Walls are inherent to creative writing, especially nonfiction. A wall of truth and memory. Truth and memory are as great of laws as fourteen lines to a sonnet. If, in your writing, you are tied to the truth, attempting to get at the truth sharpens your language, enriches images, intensifies meaning. "Tie up my hands with your chains, they are bound to set me free," said St. Augustine. Or maybe it was the band No Means No. Either way, it's one reason I stick with the term *creative nonfiction.* Even if it's oxymoronic, the "nonfiction" is what helps to make the "creative" happen.

Last winter, my mom invited me to speak to her book club about my book that had just come out. It was hard for her, in a way, to have family secrets spilled all over Amazon.com. But she was proud too. It was thanks to her that I loved literature. We had books in every corner of the house. She had been an English major. She scribbled in journals of her own. Her book club fostered in me a sense that books brought people together. One of the members of the book club, Kathy Lake, asked why I combined stories about my father's alcoholism with stories of how the Mormon settlers transformed the Salt Lake valley from an arid desert into a cradle of green. I answered, the way the Mormons transformed the mountain streams to reconfigure the valley below was similar to what my dad was doing with his drinking. Trying to change a seemingly unchangeable situation. The rivers flowed down the mountains, funneled into the Great Salt Lake. My dad drank a lot of liquor. The Mormons made reservoirs to stop the rivers before they reached the lake in order to irrigate their farmland. My father went to AA, Betty Ford, and the Minneapolis Rehab Center to try to stop the drinking. In the end, the Mormons were more successful than my dad—they transformed the landscape. But as I spoke to the book club, I understood that the content of my book—that one spends one's whole life wrestling with granite-like forces—paralleled its form, and that truth, natural force that it is, has to be contended with in writing.

When I reach for a memory, for instance, of my dad getting up from watching *Dallas* to get what I then thought was a drink of water, I envision the scene. I can hear the clinking of the ice cubes. The jug-jug of the water filling the glass. The shifting blues coming from the TV screen. In my memory, the glass is filled with water. Later, when he is sick with cirrhosis, I have to rethink my memory. Was it water? If it was vodka, how does that change things? Does it change the smell in the room? The colors coming from the TV? Yes and no. The TV still shimmers blue, but now that blue glows a little darker. The innocent sound of ice now sounds like the dum-dom-dum of mystery revealed. J. R. Ewing's words are more sinister.

That truth, or those truths, combine to make different kinds of senses. One is a new, logical sense. If my dad is sick, then maybe he was drinking. But there's another layer to that sense, an intensified meaning. That my dad, though drinking, sheltered me from what he was doing. That the drinking, at that moment, had no sinister result. That in my memory, water is water and my dad is my dad. That the truth was possibly different is what makes it interesting, puts some stress between memory and logic, and gives me reason to put the story to language. The language—*blue, Ewing, ice*—deepens the meaning and does double duty trying to be faithful to both memory and truth.

*

In writing about my dad's death, I needed an edge of "truth" not only to add meaning and texture. I needed it for a break. Toggling between a semi-ridiculous litany of liquor laws and the gut punch of finding out my dad died, I can do two things: hide out from emotional overload and situate my dad's drinking into a larger context. Who is protecting whom? What are the liquor laws supposed to prove?

Some Rules to Train Your Abundant Spirit

TAVERNS, or BEER BARS These establishments may
    sell beer no stronger than 3.2 percent by weight.
    They need not serve food.

AIRPORT LOUNGES Can serve beer, wine, and mixed
    drinks with or without food. There are only a very
    few of these. They are all located at the Salt Lake
    International Airport and are intended to give visi-
    tors a warm first impression.

BREW PUBS Serve beer which was brewed on premises.
    There are some of these in the state.

RESTAURANTS With the proper license, alcoholic
    beverages may be served with meals. Liquor bottles

must be hidden from view. Servers are not allowed to solicit or suggest drinks. Patrons must request a wine list or drink menu. If a restaurant derives more than 30 percent of its profit from alcoholic beverage sales, it can lose its license.

PRIVATE CLUBS Beer, wine, and mixed drinks may be consumed in nonexclusive private clubs between 10 a.m. and 1 a.m. These clubs by law must be nonprofit organizations, must charge a membership fee, and are barred from advertising to boost membership.

The Rules We Can't Obey

The last time I talked to my dad before he died, he called me at 2:30 in the morning, around his birthday.

Good morning.

Dad, it's two in the morning, three for you in Salt Lake.

No it's not. It's 9 o'clock. How late do people in Portland sleep in anyway?

Dad, look outside. It's dark. Call me when it's light out.

Nik, I have to tell you something. (Here, his words started to slur.)

What do you have to tell me that can't wait until morning?

Nik, I've won all the awards I'm going to win.

That's not true, Dad.

I have patents.

I know.

I don't have a job anymore.

I know, Dad. But you can get a new job. Write a book.

I'm in *Who's Who*.

I know, Dad. But think. You might have grandchildren soon. That's an award in a way.

My diamond drill bit is in the Smithsonian.

You still have us, Dad. Me and the twins. It's almost your birthday.

I know, Nik. But there are no more awards.

After I recount my last conversation with my dad, I think to myself, Perhaps you could employ some self-moderation [I tell my dad. I tell myself].

You can lead a horse to water,

but you can't make him drink.

You can lead a community to save water,

but you can't make us think.

Then, I follow that conversation with a short news article, stuck in the middle of the chapter, pulled verbatim from the newspaper.

> The water-use restrictions passed Tuesday by the Salt Lake County Council are more about leading than about making. But this action, and other examples of leadership around the state, should at least get people to be thinking about the ways in which we use, and waste, water every day. If we don't, then much more stringent conservation laws will come into play. Our leaders will have no choice. So slow down. The water you save will be your own.

Then I return to the story of my dad. Who will be saved? My own life? Maybe.

> It rained in Portland from the day of my dad's fiftieth birthday—September 22—until I went home for his funeral on October 26. I flew home to Salt Lake to blue skies and brown trees. When I saw him lying on the table in the morgue, he looked frozen. Curled in a fetal ball with just one little bruise on his forehead. They didn't do an autopsy. They didn't fill him with formaldehyde. They would have to stretch him out before they cremated him. I left him alone and went looking for something to drink. I was thirsty.

This is some of the most egregious, maybe even aggressive, brick-laying I do. Where do I turn? At the end of a short narrative, I turn to another context, something else to give me relief but also to help me understand. In the article about water restriction, I wonder what kind of laws, bounds, and stoppers could have helped my dad? Probably none. Laws try to restrict but external restriction just leads, as the *Salt Lake Tribune* wrote, "to more stringent conservation laws." If you're going to self-satisfy, you're going to self-satisfy. The laws aren't useful unless they are imposed from within.

But the stoppers that help me, that give my writing some rules, are those internalized ones that say, *you have to think about this in a different way. You have to get some perspective.* Without that, the story remains unprocessed and uncontextualized. It is still merely the writer's anecdote. It isn't an essay without that stretch. The bounds of the research make me turn my head another direction. They force me to generate another story, a deeper story even, as I try to work the rules and laws and chains of fact into the malleable world of memory.

Shelley wrote in his "A Defense of Poetry," "We want the creative faculty to imagine that which we know." Knowledge, truth, and memory are the laws, the chains, the givens against which writers flail. It is our creative faculties that turn those truths and memories into meaning. The knowing is the wall. The creative faculties, the head. If our heads, like our genres, become bent a little in the banging, it's worth it. We created something new.

But it's not just me who does this rule-making, I don't think. I can't read other authors' minds, but I can read their stops and turns. We are familiar with generative workshops, with prompts and ways to get people to write. But sometimes, I think we need ways to get writers to stop too: to begin to generate but then to stop and reach for some real information, law, or boundary or other perspective, like research or even a dictionary definition. Get them to make meaning. In an essay called "Sail On, My Little Honey Bee," Amy Leach writes fluidly. Her language flows so immediately and quickly that, as a reader, I sometimes think I might drown in the molten lava of her words. But then she stops. Exposes magma to air. And hits me like a rock to the head. Amy Leach: What stops her? What does she use as a buffer? What becomes her rock? Sound and science.

Mars has two small moons whose names mean *panic* and *terror.* Phobos looks like a potato that experienced one terrible, and many average, concussions. Phobos hurtles around Mars every eight hours, which is three times faster than Mars rotates, which means Mars pulls it back and slows it down. Slowing down makes a moon lose height; in the end Phobos will smite its planet, or else get wrenched apart by gravity into a dusty ring of aftermath. Mars's other moon Deimos is a slow and outer moon—an outer and outer moon—someday it will be a scrap moon, rattling around in the outer darkness, where drift superannuated spacecraft and exhausted starlets.

So fast moons slow down and slow moons speed up, and only during excerpts of time do planetary dalliances appear permanent. Our moon through many excerpts— the Moon—is a slow moon. Thus it is speeding up, thus it is falling up, coming off like a wheel, at one and a half inches per year. Let us now reflect upon the distancing Moon, for the Moon has long reflected upon us.

To get an idea of the relationship between the Earth and the Moon and the Sun, find two friends and have the self-conscious one with lots of atmosphere be the Earth and the coercive one be the Sun. And you be the Moon, if you are periodically luminous and sometimes unob-servable and your inner life has petered out. Then find a large field and take three steps from the Earth, and have the Sun go a quarter-mile away.

For an idea of how long your light takes to reach Earth, sing one line from a song, such as "Sail on, my little honey bee" and that is how long moonlight takes. The Earth can sing the same line back to you, to represent earthlight. "Sail on, my little honey bee." As for the Sun, he should sing as lustily as sunlight; have him discharge the song "I Gave Her Cakes and I Gave Her Ale," which is eight minutes long, which is how long sunlight takes to reach the Earth. Also the Earth may sing to the Sun and the Sun to the Moon and the Moon to the Sun, songs of representative length.

A poem is meant to be played on a lyre, and a song must have some sound. A poem must turn, and to turn you must slow down. In nonfiction, when it's working like a poem, you have to stop sometimes. See how Leach slows down, repeats the "o" sound at the beginning of the last paragraph: "For an idea of how long your light takes to reach Earth, sing one line from a song" Now, the sounds are in your ears. You are ready for voice. You are ready to hear the music. Then you gather up speed by gathering up material. The new information sounds a new rhythm. You pick up the pace. You pick up more stuff. By the time you're at the second song, "I Gave Her Cakes and I Gave Her Ale," you've made it to your next subject. You will go so fast. But you will find another turn. Maybe even a sonnet.

In Gerard Manley Hopkins's poem, also a sonnet, "The Windhover," the rhymes spring him forward. He uses the ends of sonnets' lines like a pole-dancer—to swing him around. To gain momentum.

> **To Christ our Lord**
> I CAUGHT this morning morning's minion, king-
>   dom of daylight's dauphin, dapple-dawn-drawn
>   Falcon, in his riding
>   Of the rolling level underneath him steady air, and
>   striding
> High there, how he rung upon the rein of a wimpling
>   wing
> In his ecstasy! then off, off forth on swing,
>   As a skate's heel sweeps smooth on a bow-bend: the
>   hurl and gliding
>   Rebuffed the big wind. My heart in hiding
> Stirred for a bird,—the achieve of; the mastery of the
>   thing!

Brute beauty and valour and act, oh, air, pride, plume, here
  Buckle! AND the fire that breaks from thee then, a
  billion
Times told lovelier, more dangerous, O my chevalier!

  No wonder of it: shéer plód makes plough down sillion
Shine, and blue-bleak embers, ah my dear,
  Fall, gall themselves, and gash gold-vermillion.

But what provides a buffer, a narrative, a stopping point? Exclamation points. Dashes. The word *rebuffed* makes a buffer. And *f* stops anyone anywhere. The direct address, "ah my dear"? The commentary? "Stirred for a bird." This bird is falling, which is flying, which is, as Susan Mitchell reminds us in her "Notes Toward a History of Scaffolding," that a bird falling is teaching itself not how to fly but how to sing. The rise and falls of Hopkins's poem—the lifts and the crashes are the terrors of flight but still provide one comfort—that the bird knows what he's doing. Every time the poem pauses, the bird nearly touches ground then takes off again.

As a ballet dancer knows, you have to have a floor from which to leap. You don't get to defy gravity without having some gravity to begin with. There is no kinetic energy without potential energy. You have to believe in the hardness of granite before you hit it with your hammer. Before you can shave off a piece. Before you carry it down the mountain to begin to build your temple.

The rules you make should be hard and fast. They should be your own. They should be inflexible until they don't work for you anymore, until they don't force new thoughts, or new words, or make better metaphors, or give you some perspective. Then you should make some news ones or do what Walt Whitman does and write the rules down so that you and the rules and the poem are the same thing.

Walt Whitman at the end of *Leaves of Grass:*

  This is what you shall do: Love the earth and sun and the
  animals, despise riches, give alms to every one that asks,

stand up for the stupid and crazy, devote your income and labor to others, hate tyrants, argue not concerning God, have patience and indulgence toward the people, take off your hat to nothing known or unknown or to any man or number of men, go freely with powerful uneducated persons and with the young and with the mothers of families, read these leaves in the open air every season of every year of your life, re-examine all you have been told at school or church or in any book, dismiss whatever insults your own soul; and your very flesh shall be a great poem and have the richest fluency not only in its words but in the silent lines of its lips and face and between the lashes of your eyes and in every motion and joint of your body.

On the Fugue, Alison Bechdel's *Are You My Mother?*, DFW, and the Resistance to the One Thing

1. Rainy night, windy night. Subway platform, A Train, Fifty-Ninth Street, Columbus Circle. Four bearded young men huddle by the turnstiles, lift their horns, and begin to play Bach. Four melodies, four tones, fill the tunnel at once. My eyes fix on the tracks, on the junk down there. A little rat runs through the junk. Like everyone else on the platform, I pretend I'm not a struck tuning fork. That's what the city exacts of us. We're already dreaming into the thing we're on the way to. workout, hookup, business deal, drink, dinner, that meeting with an editor. And yet something important is going on here. I know it. I suspect the men and women beside me know it. It's our secret. This isn't just music but a village. Four voices in conversation, mimicking, talking back to one another. Sometimes in sync, sometimes in argument. I think there is something beautiful moving among them, between them. The sounds lean into one another. They lift us above the trash. The one light of my train is coming up the tunnel. Soon the village will be taken down into the noise of it, but that's all right: that's a part of the pact. Perhaps the playing (and listening) wouldn't be so animated if there weren't some shared awareness of interruption. And then it occurs to me: this might not just be a village we're listening to but something nearer, inside us. It's the sound of consciousness, the song of the human brain thinking four different things at once.

2. Simultaneity: the dream of getting that on the page. The composer has counterpoint. Or more typically: harmony. In pop music, bass line, drum, keyboard, vocal, etc. Many layers in the simplest piece of music, but in writing? One voice at a time, the tyranny of the singular. Not that words aren't freighted with multiple associations, not that we don't have puns, rhymes. But how does one begin to write conscious-ness on the page? Virginia Woolf made use of parentheses. David Foster Wallace tried the footnote. As D. T. Max says, the footnote was DFW's way to capture "all the caveats, micro-thoughts, meta-moments, of [the] hyperactive mind." But all that leaping about, all those gaps in time between taking in the primary text and its subordinates. It doesn't exactly happen with the grace of the fugue, even if there is something oddly stimulating about being wrenched back and forth between two tracks. It's a little like being in the hands of a taxing trainer, who tells you to do ten lunges, ten chin-ups, ten lunges again.

3. On pages 22–23 of Alison Bechdel's book-length graphic essay *Are You My Mother?* we have tables of romantic attachments, tables of therapists. A drawing of a young mother inside a circle, cigarette poised between fingertips. Boxed interpretations of D. W. Winnicott's theories of the mother-infant relationship. A graphic representation of an exchange between the speaker and her therapist. Graphics at some (comic) odds with the fraught content of the exchange. A boxed state-ment concerning the "involuntary torrent of words and images" that came to Virginia Woolf in the writing of *Mrs. Dalloway.* Somehow these two pages manage to be orderly, meaningful, orchestrated. We're given space to process this material. But graphics set their own terms, and we're once again shunted back to the limitations of mere words.

4. ANONYMOUS: "A fugue is a piece of music in which the voices come in one after another and the audience go out one after another."

5. MICHEL FOUCAULT, *Of Other Spaces,* 1967: "The present epoch will perhaps be above all the epoch of space. We are in the epoch of simul-taneity: we are in the epoch of juxtaposition, the epoch of the near and

far, the epoch of the side-by-side, of the dispersed . . . of a network that connects points and intersects with its own skein."

6. I have a short attention span. I hope that doesn't make me sound like an idiot, but I'll risk it anyway. By that I mean a sensitivity to too-much-ness. The door swings open; too much light comes in with that flood. My eyes hurt. My brain aches. I need to pull the door closed before I can open it up again. Open-close-open-close-open: that's the story of perception to me. Which is another way of saying the story of reading, writing.

But that's only half of what I'm struggling to say. I think my resistance might be to the One Thing. In my imagination the One Thing can loom like a Giant telling me to think this way, not that. The Giant prevents multiple viewpoints, the Giant ignores the fact that there are other truths, other colors, other sexualities: in-betweenness, paradox, ambivalence. The Giant can only see what's in front of him. I need to look to the left and right of the Giant's big feet. I need the village. I need the space between oncoming trains in order to hear the music in the tunnel.

7. No surprise we perceive in short bursts given the flood that's coming toward us: 30 percent more information than thirty years ago. DFW anticipated it himself, from years back, when he talked of footnotes: "They might make the primary text an easier read while . . . [mimicking] the information flood and data-triage I expect would be an even bigger part of U.S. life fifteen years hence."

8. My best friend has brain cancer. My mother has dementia. Though they are decades apart in age, they share some of the same symptoms at the end, a loss of tact, a tendency to mash one layer of time into the next. They die within weeks of each other, one at the beginning of the summer, one at the end. The deaths of our beloveds are to be expected in every life, but I'm stunned by these losses, especially by the loss of my friend, who is unexpectedly easier to miss than my mom, who was gone long ago. In the months after her death, I start to write

a book about her. She would love a book about her—a love song of sorts—even though it feels like hell to do it. I don't want to say my friend is dead, I don't want to say: the world is dangerous, brutal now, ugly. I want to write about joy. I try my best to represent my friend in emblems—"moments of being," as Virginia Woolf would call them— but the emblems aren't enough. They're not the whole story. The whole story is: a climate out of whack, rising water, a tsunami, an uncapped oil well slopping beaches, mangroves. Dolphins dead in the marshes. What's outside the body is also inside, which is why the book must move back and forth between two tracks. The structure doesn't quite resound with the simultaneity of the horn players, but I'm once again dealing with the fact that words aren't wind.

9. MICHAEL HAMMER, "What's in a Name: Fugue": "In a few seconds, this voice will be joined by a second voice, imitating it, at what we call a fifth higher. . . . Now, it is one of the secrets of fugue writing that you have to know the best way to bring in that second voice—exactly as the first, or by 'fudging' it a little. There are rules for that, too. Then, after a brief bit of 'connective tissue' we arrive back in the original key, and a third voice enters, again with the subject. If there are four, or five, voices (Bach once wrote one with six!) the same thing happens with their entrances, alternating between the original notes and five notes up from the first. The whole section is called the subject area. During the arrival of the additional voices, the old ones keep on 'singing' but they do not have to keep to any particular tunes, because the newly arrived ones are not going to keep imitating them. It is only the subject that is important. . . . When all the voice entrancing has been accomplished, they all begin to dance around according to the inspiration of the composer. This more optional section is usually referred to as an episode, as in 'I'm having an episode, and if you don't go away I may have another one.'"

10. What else could I do? If I had a stack of transparencies, I'd print one passage per page, hold them up to the light, so you could see each text burning into the next.

On *The Squared Circle: Life, Death, and Professional Wrestling* by David Shoemaker

I know. I know. Bear with me here.

Professional wrestling is not pretty. At its worst, it is carnival schlock: shirtless men throwing each other around with all the grace of a Buffalo Wild Wings on a random Thursday—loud to the point of white noise, the scent of thrice-used canola oil and whatever it is we've decided testosterone smells like these days—men in football jerseys and jorts cursing the name of the name on their backs, all things bulbous and grotesque.

At its best, well, it's still probably a Buffalo Wild Wings, but an extremely efficient one: the waitresses move with a beautiful quickness, the sauces are innovative enough, and even though it is incredibly predictable in its existence, at times it surprises you—there is one extra light beer on draft, or you can make out a faint habanero flavor through the kick. There is comfort in knowing what you are going to get, and yet there is pleasure when things are unexpected.

The Squared Circle: Life, Death, and Professional Wrestling by David Shoemaker is a book of essays about professional wrestling. If you know anyone who loves or has loved professional wrestling at any moment in their life, you owe it to them to get them this book: it is filled with incredible insight into the business of professional wrestling, as well as loving nods to all of the madness that surrounds the spectacle. It is a book of beautiful nostalgia: odes to fallen wrestlers, who far too often turned to drugs and alcohol after their time in the limelight—beautiful observations that go well beyond the "whatever happened to?" questions brought up when someone who used to watch every Monday night starts reminiscing about their adolescence. There are asides to the tropes surrounding wrestling as well: a history of televised weddings, a list of "evil foreigners" brought in to take on our all-American heroes. Trust me, if anyone you know loves wrestling, they'll love this book.

But let's be fair: there is disconnect between the concept of a "professional wrestling fan," and one who reads essay collections and appreciates the concept of poetics.

Todd Kaneko in the *Superstition Review* has an amazing experiment where he demonstrates the unseen parallels between poetry and professional wrestling: "[_____] is a real thing in the real world, despite what some of [_____]'s biggest detractors might say."

I kept this post in mind while reading Shoemaker's book: that above all, this book is a treatise on how to approach an essay. In some semblance, Shoemaker is attempting to demonstrate the realness in something that is so absurd that it seems fake: the idea that grown men and women are entertained by fake fighting, despite knowing that everything unfolding in front of them is an artifice. All essays are attempts to categorize the unbelievable: to attempt to make sense of something so unfathomable that it has to be true—from the preposterous to the trite. In a collection of essays, the book itself is the final essay—Shoemaker acknowledges this in the introduction.

> "History" is mostly quartered to the realm of wrestler reminiscence, which would be factually problematic on its own, but couple that with the industry's desire to mythologize everything and to keep up with the façade of fakery that undergirds the sport and you end up with a lot of facts that contradict each other. What follows is my best effort to sift through them, organize them, break them down, and put them back together in something approaching truth. If all that follows isn't true in the plainest sense of the word, it's an honest effort at it. And

at a minimum it's a look at reality through the distorted lens of pro-wrestling unreality. It's the truth about a century of misdirection and lies.

What unfolds is an experiment in truth-telling: to acknowledge the world that has been crafted, but also to try to dissect the scaffolding and to figure out what holds everything upright.

To me, the beauty in essay is acknowledging the form of the essay—the most influential essays, to me, are the ones that bring the author into the work—"The Search for Marvin Gardens," "The Glass Essay,"—in an attempt to talk about the difficulty in talking about the subject. Here, Shoemaker acknowledges the artifice of professional wrestling in a way that professional wrestling does not acknowledge in its own falseness, and the result is tremendously entertaining and fascinating. We might not want to know where these things come from in the same way we do not want to see the chicken wings being spun or where all the cable wires lead to—that there is comfort in having exactly what we have. Shoemaker lets us know that it is necessary for us to know where these stories come from: that anything with that much mystery needs to be dissected.

PAM HOUSTON

On Rick Reilly's "Need a Fourth?" from
Sports Illustrated, March 31, 1997

For many years I read *Sports Illustrated* weekly, cover to cover, in the bathtub. And not just Tom Verducci's signature baseball features, or Gary Smith's memorable essay on reluctant superstar Mia Hamm, or his powerful piece on the death of Devaughn Darling, or George Plimpton's historic "The Curious Case of Sidd Finch." I read everything. From the letters to By the Numbers to This Week's Sign of the Apocalypse to Faces in the Crowd. I'm a workaholic, like my father, and his only son. He taught me to love the games' many intricacies and complicated dramas, and like him, the only real leisure time I allow myself is watching, participating in, or reading about sports.

For years Rick Reilly owned the back page of *Sports Illustrated.* His column, which predated the current Point After, was called Life of Reilly, and the short pieces were always either funny ("The Ten Travails of Tiger," for example, this before Tiger Woods actually had any travails) or feel good ("The Biggest Play of His Life" about the high school football captain who came out of the closet to unanimous team support). Sometimes they were both. Sometimes *Sports Illustrated* gave Rick more space than the back page, and his essays were allowed to be funny and feel good and something more, as on March 31, 1997, when Reilly wrote "Need a Fourth?" about former NFL star O.J. Simpson, suspected murderer of the mother of his children and golf addict, postacquittal, now banned from his tony country club, hanging around the Rancho Park Public Golf Course in Los Angeles, trying to scare up a game. "Three players will be waiting for the fairway to clear," Reilly wrote, "waiting to hit their first drives of the day . . . when the starter will crackle over the public address system, 'Sending a single to join you.'"

With a few notable exceptions, in university English and literature departments in America (which have ceased to be about English and literature at all), anyone who is knowledgeable or enthusiastic about sports is widely pitied. It is O.K. to utter a sentence like "Manchester United can beat Arsenal to get back on top" or anything else sporty that can be said in a British accent. In some academic circles it is even O.K. to like the Boston Red Sox, or at least it was, until they began winning, and spending more money than God on players, and changing their image from a long-suffering symbol of the striving proletariat masses into a super-efficient cog in the machine of the Man. But if you actually own season tickets to the Denver Broncos. If you make it a point to go to Phoenix for Cactus League baseball every spring break. If you once got your nose broken by a punch delivered by a young man in a Saint Louis Blues cap when you were both sitting behind Patrick Roy's goal in the third period of a late-season home game that had play-off ramifications for your Colorado Avalanche, just because you tried to school him in away-fan etiquette, it is best to keep that information out of the mail-room chatter.

According to Reilly, in 1997 O.J. Simpson was a pleasant, if emotionally charged, presence on the public course where he played at least one round a day without fail, described by the plumbers and contractors who welcomed him as a fourth as polite, gentle, and warm. He got no preferential treatment there; if he wanted a tee time, his options were to call the computerized system at 5 a.m. a week before and be put on hold for over an hour or to just show up and put his name on the singles list. When Reilly asked one of the guys who wound up playing with O.J. semi-regularly, ad salesman Ken Smitely, what his wife thought of him playing with the Juice, Ken thought for a moment and said, "Let's put it this way: your wife isn't going to like every friend you have."

When I have tried to explain my love of sports to my creative writing colleagues (and only, ever, to the ones I genuinely like), I use all the predictable arguments. Copious amounts of narrative tension. Multiple layers of understory. Ever-changing probability and outcome. Think Bob Costas's coverage of the Olympics. Think of the 1997 Broncos, who entered the play-offs as a wild card and beat team after team in a series of away games that led to them besting Brett Favre's Packers in Super Bowl XXXII. Think of Favre, the heavy favorite, unable to overcome his lifelong hero worship of Elway, and Elway, winning his first Super Bowl in his storied career's penultimate season after three Super Bowl losses in the days when he was younger, stronger, healthier, but not nearly as smart. Think of A-Rod, who got paid more money this year than the entire Houston Astros baseball team NOT to play baseball. People who hate sports believe them to be simple. Sports can be a lot of things, many of them unsavory (violent, greed-driven, sexist, racist), but if you take the time to know anything about them, simple is one thing they are not.

O.J.'s life in 1997, however, was oddly pared down. He couldn't get a job, a book deal, endorsements, or public speaking gigs. His house was in the process of being sold, and he was considering moving to Florida, but Florida didn't much want him either. In one of the most brilliant moments in the essay, Reilly called him "a human unplayable lie." Juice described himself at the time as having zero net worth, making "just enough [money] to play relatively new golf balls." "If I didn't have golf," he told Reilly, "I'd be in Bellevue." So he teed up once, sometimes twice, a day, and passed a little more time flirting with twenty-somethings in the Rancho bar. One young woman told Reilly that O.J. asked her if she believed in "love at seventh sight," and she said, "O.J., if I went out with you, my parents would kill me. And my girlfriends would kill me. And then you'd kill me. And then where would I be?" Everyone was relieved when O.J. laughed. According to Reilly, the former running back was even known to tell the occasional O.J. joke on himself. His favorite: "O.J. and Al Cowlings are in the Bronco. And O.J. is pissed. He goes, 'I said Costa Rica, mother ——! Not Costa Mesa!'"

Rick Reilly, who has published ten books of essays and been voted National Sportswriter of the Year eleven times, still gets asked—to his constant irritation—when he is going to get out of sports and write about something that matters. At Sports Authority Field at Mile High, when the Broncos play, well anyone, really, but lets say the New England Patriots, and Tom Brady hurls a pass thirty yards into the air to his big tight end Gronkowski, and Gronkowski takes his eye off the ball for only a second, and the ball tumbles to the field on a third and eleven, uncaught, and the announcer says, "And Tom Brady's pass to Rob Gronkowski is . . . ," 75,002 people will shout, in unison, "IN-COM-PLETE!" I don't know too many situations where you could get 75,002 people to do anything simultaneously—though plenty of nefarious possibilities ("HEIL HITLER!") jump quickly to mind, and while it would be cool if instead of "IN-COM-PLETE" they said, "ADDRESS CLIMATE CHANGE" or "FEED THE HUNGRY," the sheer force and volume and regularity (every time an opponent drops a pass) of the chant means that at least to some people, sports matter a great deal.

"If you can talk sports," my father used to tell me, "you can talk to just about anyone." And while my decision to pursue a career in the arts has proven plenty of exceptions to that statement, I can attest to the truth of it in this slightly amended form: "Since I can talk about sports, I have something to talk about with all the people with whom I don't have something else to talk about." To this day, one of my greatest pleasures is to go into a sports bar and make everyone I am talking to forget I am a girl.

When Reilly asked O.J., back in 1997, how he felt about spending his days with a bunch of "plumbers with loops in their backswings and Pabst Blue Ribbons in their golf bags," Juice said, "It's my life now. [It] could be worse." And he was right, it could and would be worse. Significantly. Currently, the 1968 Heisman Trophy winner is serving a nine to thirty-three year sentence in the Lovelock Correctional Center in Nevada for a kidnapping and assault he committed in 2008 when, one imagines, daily golf on a public course had stopped being enough.

What makes an essay stay inside a person—with uncanny accuracy—for sixteen years, especially a person like me who reads constantly? Precision, humor, the unexpected turn, the suggestion of depth under a rich, well-made surface. Rick Reilly's "Need a Fourth?" has become part of my inner lexicon for all of these reasons and also because I love the super sly way it gets at the heart of what it means to be an American.

And by that I don't mean O.J.'s super-funded acquittal or his series of mistakes in Vegas that followed. I'm thinking instead of those good old boys out on the browning, poorly trimmed public courses, guys who work hard for forty or fifty or sixty hours a week for an indecent wage and finally make it to the first tee and look up through the coastal fog to see the disgraced hero who is about to join them, a bunch of guys, who Reilly points out, "if given the choice between playing and not playing . . . would tee it up with Mussolini." Soon the four of them will be talking about three woods and nine irons, the hole in one somebody shot straight out of the bunker on thirteen, that time they got to play the Links at Spanish Bay and their wives went along and filmed the whole thing. "From what I've seen of him, I don't think he could take the mother of his children," Smitely told Reilly one day after O.J. shot a seventy-six. And on one March morning, in 1997, maybe sports could be as simple as that.

On Jim Bouton's *Ball Four*

I readied the relic and began the ritual.

Yes, every year at the start of spring training, I read Jim Bouton's *Ball Four*, and no—as I hear the sound of readers rifling past these pages—don't worry: this isn't going to be another intellectual's paean to "America's Game."

In fact, this is one of the great things about *Ball Four*: It wasn't trying to be great, few pretensions of profundity—it was just the diary of a witty non-star navigating a single, insignificant season. Nonetheless, it's considered one of the greatest sports books of all time, or as David

Halberstam proclaimed on the jacket copy, "A book . . . so deep in fact that it is by no means a sports book" (though I'd suggest a sports book can be as deep as any other).

It is, for example, the only sports book selected for the New York Public Library's Books of the Century, sidling in conspicuously right behind *Catch-22* and *In Cold Blood.* I imagine *Ball Four* looking around awkwardly, adjusting its cup and reflexively spitting tobacco, amidst such august company; I love the juxtaposition of its subhead, *My Life and Hard Times Throwing the Knuckleball in the Big Leagues,* and that of its predecessor, *A True Account of a Multiple Murder and Its Consequences.* But the gravitas gap between the two isn't as yawning as it might seem—both books were similarly genre-altering.

It'd be a lie, though, to say I initially sought out *Ball Four* for literary merit; I borrowed it from a friend in the middle of a SAD-inducing Minnesota winter. Cracking the cover in February, I was immediately pulled in, and by the time I finished the book, it was early April; *Ball Four* both reminded me of, and delivered me to, warmer weather.

There's no excuse for the ritual now that I live in Arizona—except to say that SAD can still happen in sunny climes, but no one is going to feel sorry for you. One must self-medicate privately, be it with books or booze or both. Or baseball.

*

When initially released, *Ball Four* was noted more as a cultural event, a scandalous expose à la *Smoking Gun* or *TMZ,* than as capital-L *Literature.*

Jim Bouton had been a bionic-armed fireballer for the Yankees in their golden age, winning twenty-one games in 1963, eventually conquering numerous World Series; he hurled the ball so hard his hat would fly off his head as he finished a pitch. *Phenom.* Then, after three seasons, he blew out his arm—forfeiting fastball and career trajectory.

He muddled about in many middling leagues, and by 1969 was trying to make a comeback as a knuckleballer (considered an embarrassing gimmick of a pitch) for the Seattle Pilots, an embarrassing expansion team that lasted for one embarrassment of a season. But Bouton, always known as outspoken and intelligent, was asked by journalist Leonard Shecter to keep a record of his year.

The single season of anecdotes—casually iconoclastic, carefully culled by Shecter—became the book. And then it exploded.

Some classify American sports writing as pre–*Ball Four* (respectful reportage if not outright hagiography) and post–*Ball Four* (mythos slip, and the public sees "the truth"). Both seem overly extreme, but so were the results for Bouton. The book launched/ruined his career.

*

Much of the scandal surrounded Mickey Mantle—the man who wore, yes, the mantle of "America's Sports Hero." He already held the image of being the boy who never grew up; the back of his baseball card contained such info as: *Bats: Switch; Throws: Right; Drinks: Excessively.*

Ha ha, we get it, what a lovable character—but in *Ball Four,* the public saw Mantle actually

> 1. "beaver shooting," a baseball term for sexually spying on women. In *Ball Four,* pro players race around beneath bleachers as the national anthem distracts nubile fans, the boys of summer looking up for glimpses of *you know.* Also, there is a memorable scene where Mantle leads a group of Yankees around the top of the Shoreham Hotel, scouting for stewardesses before half-closed blinds.

> 2. hung over. "I remember one time [Mickey Mantle had] been injured and didn't expect to play, and I guess he got himself smashed. The next day he looked hung over out of his mind and was sent up to pinch-hit. He could hardly see. So he staggered up to the plate and hit a tremendous drive to left field for a home run. When he came back into the dugout, everybody shook his hand and leaped all over him, and all the time he was getting

a standing ovation from the crowd. He squinted out at
the stands and said, 'Those people don't know how tough
that really was.'"

The public's shock now seems shocking. Compared to modern sports
scandals like the Cowboys' "White House" or the Vikings' "Love Boat"—
mountains of cocaine and prostitutes flown in from companies that
exclusively service pro players—Mantle's indiscretions seem almost
cute, Rockwell Americana. A man paid to play a child's game was a
bit of a Peeping Tom and a boozer? The clutching of pearls—why?

But it *was* a big deal. Celebrity indiscretions may now seem routine,
and were routine then as well, but the reporting of them? *Ball Four*'s
release blackballed Bouton from baseball; players hated him for telling
private tales, violating a clubhouse omerta; owners found Bouton bad
for business; commissioner Bowie Kuhn called the book "detrimen-
tal to baseball" and demanded Bouton sign a statement declaring the
book a work of fiction.

A curious thing to consider within the current "truth in nonfiction"
debate.

Anyhow, Bouton refused, effectively ending his relationship with
baseball while simultaneously launching a long career as a media
personality/raconteur. Bouton had become an irrelevant inning-eater
in baseball pre–*Ball Four,* then went on to achieve a fame greater than
many megastars post–*Ball Four,* so his castigation could almost come
across as karmic gain.

But what denouncers didn't understand, and what makes the book
still endure, was this: *Bouton loved baseball.*

One of the great regrets of his life was that Mickey Mantle refused
to ever converse with him again. And Bouton was never invited to
Yankees Old-Timers' Day, a hallowed tradition. Even with all the noto-
riety brought about by *Ball Four,* Bouton attempted a comeback years
later, a too-old man throwing his ridiculous pitch that he still couldn't
master, just for one more chance to play the game; it was that love that
was lost and was lost, and you know you're a fool to pursue and pursue,
but what can you do? Lost amidst the "scandalous" revelations about

Mantle was that, overall, the book brushed an endearing portrait of the man. And more importantly, the Game.

A mash note would have been boring, but so too a hatchet job. Instead, Bouton told the total truth about his inamorata; as any part of a romantic pair can attest, this is noble—and oft disastrous.

*

Nothing is so good that some Super Fan can't ruin it for you with zealotry.

I worry my overreverence wrecks the most entertaining aspect of *Ball Four*—it infuses the reader with the day-to-day experience of being a ballplayer (if that ballplayer were effortlessly hilarious and profound).

Here's Bouton, saying things we wish ballplayers would say about

> God: "The philosophy here is that religion is why an athlete is good at what he does. 'My faith in God is what made me come back.' Or 'I knew Jesus was in my corner.' Since no one ever has an article saying, 'God didn't help me' or 'It's my muscles, not Jesus,' kids pretty soon get the idea that Jesus helps *all* athletes. . . . So I've been tempted sometimes to say into a microphone that I feel I won tonight because I don't believe in God, just for the sake of balance, to let the kids know that belief in a deity or 'Pitching for the Master' is not one of the criteria for major-league success."

> Infidelity: "A young girl asked one of the guys in the bullpen if he was married. 'Yeah,' he said, 'but I'm not a fanatic about it.'"

> Positive thinking: "When I pitched in the World Series in '63 and '64 I won two out of three games and the only thought that went through my mind before and during the

game was, 'Please don't let me embarrass myself out there.' No thought of winning or losing. If you told me before- hand that I would lose the game but it would be close and I wouldn't be embarrassed, I might well have settled for that. I was terrified of being humiliated on national tele- vision in front of all my friends. Now, that's certainly not positive thinking, and yet I was able to win ballgames. Maybe there is a power to negative thinking."

Teammates: "It's difficult to form close relationships in baseball. Players are friendly during the season and they pal around on the road. But they're not really friends. Part of the reason is that there's little point in forming a close relationship. Next week one of you could be gone [traded or sent down]. Hell, both of you could be gone. So no matter how you try, you find yourself holding back a little, keep- ing people at arm's length. It must be like that in war too."

But I needn't have cherry-picked. Every page contains something that stops the reader short.

I will now open the book at random and transcribe the best para- graph. April 26: "When I called my wife after my third save there was a gathering of Vancouver Mounties outside the phone booth. So on the bus today I was asked if I always call home after a save or win and I said yes, I did. And Greg Goossen said, 'Big deal. It means about three phone calls a year.'"

*

An analog blog.

That's the basic structure of the book—the section breaks are dates, singular entries spanning November 15 to October 2—but it never feels "bloggy" in the pejorative sense. It has all the advantages, entirely real slices of the day-to-day, without the drawbacks: the mundane rarely reads as myopic.

Ball Four combines two elements that currently seem antipodal: rigorous journalistic editing and shoot-from-the-hip journaling.

Bouton recorded his thoughts via paper scrap and audiotape—which were then transcribed by "Miss Elisabeth Rehm of Jamaica, NY." If *Ball Four* feels overlooked of late (did I mention that *Time* once listed it as one of the one hundred greatest nonfiction works of all time?), Rehm really lacks acclaim. Certainly Shecter, the editor, got short shrift. He took over 1,500 pages of text and turned them into an unassuming 398. Then he died three years later, before the big plaudits, but after major sportswriters like Dick Young decried Shecter as a "social leper."

Could *Ball Four*'s construction be a useful model—a way to keep the allure of the diary, while avoiding what George Saunders warned about, when I overheard him after an interview at the Fitzgerald Theater: explaining why he didn't blog, he said something to the effect of, *It doesn't seem like the problem with current writing is that there isn't enough of it.*

Yes! And yet, and yet . . .

*

The journal, allowed to steep for a year, then edited by an outsider, *can* catch amazing moments—like this era-encapsulating gem (I should note that Bouton was one of the more socially progressive players in the game):

> When I was a kid I loved to go to Giants games in the Polo Grounds. And a little thing that happened there when I was about ten years old popped into my mind today. There was a ball hit into the stands and a whole bunch of kids ran after it. I spotted it first, under a seat, and grabbed for it. Just as I did, a Negro kid also snatched at it. My hand reached it a split second before his, though, and I got a pretty good grip on it. But he grabbed the ball real hard and pulled it right out of my hand. No

complaint, he took it fair and square. I thought about it afterward, about what made him able to grab that ball out of my hand. I decided it had to do with the way we were brought up—me in a comfortable suburb, him probably in a ghetto. I decided that while I *wanted* the baseball, he *had to have it.*

Also, I wonder if this passage was the inspiration for the Best Baseball Writing Ever (sorry, Bouton, you're in second place), which is Don DeLillo's novella *Pafko at the Wall,* which later became the prologue for a little pamphlet called *Underworld.*

A highly similar event, which occurs at the Polo Grounds, forms a core plotline. If you haven't read *Pakfo,* I recommend it every bit as much as *Ball Four.* Treat yourself to some totally transporting prose, with the added benefit of being able to

A. claim credit for reading *Underworld,* without working your way through the full doorstop
B. ingest an ending passage every bit as beautiful as the close of *The Great Gatsby*

*

I was only being a bit hyperbolic at the open, pretending *Ball Four* to be a religious relic.

I have an original copy. It was given to a man as a Christmas present, and that man later died in his forties. The book was then given to his young son, and that son ended up reading it ritualistically at the start of each baseball season. I am not that son.

Rather, that son, my closest friend, lent me the book. Note: *lent,* not *gave.* I'm no thief, though my foible is equally unforgivable when borrowing books: I am forgetful and disorganized.

After three years, I realized this particular sin of oversight was damning, even by my lazy standards, and I called and confessed. "Keep the book," he said. He's not passive-aggressive—the opposite, actually.

Though thoroughly/modernly in touch with his emotions, he's admirably unsentimental and already has many mementos.

Maudlin displays, for him, would be a far greater crime than petty theft, which is why I must ask forgiveness for a vice I'm about to indulge (which, as any Catholic could tell you, means no forgiveness at all). It's not that the posting of this inscription is so striking:

Oddly, it's *this,* in the crease of the following page—which I only noticed for the first time two hours ago:

A person buys a book as a gift, then decides to scribble a quick inscription; they start on one page, then opt instead for the previous. No big deal. And yet.

Listen, *I'm not getting misty here;* I've already co-opted a ritual and book, so co-opting a calamity would be strike three. My copy of *Ball Four* should cause no crocodile tears, and though I feel an odd guilt, it's tempered by knowing my friend's mother is even tougher than he (apple/tree trajectory, etc.).

But I must admit, after an unintentional defense of blogs, I equally esteem the book, *this* book, as physical object. Believe me, I don't want to seem old-timey (he says, after using the verb *esteem*). I'm in my midthirties, which means nothing more than a desire to seem not in my midthirties—but goddamn:

Sometimes marginalia can cause as much time travel as the text.

*

Bouton treats his tape from Mickey Mantle like a religious relic.

It turned out that Mantle's boozing wasn't cute—it was a lifelong problem. Only after going to the Betty Ford Center late in life did he finally get clean. And right as he left the clinic, he learned his son had died—died from addictions modeled by the father. Many observers assumed this would plunge "The Mick" back into boozing, but instead Mickey Mantle lived his last remaining year sober; some would say this was every bit as heroic as any of his home runs, and I don't know if that is hyperbolic or not.

"In the final year of his life, Mickey Mantle, always so hard on himself, finally came to accept and appreciate the distinction between a role model and hero," said Bob Costas at Mantle's funeral. "The first, he often was not. The second, he always will be."

*

Bouton, who first expressed that distinction, however inchoate, wasn't invited to speak at the funeral; but far from being bitter, he just seemed to miss the man as a friend. Bouton's own actions, pre-eulogy, didn't come out until much later, prompted by interview:

> When Mickey's son Billy died, I wrote him to say how badly I felt, how I remembered Billy running around the locker room in spring training, and how awful it must be to lose a child. I never expected Mickey to respond. He's pretty shy. But about 10 days later, Mickey leaves a message on my machine: "Hi, Jim, this is Mick. I got your note and I appreciate it. Also, I want you to know I'm O.K. about *Ball Four.* One more thing; I want you to know I'm not the reason you're not invited to Old-Timers' Day. I never said none of that. Take it easy, bud."

Thirty-five years after Bouton's book, the two were reconciled—even though they never spoke directly, and even though the Yankees continued to shun Bouton. It was enough. "I still have the tape," Bouton said.

The tape is locked away, to be willed to his sons upon his demise.

*

Two years after Bouton wrote the message to Mantle, Bouton's daughter Laurie died in a car crash at the age of thirty-one.

In *Ball Four,* Bouton had written, "The Unsinkable Molly Brown is what we call Laurie, our youngest. She's only three, but a tough little broad. This spring alone, for example, she's been bitten by a dog, hit in the head by a flying can of peas and had nine stitches sewed into her pretty little head. Nothing puts her down." But in his eulogy, related in the *New York Times,* he didn't highlight toughness; he talked of how she wanted to be a nurse, with dreams of putting flowers in patients' rooms and throwing open curtains to bring sun into people's lives: "But that dream ended," he said, "when she discovered in nurse's school she had to dissect a frog, and she couldn't bring herself to do it. And a dead frog at that." He smiled and then began to cry.

*

After the funeral, one of Bouton's sons, Michael, wrote an open letter in the *New York Times* to George Steinbrenner, owner of the Yankees. After explicating familial grief and his father's reconciliation with Mantle, Michael laid out a point-by-point argument for Jim Bouton's inclusion in Old-Timers' Day, noting what it would mean for the family. Michael Bouton was a philosophy student, and, as Jim would later note, "it took a philosophy student to write that letter."

Steinbrenner reluctantly relented on the ban.

So in 1998, Bouton took the field again, and family and fans cheered. A hat had been specially fitted for him so that it would fall off his head postpitch, just like in the old days. Bouton appeared genuinely happy, though the event bittersweet—but it's hard to describe his timbre, as he said into the microphone, "This is for Laurie."

*

If I were to admit that transcribing such words as these makes me misty, I would note that it only happens when rewriting the words of others, never when composing my own, which would be weird/ right; for an essay like this, I might also note that this is interesting— and perhaps implies something about how nonfiction narrative traffics in the exact same effects as fictions and drama. The same sort of suspension of disbelief, and protagonist empathy, is required. To care. I might imply, even, that the enjoyment of sports in general also operates similarly—that the enjoyment of a great game and a great movie and a great novel is somewhat the same experience. Say I watch *Hamlet* (a good version); one would hope that I know I am not the melancholy Dane, nor am I related to him in any way. One would also hope/assume I know I'm not the protagonist when reading a novel or, say, *Ball Four.* So why do I get sad when Hamlet (in a good version) dies, or Gatsby dies, or Bouton loses everything? Yes, these *are* all very different expressions—but for a reader? We're maybe more sympathetic/crass than assumed. I'm not saying these situations are the same, just similar.

And if I were to write those things, I would bring up something else: in a recent scientific study of European soccer (football), fans of the losing team revealed a greatly diminished testosterone level, tested as they left the stadium. "How pathetic," was the sentiment amongst a few I knew—and I had to agree; the sadness of a losing sports fan is silly, I know! It is every bit as silly as the sadness resulting from novels, plays, etc. "Jocks versus nerds" is an embarrassing dynamic to believe in for anyone over the age of seventeen, and yes, "I was the latter," I'd yell.

*

And hear Bouton . . .

> You're much better off in athletics if you do things instinctively. I suppose that's what they mean when they say baseball isn't a thinking man's game. If you have to think about it, you tend to do things mechanically rather than naturally.
>
> I've always felt there were three kinds of athletes. First, there's the guy who does everything instinctively and does it right in the first place. I think Willie Mays is that kind guy, and so was Mickey Mantle. I don't think these guys can articulate what they're doing, they just know what to do and they go out and do it.
>
> Second, there's the athlete who's intelligent. If they're pitchers they try to figure out the mechanics of rotations and the aerodynamics of the curve ball . . . Jay Hook comes to mind. He was a pitcher with an engineering degree. . . . He had all the tools. . . . But he was always too involved with the mechanics of pitching. Ballplayers often say, "Quit thinking, you're hurting the club." I really

believe you can think too much in this game, and Hook always did.

The third kind is the one who is intelligent enough to know that baseball is basically an instinctive game. I like to think that's me.

He might suggest sermonizing is silly; if one doesn't know how to end, and lauding a long work has turned into logorrhea, just use the author's own words.

*

Bouton talks at the end about major leaguers, now stuck in the minors, clinging on way too long to their dreams—they're full of odd hopes in inferior games—and wonders if he could ever be so foolish. And admits: yes. "You spend most of your life gripping a baseball and in the end it turns out it was the other way around all along."

PHILLIP LOPATE

On a Little-Known Gem by Max Beerbohm

The sometime-caricaturist, drama critic, and novelist Max Beerbohm once declared: "What I really am is an essayist." By 1920 Beerbohm had hit his stride, publishing his best essay collection, *And Even Now,* that year. (With mock conceit, he had titled his youthful, thin debut *The Works of Max Beerbohm.* Thereafter, he tagged each subsequent gathering of essays with an afterthought—*More, And Even Now, Yet Again*—like a postscript apology for still taking up the reader's time.) *And Even Now* especially should be singled out as one of the most consistently superior essay collections published in the twentieth century. "More of a personal manifesto than any of its predecessors," noted his biographer, David Cecil, it included some of his most famous, frequently anthologized essays, such as "Going Out for a Walk," "Laughter," "Hosts and Guests," "No. 2, The Pines," and "How Shall I Word It?"

Tucked among these was one of his funniest essays, "Quia Imperfectum," which, I feel, has been unjustly neglected. Perhaps the Latin title put people off: it means "Because Imperfect." Beerbohm, though usually self-mocking when it came to his intellectual range, prided himself in his schoolboy mastery of Latin, which he considered essential "to the making of a decent style in English prose." By giving this piece a Latin title, he was perhaps flattering his cultivated English quarterly readers' presumably classical education. Or maybe he was making fun of that snobbishness, since the subject of the essay turns out to be the unachieved, the imperfect, and the monstrously tony.

The essay begins with a leisurely preamble:

> I have often wondered that no one has set himself to col-
> lect unfinished works of art. There is a peculiar charm
> for all of us in that which was still in the making when its
> maker died, or in that which he laid aside because he was
> tired of it, or didn't see his way to the end of it, or wanted
> to go on to something else.

One may note a few things in this opening: the straightforward clarity
of the first sentence, followed by the slyly complicated, diminuendo
spiraling of the second, from the most dignified explanation for the piece
being left unfinished, death, to the less dignified fatigue, confusion, and
finally boredom. The universalist assertion ("all of us") temporarily
unites Beerbohm with his readers, noteworthy because he will just as
often push us away with his contrarian singularity.

He then rambles through some examples of works left incomplete,
from Coleridge's "Kubla Khan" to the statues Michelangelo never
got around to finishing in the baptistery, to Racine's abandoned play,
Asquith's plan for the reform of the House of Lords, Leonardo's St.
Sebastian, etc. There is some hint of raillery in these paragraphs, at
least a provocative lack of respectful tone in speaking of these geniuses,
but we don't know where he is going with this yet: we don't see that it is
meant to set the stage for where he turns next, his takedown of Goethe.

At the bottom of page 2 he lights on his main focus, "a certain huge
picture in which a life-sized gentleman . . . ," etc. New paragraph: he
starts to have some fun: "The reader knits his brow? Evidently he has
not just been reading Goethe's *Travels in Italy*. I have." He is no longer
in league with the reader, but cheekily one-upping him. He continues:

> Or rather, I have just been reading a translation of it,
> published in 1883 by George Bell & Sons. I daresay it isn't
> a very good translation (for one has always understood
> that Goethe, despite a resistant medium, wrote well—an
> accomplishment which this translator hardly wins one

to suspect). And I daresay the painting I so want to see and have isn't a very good painting. Wilhelm Tischbein is hardly a name to conjure with, though in his day, as a practitioner in the "historical" style, and as a rapturous resident in Rome, Tischbein did great things, big things, at any rate.

The word "rapturous" is a mischievous tip-off: Beerbohm keeps puffing up these historical figures, then pulling them down. He has dropped his superiority toward the reader for not having been in the midst of reading *Travels in Italy* and is now colluding with the poor, puzzled, intimidated but (deep-down) skeptical average person who wonders if all these artists are really what they're cracked up to be. A self-professed little man and minor writer himself, Beerbohm is saying, in effect: Don't be intimidated! I am going to take you by the hand and show you what assholes they really are.

He starts by zeroing in on Goethe's vanity. "Goethe has more than once been described as 'the perfect man.' . . . But a man whose career was glorious without intermission, decade after decade, must sorely try our patience." He enumerates: "he was never injudicious, never lazy, always in the best form—and always in love with some lady or another just so much as was good for the development of his soul and his art, but never more than that by a tittle." Of course this is unfair, but the irreverence is tonic.

He then mocks Goethe's unquestioning acceptance of a flunkey's dedication as his due:

> Men of genius are not quick judges of character. Deep thinking and high imagining blunt that trivial instinct by which you and I size people up. Had you and I been at Goethe's elbow when, in the October of 1786, he entered Rome and was received by the excited Tischbein, no doubt we should have whispered in his ear, "Beware of that man. He will one day fail you." Unassisted Goethe had no misgivings.

Beerbohm loves to play the seductive game of bonding with his readers' "trivial instinct," while mocking the grandiose self-confidence of larger-than-life figures. "Goethe, you may be sure, enjoyed the hero-worshipful gaze focused on his from all the table of the Caffé Greco." He also has fun mocking the opportunistic painter ("Pushful Tischbein!") who latches onto the great writer and starts to paint his portrait in the hopes it will lead to some juicy commissions.

The rest of the essay plays out as a narrative, with Beerbohm quoting from the surviving letters and diaries and speculating as he reads between the lines. The flunky abandons the great man, preferring to chase some beauty. "Incredible!" Beerbohm writes with mock-astonishment. "We stare aghast, as in the presence of some great dignitary from behind whom, by a ribald hand, a chair is withdrawn, when he is in the act of sitting down." One can almost hear Beerbohm giggling spitefully in the background as the condescending Goethe gets his comeuppance, but what makes the essay so effective is the tone of formal propriety and scholarly historical research maintained throughout. So much of Beerbohm's humor is based on vocabulary and levels of diction, ranging from archaic to modern, always with an ironic whiff of parody that is difficult to pinpoint but apparent nonetheless.

Lord Cecil, his attentive biographer and anthologist, summarized Beerbohm's approach thus:

> Irony is its most continuous and consistent character; an irony at once delicate and ruthless, from which nothing is altogether protected, not even the author himself. Ruthless—but not savage: Max could be made angry—by brutality or vulgarity—but very seldom does he reveal this in his creative works. His artistic sense told him that ill-temper was out of place in an entertainment, especially in an entertainment that aspired to be pretty as well as comic. His ruthlessness gains its particular flavor from the fact that it is also good-tempered. On the other hand it is not so good-tempered as to lose its edge. Max's irony is never that sort of "kindly" irony that softens and sen-

timentalizes. His artistic sense tells him that softness, as much as savagery, would destroy the clear bright atmosphere needed for his entertainment to take place.

In short, though his thoughts might disconcert, his formal shaping of each essay still aimed to give pleasure, and succeeded. So he rounds out this particular piece with some appropriate further musings on Goethe's conceit and the charm of artistic incompletion. The essay, as we know, is a form that resists airtight perfection and invites impurities or digressions, so Beerbohm may also be commenting self-reflexively and even approvingly on his chosen métier. The irony is that, as Virginia Woolf remarked: "Mr. Beerbohm in his way is perfect . . . and then, as if one could swallow perfection and still keep one's critical capacity unsated, one looks about for something more. . . . For a second he makes his own perfection look a little small." Still, perfection is not such a bad thing. Quia perfectum.

On Eliot Weinberger's "Wrens"

I'm looking for company. When I first read Eliot Weinberger's "Wrens," I wanted to hand it to other people, watch their faces while they read, and be there when they looked up at the end. But I've been a little lonely in this regard. If you don't mind, then, can we get right to the essay? I'll meet you on the other side:

Wrens

Wrens live almost everywhere; they eat almost anything; they adapt to most climates—converting, for example, from polygamy to monogamy where food is scarce. There are twenty million of them in the British Isles alone. They build their nests almost anywhere, even in the beard of Edward Lear's Old Man with a Beard. The pastor-naturalist Rev. Edward A. Armstrong wrote that he found a nest in a human skull, but he didn't explain how.

Yet the prolific and anonymous wren is not simple. In many of the European languages, its name means "king of the birds" or "winter king." Killing one was bad luck: you'd break a bone, break out in pimples, get struck by lightning; the fingers on the hand that did the deed would shrivel and drop off; your cows would have blood in their milk.

Once a year, an exception was made. In most of France, Ireland, and the British Isles, there was a ritualized wren hunt that is recorded in Medieval texts, is undoubtedly much older, and was widespread until recent times. Though it varied from village to village, the essential ceremony was the same:

Sometime around the winter solstice—on Christmas or St. Stephen's Day (December 26) or New Year's Eve or New Year's Day or Twelfth Night—boys or young men would blacken their faces and dress up in crazy clothes— women's dresses or pyjamas or suits of straw—and, accompanied by fife and drums, would go out to beat the bushes for a wren. The boy who successfully caught one was named King of the Hunt and often required to perform tasks such as jumping naked in a lake. The slain wren was hung on a pole with its wings outstretched or carried on a bier decorated with ribbons and mistletoe or even in a miniature house complete with doors and windows. Its size was exaggerated: the boys pretended to stagger under the weight of the pole or bier, and in some places the bird was bound with heavy ropes and placed in a cart pulled by four oxen.

The Wren Boys then proceeded from house to house, singing songs and collecting coins. One of the versions of the song went:

The wren, the wren, the king of all birds,
St. Stephen's Day was caught in the furze;
Although he is little, his family is great,
I pray you, good landlady, give us a treat.

The money paid for a banquet and a dance that night, one that usually featured transgressive games or rituals for the newly wedded and the still unmarried. The next morning the wren was solemnly buried.

That the little wren comes from somewhere far in the past is evident in the stories about it. The wren is a subverter of Christianity. As St. Stephen was about to escape from jail, a wren landed on the guard's face and woke him up, leading to the saint's martyrdom. The Irish St. Moling cursed all wrens because one ate his pet fly "that used to be making music for me." St. Malo chose to freeze rather than wear his cloak for a wren had built a nest in it. Wrens are sometimes known as the "bird magician" or the "Druid bird."

The wren, in countless stories, is the enemy of the eagle, whom it usually outwits. The soaring eagle is the quintessential symbol of the sky, storms, and the sun. The wren—which doesn't fly high, which creeps into mouse holes and crevices—is an emblem of the earth. (In Greece, Trochilos the wren was the son of Triptolemos, the inventor of the plow.) And more: through the gender reversal so common in folklore, the wren, though "king of the birds," is female. She is Jenny Wren or Kitty Wren, the wife of Cock Robin, the universal bringer of fire. The wren is pagan, chthonic, female.

Four to six thousand years ago in these same parts, two distinct kinds of megaliths were constructed: circular passage graves with a single entrance and rectangular gallery graves with two entrances. As each is confined to various large and specific geographical areas, and as they rarely overlap, it is believed that they represent two distinct cultures or religions.

In the 1950's, the Reverend Armstrong mapped all the places where the Wren Hunt occurred and discovered that it was largely absent from the areas where gallery graves are found. In Ireland, the area of passage graves and Wren Boys and the area of gallery graves and no Wren Boys corresponded almost exactly with the national entities now known as Ireland and Northern Ireland. Wrens go deep.

*

Right? Yes? Did you feel a cliff fall away at your feet? Or an invisible architecture materialize before your eyes? Here you were, standing in it all along?

To me, the ending has the lightning-bolt feeling of truth revealed (is that right? do these conflicts go back and back and back? what other codes have I failed to crack, have I not even recognized as codes?). But it also has the drama and dread of a new myth coalescing. We feel the subversive delight of telling stories about the world, an effort both to describe and manipulate. This is Weinberger's particular genius in the essay: finding the nexus between natural and cultural history, and then creating that fusion in his own telling.

Camouflaged like the plain, small wren, his stealthy project begins with wren data—habitat, diet, statistics. We suspect we will be able to write a school report about wrens by the essay's conclusion. But the "live almost anywhere" and "eat almost anything" are almost comically vague, and, by the end of the paragraph, we're in the painting of a beard and then a human skull ("but he didn't explain how"). We remain in the human skull as Weinberger mines the anthropological history of the wrens. Cross-dressing Wren Boys, the campy exaggerations of the wren processionals, martyrs yoking wrens to their tableaux—we feel the weight of humankind coming to bear on the miniscule skull, the hollow wing bones of a wren. Wrens go deep, indeed.

*

The book in which "Wrens" appears, *An Elemental Thing*, is bewildering and transporting, moving like water through centuries and continents. At times it's as if I'm reading a new language, the vocabulary of which I understand in the light of day, but the arrangement/geist/residue of which I only understand when I'm asleep. And that is an essentially private experience—no one wants to hear your dreams. Except that Weinberger is writing about cultures, history, the movements of ideas through space and time, through syntax and metaphor, ritual and art.

PATRICK MADDEN

On Charles Lamb's "New Year's Eve"

On or about New Year's Eve every year I reread Charles Lamb's "New Year's Eve," a perfect essay, which in a spill of language and punctuation turns an occasion into a meditation, in this case, on mortality, that inexhaustible topic and perennial favorite of writers from all ages. I love it for how it hooks not just my gut but my mind, not with drama or story but with idea, and because at nearly two hundred years old, it still speaks to a universal feeling sparked by the arbitrary turning of the calendar loaf. Also because it reminds me, as any memento mori should, that I will die.

I don't like the idea of my death, and I believe it to be a long way off, but I like to rage with Lamb against it and to think that each December 31 as I read, I am resurrecting the melancholy, impertinent writer, who pleads once more to arrest time—

> I begin to count the probabilities of my duration, and to grudge at the expenditure of moments and shortest periods, like miser's farthings. In proportion as the years both lessen and shorten, I set more count upon their periods, and would fain lay my ineffectual finger upon the spoke of the great wheel. I am not content to pass away "like a weaver's shuttle." Those metaphors solace me not, nor sweeten the unpalatable draught of mortality. I care not to be carried with the tide, that smoothly bears human

life to eternity; and reluct at the inevitable course of destiny. I am in love with this green earth; the face of town and country; the unspeakable rural solitudes, and the sweet security of streets. I would set up my tabernacle here. I am content to stand still at the age to which I am arrived; I, and my friends: to be no younger, no richer, no handsomer. I do not want to be weaned by age; or drop, like mellow fruit, as they say, into the grave.—Any alteration, on this earth of mine, in diet or in lodging, puzzles and discomposes me. My household-gods plant a terrible fixed foot, and are not rooted up without blood. They do not willingly seek Lavinian shores. A new state of being staggers me. Sun, and sky, and breeze, and solitary walks, and summer holidays, and the greenness of fields, and the delicious juices of meats and fishes, and society, and the cheerful glass, and candle-light, and fireside conversations, and innocent vanities, and jests, and *irony itself*—do these things go out with life?

—that by my reading I am bringing about his wish to stand still at the age of forty-five, on the eve of 1821, reviewing the events of the past twelvemonth, revisiting the graveyard to taunt the buried-under-stones: "I am alive. I move about. I am worth twenty of thee. Know thy betters!"

It is helpful to know that Lamb wrote his essays in persona, as an Italian clerk named Elia, who shared some of Lamb's biography but not all of it, yet he sometimes, as in this essay, slips away from his character in order to comment upon it. Thus his delightful passage of self-ridicule:

No one whose mind is introspective—and mine is painfully so—can have a less respect for his present identity, than I have for the man Elia. I know him to be light, and vain, and humorsome; a notorious * * *; addicted to * * * * : averse from counsel, neither taking it nor offering it;— * * * besides; a stammering buffoon; what you will; lay it on, and spare not; I subscribe to it all, and much more.

This is, I think, a worthy lesson to essayists today, or to humans today, to make light of ourselves and puncture our propensity for pomposity. When I read "New Year's Eve" in the atmosphere of promises to lose weight, read more, work less, do better, I think that there is no better resolution than to be humble, which Lamb also achieves in signing off with what I take to be a salute to those who'll outlive or come after him, undermining his prior glee at outliving the earlier dead. "And now another cup of the generous," he offers, "and a merry New Year, and many of them, to you all, my masters!" He seems to be winking right at me, who am worth twenty of him, because I am alive.

For no reason other than the childlike joy of it, I want to end by mentioning a wonderful coincidence I once discovered thanks to "New Year's Eve." I love Lamb's opening thesis-like sentence, that "every man hath two birth-days: two days, at least, in every year, which set him upon revolving the lapse of time, as it affects his mortal duration," an eloquent phrasing of a kind of existential situation familiar to many of us, yet, as I found out, not quite as universal as he and I were wont to believe. One early January day, after I'd assigned my students to memorize a passage of Lamb's prose and I'd happily recited the first paragraph to them, a student spoke up to argue with the premise. Not everyone, she said, has two birthdays. She had just the one, January first. In chorus, two other students spoke up. They, too, were born on New Year's Day. Of the twenty-two students signed up for History and Theory of the Essay, three of them gave the lie to Lamb's notion. As I've written elsewhere, the odds of shared birthdays in relatively small groups are remarkably, unexpectedly good. Given the twenty-three people in the classroom, we had a better than 50 percent chance that two of us would share a birthday. That three would share a birthday (any birthday) was about 15 percent probable. But three people all born on the essayistically (and calendrically) important first day of the year: the answer to this problem slips away from my grasp of mathematics in a way that suggests the unknowing open-endedness surrounding all great essays, and it leaves just enough mystery as to seem miraculous.

ELENA PASSARELLO

On the *Book of Days*

I am never eager to make resolutions on January 1. I'm pretty crappy at resolve on any date, and I find it difficult to come up with New Year's resolutions that excite me enough to try and keep them. If I do think of a thrilling resolution, it usually turns out to be impossible. The last New Year's resolution I made in earnest was in 2009, when I swore to see a moose by December. I never did, despite my limited efforts. I also made the resolution in March.

One thing that does excite me about the first of the year, though, is the opportunity to adopt a new principle for organizing that year. I think this is why I get a bright new coat every after-Christmas sale season; I imagine the world seeing a punchier arrangement of me walking about. And I *love* to get a blank calendar and notebook, which I never immediately treat like my old calendars and notebooks, instead devising for myself a fresh course of annotating and remembering and thinking. It is the idea of not just commemorating the year, but curating it, that charms me.

An amplified version of this charm is available in Robert Chambers's *Book of Days*, a 1,672-page, single-spaced home reference that could be considered the world's wordiest—and most essayistic—calendar. First published in the 1860s after a writing and indexing process that nearly killed him, Chambers's book is subtitled *A Miscellany of Popular Antiquities in Connection with the Calendar, Including Anecdote, Biography, & History, Curiosities of Literature, and Oddities*

of Human Life and Character. It is more than an almanac, encyclo-
pedia, or annual, because to peruse it is to step inside a singular and
biased mind. It is one polymath's vigorous and desperate attempt to
organize time for the benefit of a larger audience.

The book moves through the days like a factoid magnet, capri-
ciously attracting notes on holidays, important births and deaths, facts
of the natural and folkloric world, and—my favorite—what Chambers
calls "curious, fugitive, inedited pieces."

January 1, for example, begins with an essay on birthday boy
Edmund Burke—"A wonderful basis of knowledge was crowned in
his case by the play of his most brilliant imagination." This appears
near a discussion of the Scottish New Year's tradition of "first foot-
ing" (which turned deadly in 1812, as Chambers somewhat gleefully
reports). Then comes an entry with only the loosest of connections to
the date: a four-hundred-word reflection on understanding the "happy"
in "Happy New Year"—"God certainly has not arranged that any such
highly intelligent being as man should be truly happy." January 1 ends
with a loving profile of Old Hobson (1544–1630), a proto-mailman who
seemingly made the book because he lived for eight decades and was
good to his horses.

Other days treat readers to an explanation of how snow crystals are
made (in the January foreword), a play-by-play of how villages shame
bad husbands (October 29) or bad wives (February 1), and a diatribe on
the ring finger (February 3). The different guide words at the tops of the
pages are delightfully mixed:

> "Animal Comedians" (February 24)
> "Priests' Hiding Chambers" (March 28)
> "A Brace of Cavalier Poets"(April 29)
> "Whipping Vagrants" (May 5)
> "A Balloon Duel" (June 22)
> "The Prophesies of Nostradamus" (July 2)
> "The Legend of the Pig-Faced Lady" (August 23)
> "Michelmas" (September 29)
> "Lighting Old London" (October 3)

"Mermaids" (November 24)
"Primitive Styles of Ice Skating" (December 30)

When read more carefully, the book gives an intriguing picture of Chambers as curator; there is a lovely personal stamp on his organization of information, which grows with each passing day. He seems obsessed with both public humiliation and hot air balloons. He is also prone to commentary; Chambers does not appear to revere either Henry VIII or Montaigne, though he is cool with Thomas Cromwell. He is nervous to report any scatological detail. His book tells us not just all these facts, but of the man who decided that March 23 is best represented by only four things: singing in the Sistine Chapel, an analysis of the handwriting of the Castilian king Pedro the Cruel, a fire that destroyed Kensington manse, and this one time in Edinburgh that a lady swallowed a padlock.

But why *not* use this quartet to mark a day in March? And why not match a sober recounting of the Battle of Hastings with a celebration of the pun and a history of the back scratcher? These groupings are the true pleasure of the book. What they allow isn't the chance for readers to learn the most important contributions to humanity that occurred on a specific day, but to stitch their own senses of significance and companionship among the motley raw materials Chambers offers.

And there is an accuracy to this essayistic coursing of human events; I imagine that many days in my 2013 will be, more or less, a ragged and confusing assembly of epic battles, plays on words, and itchy backsides. There are so many possibilities as to where the next 365 days will take us all that a mismatched bunch of high and low points in history seems the only way to offer proper companionship.

I know that the book is not an anomaly; Chambers takes organizational cues from earlier reference almanacs (though few were as exhaustive and none were as idiosyncratic), and many other books of days have followed his lead since 1864. A British publisher even released an updated version of the book eight years ago, but the inclusion of new facts watered down Chambers's voice, and something about pairing discussions of balloon dueling with Spice Girls record sales numbers leaves me cold. One could also argue that reading a few pages of the book mimics more contemporary fact-based reading pleasures, like falling down a Wikipedia wormhole or perusing someone else's Pinterest board, but I say nuts to that.

Though I loathe resolving, I think I might vow—or at least strongly suggest to myself—to open the *Book of Days* every day of this year, and to read just a little. The whole tome is, of course, indexed online, but I got a 112-year-old print version from my library, and it is so much more satisfying—Chambers and his brother laid out each busy page gorgeously, so it hums with tightly-packed words and fine-ink illustrations.

And I swear the entries keep changing, like in a Hogwarts book. I just turned back to that page with the hot air balloon duel and discovered a story of a codfish found in the river Cam with a book of religious treatises in its belly. I know that anecdote wasn't in there when I last landed on the page (but then again, the print is really small). And that magic is just another joy to be had in Chambers's book: this attempt to curate the timely world into meaningful volumes, years, months, days, anecdotes, and meditations; this Russian doll of essays and essaying.

ERIN ZWIENER

On the False Glint of Fool's Gold and Cliché

Maybe romantic is going out to Wyoming and roping a wild bronco. But after you get out of the hospital, you have to feed the son of a bitch. He bites and kicks and doesn't take kindly to the saddle, and after you get out of the hospital again, you neglect and abandon him, and the PETA people haul your ass into court—there is no romance in court, ever.

—RICHARD SCHMITT, "SOMETIMES A ROMANTIC NOTION"

Forty horses stretch in a line along the wide path, one wrangler (at minimum) for every seven dudes per our insurance policy. The wranglers, professional horsemen and horsewomen, are easy to spot. We wear cowboy-cut jeans, palm-leaf hats, boots, and fire-engine red or denim pearl snap shirts. Fringed chaps wrap around my thighs, and I enjoy correcting the guests about the pronunciation of the leather leggings. "Ch-ap is what happens to your ass when you don't wear sh-aps. It's related to chaparral, brush country." Some guests have gone shopping before arrival, trying to look the part of a westerner. Little girls wear pink pointy-toed boots, women tie bandanas glinting with rhinestones around their necks, and men ride with one hand clutching their ill-fitting, ill-shaped straw hats.

It's a routine we repeat every week. A new batch of dudes arrives on Sunday and fills the rickety bleachers. Lee Greenwood belts out "God

Bless the USA" as the wranglers stream into the arena and perform a choreographed routine of loops and x's. I ride a svelte bay gelding and carry a Colorado flag that flutters behind me as we gallop. At the end of the performance, the horses line up in the center of the area facing the audience. My gelding stands like a statue while I hold my hat over my heart for the National Anthem, and the guests applaud.

Then we heave the guests onto the presaddled horses waiting in the corral and take them on what we call a trail ride. But the "trail" travels through one pasture, behind a subdivision of summer homes, across the country road, and around a pond in a second pasture. Nothing remote or impressive if you're used to Colorado, but our dudes come from Los Angeles, New York City, and Atlanta.

The first section of the path abuts another large field full of horses. One bay with an arched neck gallops the fence line, calling to the sedate, dude-bearing mounts. He tosses his head, shakes his black mane, and kicks his hind legs in the air.

"Can anyone ride that bronco?" one woman asks.

"That's the horse they put the bad guests on," her husband answers, shooting a look at his oldest son.

"That's right," I say. "Better do everything I tell you to, or we'll put you on him tomorrow."

The boy's mother laughs but scrunches her face in a way that tells me I've worried her. My first job is to keep everyone alive and healthy. The ranch horses are used to beginners and tend to be slow-going, but animals are unpredictable and humans are always looking for new ways to find trouble. I give tips on sitting comfortably in the saddle and bark at children to not throw acorns at one another. I watch the dudes to determine who is coordinated (and obedient) enough to go on rides up into the mountains. My second job is entertainment, and I chatter about horses, backcountry, wildlife, and country-western dancing.

When we return to the ranch, the bay gelding is still frolicking. After the guests are safely back on the ground, I ask, "Do y'all want to see me break that crazy horse to ride?"

The woman tells me seriously, "No, we don't want you to get hurt."

"Oh, I'm pretty sure I can handle him." I answer.

I grab a soft cotton rope and duck through the wire into the pasture while the dudes gather near the fence line. The bay gallops my direction, and I flail the rope toward his face when he nears. He pivots on his hind end, kicks his heels in the air, and gallops away. When he slows to an energetic trot, I move so that I'm perpendicular to his shoulder, and he starts to circle me, his delicate head lowering. When he slows to a walk, I drop my eyes to the ground and step backwards. He stops, and I back up farther. The bay steps toward me warily.

I give him a moment to settle, and then pad up to his shoulder with quiet heel steps. He shudders when I pat him firmly on the neck but doesn't move away. I ease the rope around his neck and leap onto his back while the crowd gathered on the other side of the fence gasps. The bay rears up, lifting his front feet and striking like the Lone Ranger's Silver, and I dig my fingers into his mane and press my chest into his neck. When he touches down, he shoots forward at a full run. I coo at him until he slows to a relaxed lope, and lay the rope against the right side of his neck. When the gelding curves his spine and turns to the left, I praise him loudly and direct him toward the watching guests.

I swing off directly in front of them, give the bay an approving rub, remove the rope, and turn to my onlookers. The bay tries to use my back as a scratching post, and I scold him.

"Not too bad for the first ride," I say.

The guests are in awe of me, their own private Annie Oakley and fearless tamer of wild horses. None of them recognize the bay from our drill team event that morning, one of two horses on the ranch that can carry a flag without spooking, and they won't recognize him when we run short of kids' horses on Wednesday and pack an eight-year-old on him. A horse that I have owned since I was thirteen. A horse that I taught verbal commands such as "up" for rear and "let's go" for gallop. I make the best tips of any wrangler on the ranch.

*

Even as I tell this story, I fall back into the shtick, give into the temptation to let the story run away with me. I was just starting to teach Razi, that bay gelding, to rear that summer, so his bronco display wouldn't have been as dramatic. I used a halter with a lead rope instead of just the rope. We've never mastered riding with just a neck rope despite my best efforts. The girl who rode Razi when we ran out of children's horses was eleven, not eight. Our guests came to Colorado for the fir and aspen-clad mountains, the blue lakes, the clear air, but they came to a dude ranch for the romance of the Wild West. So we gave it to them. Other wranglers told stories about competing in the National Children's Rodeo (doesn't exist), a beloved horse waiting for them at home (imaginary), the year they spent living in the wilderness (totally fictitious), a promising bull-riding career given up because of injuries (one ill-advised leap onto a bull in a pasture), childhoods on a ranch in South Dakota (born there, but the family moved to Phoenix before the wrangler in question could walk).

In his essay "Sometimes a Romantic Notion," Richard Schmitt discusses the human penchant for clichéd drama, an appetite for tales that are plucked and clipped and primped until they fit into an elegant frame. He tells his own story of "running away to join the circus" as a teenager, except he was already a runaway, a minimum wage brick scrubber sharing an apartment with a junkie who rested his hopes on a white Ringling Bros. train. From Schmitt: "People say 'run away to join *the* circus' as if there is only one, and as if there is no doubt about joining it. As if the option resides solely with the runaway. One is fed up; the need to escape strikes; you find this entity called *circus* and presto, you are embraced."

"Never let the truth get in the way of a good story." An ever-tempting piece of barroom cowboy advice. Romanticizing our past and ourselves is a trap for memoirists in particular but other nonfiction writers as well. What makes something romantic anyway? Unfamiliarity? Inaccessibility? Romance is a trope that we substitute in for reality, cowboys or circus performers with the manure wiped off their boots before they're allowed in public.

Schmitt discovered that finding gainful employment under a big top was more complicated than he'd imagined. "One didn't simply decide to join the circus and have them issue you a bandanna and a tambourine." Instead of focusing on the glitzy culmination of his circus career as high-wire act, the essay follows the teenage Schmitt searching up and down the train for someone to hire him and observing the workers and his surroundings with a honed gaze. "The spit polish and flash of the first few cars gave way to peeled paint and sooty squalor. There were garbage bags. The windows weren't washed. . . . Stockcars, pervasive zoo odors, heavy wooden ramps soiled with various types of dried animal crap . . . a hunched troll-like figure crawling from the black belly of the train, dragging a fat rubber hose, the type used for pumping septic tanks. An old man covered in soot and rail cinders. His face resembled a tire tread in dried mud." When he did find the right people, they had no work for him, at least not there in Providence. He could try Albuquerque. A romantic notion has a gleaming surface, but it lacks the depth and humanity of life.

But what harm in just a notion? It's such an impulsive little word, with none of the vigor of opinion or the steadfastness of conviction. A notion will pass like the latest fad, so why not indulge it for a moment before moving on? From Schmitt: "Notions are fleeting; they go away. One minute you are making a tiger vanish, the next moment he is having you for dinner. Being eaten by tigers is not romantic."

In sewing, notions are all the tiny items, the afterthoughts one grabs at Jo-Ann's after they've selected a pattern, a fabric, and a trim. They're the simple structural items that differentiate a professional-looking garment from an amateur one. Cider-hued thread for traditional jean-pocket stitching, midnight blue for an edgier, urban look. Goofy red buttons for clown costumes. Pearl snaps for a western shirt. Plastic stays to make a high-wire performer's collar permanently stiff. Notions also include basic tools. Scissors to make a bolt of cloth match the pattern. Pins that hold the fabric together for sewing. Bobbins that whirl out thread on the machine. Needles to prick and thimbles to protect. A seam ripper to correct mistakes and try again. Without notions there can be no stitching together of satin or scenes.

Notions are the connective tissue of essays, that singular vision that takes a jumble of parts and transforms it into a whole. Some notions may show in the finished project; others may be pulled out like pins when the piece is sewn together, but they are just as integral to an essay as narrative, voice, metaphor. Enter an essay with the wrong notion and the components won't stick. Or perhaps they'll stick but look as garish as a pair of leopard-print capris. Schmitt's steadfast gaze on the grimy details reminds us that despite the temptation of cliché, the austere underbelly is more fascinating than polished façade, that we as essayists should look past the first glint and dig for a more ambiguous treasure.

The Present of Our Past

On Alexander Stille

In the ancient agora in Athens, a re-creation of the Stoa of Attalos occupies the same ground where it stood in antiquity. Among excavated ruins, just off the route of the ancient Panathenaean procession up to the Acropolis, it was re-created down to the last details by archeologists from the American School of Classical Studies in Athens in the 1950s. Inside is a small museum of objects retrieved from the local earth. There I saw the fragile skeleton of a child buried near this spot around 1000 BC, in the Protogeometric Age. Her grave is reassembled in a glass case: the flat stones that formed the edge of the tomb, her head now a half skull filled with packed dirt, the thin bones of her arms, pelvis, and legs still plausibly showing the shape, still the inner outline of a small girl. And little jugs for wine and oil, two bronze bracelets, a ring, the pins that fastened the garment she wore on her journey to the underworld. Those burial jars, the pin that once secured the vanished cloth: they spoke of a kind of grown-up dignity particular to her time and place.

How touching it was to see her small bones in that reconstructed context. It would be wrong to call her an object of art, but she seems to offer something more than scientific knowledge: the opportunity to feel simultaneously our transience on earth, the importance of being alive in our own moment, and the particularity of hers.

Thousands of miles to the west, at the Getty Villa in Malibu, California, the intricate floor of a circular display space is composed of twenty-two concentric circles, four thousand triangular pieces of black or yellow marble, with a touch of rosso antico and green porphyry at the center. It's a marvel of illusionistic paving. Like the Stoa of Attalos, it was copied stone by stone from the original—this time the belvedere floor of a villa discovered a hundred feet underground in the course of excavations at Herculaneum, an ancient city covered by lava in the eruption of Mount Vesuvius in 79 AD that also obliterated Pompeii.

The villa's excavation was carried out in 1750 on behalf of the king of Naples, and the workers were slaves, convicts in chains. The *Guide to the Getty Villa* adds parenthetically that their chains were removed so they wouldn't damage the ancient mosaic floors. This eighteenth-century cruelty allowed the stones to be lifted out piece by piece and reassembled in the king's museum at Portici, near Naples. Two centuries later, that floor was re-created, piece by beautiful piece, in Malibu, to satisfy the vanity of an American millionaire.

In his wonderful book *The Future of the Past,* Alexander Stille writes about the way the future (us) is always taking up its own concerns as it goes about honoring, preserving, and collecting the past. He writes about nature in Madagascar and oral poetry in Somaliland, about the vanished and the vanishing, and the resurrected. He writes about the Sphinx as a monument constantly undergoing change— from the organisms and animals inside it, from the water moving through it. He writes about trying to save the Ganges from pollution while respecting its cultural position in India, and about the efforts of one American priest living in Rome to live spontaneously in the city's present through the Latin language, to share the ancient tongue's lovely conjunction with the place. And he asks if our efforts systematically to understand the past paradoxically makes it recede.

Stille allows his questions to remain open, as he gets close to those who live with them every day: an American scholar who spent weeks mapping the stones in the paws of the Sphinx; Somalia's most beloved poet, who regrets his own literacy; an archeologist in Sicily who hears in an inscription on ancient treasure taken from its ground, "an ancient voice crying out at a moment of incredible difficulty, similar to what happened in Bosnia or Kosovo." The meaning of the old things is not just in the past, but for the present.

This meaning is what I have been looking for in the places of the past and in the museums of the present. One ravishing space now at the Getty Villa is its triclinium (which would have been the dining room). Part of a recent lavish renovation of the 1970s original, the room is decorated in marbles from Egypt, Tunisia, Sparta, and Turkey. It incorporates design elements from three different villas at Herculaneum. Resting on a bench there, one's eye falls on an almost sickening display of gorgeous luxury. It's simultaneously an evocation of the past and a denial of the actual experience of visiting what's left of that vanished world, with its flaking columns and unlit frescoes. Here in the imagined loveliness of Piso's time, how distant we are from the delicacies Piso served there as the long first-century afternoons drifted into evening: flamingo tongues, ibex, and even field mice (fattened in little cages).

The past is a foreign country of ancient voices, slave labor, buried children, and field mouse stew. We stalk it like hunters immersed in a world of animals, at once predators and prey. It's a dark cave into which we shine the flashlight of the present, exploring what it is to be human by feeling our way: re-creating, reassembling our understanding of what is true. Rationality and pleasure together nose us into that dark space, trying to bring the past back from the underworld to speak to us. This reconstruction of Roman leisure on a California shore is missing the gravity of the child's skeleton, that delicate memento mori among the fortuitous remains of urban life. Nevertheless its particular aesthetic reality creates a rich experience of immediacy, loss, and grandeur.

Displayed in another room at the Getty Villa is an eerily satisfying group of terra cotta figures, Orpheus and the Sirens, the work of an unknown Greek artist working in southern Italy. How incongruous perhaps this display of Greek and Roman antiquity by the Pacific shore, and how much I would not want it sent back to its proper context in Italy! I don't think my compromised desire is incompatible with paying proper respect to the people and places where art flourished.

The scientific desire to know them and thus enrich our perspective on our own shifting place in the continuum of time is only part of what has us digging in the old earth, and filling our museums.

Running side by side with human rapacity and exploitation is that marriage of skill and imagination we call art, without which we would indeed be the poorest of bare, forked creatures. Art offers a way of being in the present—briefly unannexed to the dead, even while connected to the past and the future. Stille's book is deeply engaged with how the past is constantly shifting, as its story is constructed. Yet I am still engaged in art's shiftlessness.

Our human intelligence gives us the power to go "back through history up the stream of time," said Robert Frost, but the point is not "chiefly that you may go where you will, / But in the rush of everything to waste, / that you may have the power of standing still." Frost's poem is called "The Master Speed" and that speed is indeed just the capacity for stillness, for self-abandonment in the moment, for being free of past and future, of narrative or progress, of time and death. Predators, slaveowners, mourners, and creators, we plunder and rebuild. Alongside the vanishing particularity of our graves, though, it is the still and suddenly expansive moments of delight that free us from the brevity of our tales.

ANDER MONSON

A Fat Man Story

on H. L. Mencken's "A Neglected Anniversary"

This fine morning on the first of April, I write from my bathtub here in Tucson, Arizona, to you.

And in fact I'd like to discuss the bathtub, introduced to America in 1842 in Cincinnati in its modern form, then made of mahogany and lined in sheet lead, and later popularized by President Millard Fillmore. All this is from the mouth of one of my favorite essayists H. L. Mencken in his essay "A Neglected Anniversary," published in the New York *Evening Mail* in 1917. The *Evening Mail* is no longer extant, of course, having undergone a series of fattening mergers and finally folding its adulterated bulk in 1967.

For some reason I always picture Mencken as fat. Maybe it's the initials. Like A. S. Byatt, W. G. Sebald, or B. T. Overdrive, initials suggest the fatness, possibly adorned with a timepiece in a front pocket, or at the least a classist smirk on one's face. When I was chubbier and younger, more closely approximating a basketball or a Hutt, I am ashamed to say that I aspired to this air of eminence: I went briefly by A. S. Monson, and then Ander S. Monson, on account of the middle initial made me more distinguished, like Franklin W. Dixon (author of the Hardy Boys novels—also, as I found out sometime around fifth grade, a composite: there was no Dixon but a legion of underpaid, mostly female writers; but the middle initial remained, however false, and impressed itself on me), and also my burgeoning corpulence.

It remains an embarrassment. The initials, not the fatness—though I still live in the shell of the fatness—because that never really goes away, our sense of our fat former or maybe present selves hovering like the outer boundary of our electron shell even as we've now found somewhat leaner days. As essayists we would do well to cleave to our embarrassments, for therein might we open ourselves to others. Are you listening, Mr. Mencken?

So as fat as I am or was, thinking of Mencken this morning, I write this missive to you from my bathtub, across which I've spanned a two-by-twelve with my laptop perched atop, on which I type carefully, not wanting to allow a stray splash to render it inert. There is risk, then, in every character I depress to transmit this truth to you.

I've always been a sucker for the bathtub in all its iterations. I love immersion, one of the greatest pleasures of the human, and the bathtub is immersion's domestic home, unless you have a Jacuzzi, a sensory-deprivation tank, a space station, or a pool. Immersion is, after all, what we hope for in our fiction, even in our nonfiction: we hope to be caught and carried under, to suspend our disbelief, as we say, for a moment, to go all-in, to catch some extended air, to follow a story wherever it may lead, to give our brain over to another's for a moment. Immersion is what allows art to work its magic on us, for us to be moved without moving, to believe without leaving, to be changed without changing our clothes or ourselves. It's in the losing of ourselves for an hour to the art thing (as Mark Ehling has named it, in this space, "an art feeling") that allows us to experience a whiff of transcendence.

Or maybe that's just the Taco Bell Cool Ranch Tacos I'm still smelling, which, I must admit, were pretty good. They taste just like a cool ranch. I can feel myself getting fatter. Keep typing, chunko.

*

The observant may notice that today's date is April 1. I woke up this morning anticipating my far-too-big bowl of cereal on my favorite day of the year, April Fool's Day, in which we fool and venerate the fooled. We ask for it, we dupes: we chuckle heartily, our hearts clucking their amusement at our credulousness. Today is the day in which we should celebrate the art of critical thinking.

It is also a day for Doritos Locos Tacos Doritos (this is sadly not a joke). Or at least Doritos Locos Tacos. Or at least just Doritos if you don't want to get all loco on them. Or maybe a Jumbaco. At first I thought it sad that Taco Bell maintained locations in Tucson, Arizona, where I now live. Given the number of taco carts and trucks and local fast-food Mexican, how could it compete? Then I realized it's not really competing: it's not Mexican. It's barely anything at all. I don't feel so bad about eating there now, particularly since they've upgraded all their foods to be made with Doritos (that last part's a lie . . . for now: can't you see this is the future we've been asking for? Why settle for corn or flour tortillas when you can get everything, your drink included, terrorized with superflavor-detonating nacho crystals?).

It's a little early for the heartburn, but thinking of it and typing so hard are causing my plank to rattle and my stomach to get all churny.

I wonder: Have you been duped? Have you believed? Have you ruefully been forced to question the authority you grant to NPR, to CNN, these initialed fatties of the media, to the *Economist,* to the *New York Times,* to the BBC, all these we trust to proffer (not to profiteer) information?

Today is a day to celebrate being lied to. We are being lied to. We should take the opportunity to enjoy it. Crack a beer. Adjust your lie. Our golf is winter rules, which as any duffer knows, means you should feel free to kick your ball back in the fairway, you know, for fairness.

We want the lie. We need the lie. The lie is entertainment. The lie is narrative. We're reassured by being told a thing even if it is false. The lie is where the human is drawn. The lie is wholeness, seamlessness, the convenient arrangement of events into a story that can mean. The lie is manipulation; the lie is art.

*

Clever reader, by now you may suspect my bathtub story's rub is false, that Mencken's bathtub story is false. You would be correct. Not that

Mencken didn't write these things: he did. That's not the joke. The joke is that they simply were not true. It's not much of a joke, but I'll come back to that. I'm not convinced it's all that much of an essay either. But it was great fake news.

"Fake news has been with us for a long time," writes Robert Love in "Before Jon Stewart," his riff on the history of fake news in which he details late-nineteenth-century papers' penchant for publishing sensation and *story* [my italics] over fact. Fake news is with us now: today, more obviously, but weekdays when the *Daily Show* is on, when the *Onion* publishes, when we are credulous. While we no longer consider fake news from real news organizations O.K. (except on April 1), fake news from fake news organizations is just fine—great, in fact. Often it delivers real news. And for sure we like the taste of story. We always did, but in a disintegrating, disconnected world, we're suckers for a story. We like sensation, that slowness, that transporting feeling. We want—we must believe in—fact, but I don't think that it's as important to us as feeling something is.

But by emphasizing story we are asking for it, people. I don't mean to say that it's not possible to fact-check a story or ground a narrative in fact—it is, but by asking it for *story,* by constructing it to mean, to make us feel, we're leaving the realm of strict phenomena and are heading into interpretation, subjectivity: we're coasting toward an art feeling, a feeling of glorious emotional fatness. I ask that we remember this, our own hunger, our own desire, when we want to closely probe the things that offer us that art feeling, wondering just what we sacrifice to get it.

*

Here's Robert Love again:

> Hoaxes like this seem so *Colbert* now, like mutant cousins to his notion of "truthiness." But hoaxers are historically not comedians; they are, like Mencken, journalists who write entertaining stuff that sounds vaguely true, even though it's not, for editors who are usually in on the

joke. The hoaxing instinct infected newsrooms throughout the early days of modern newspapers to a degree
that most of us find puzzling today. Newspapers contained hundreds, if not thousands of hoaxes in the late
nineteenth and early twentieth centuries, most of them
undocumented fakes in obscure Western weeklies. The
subjects were oddball pets and wild weather, giants, mermaids, men on the moon, petrified people (quite a few of
those), and (my favorite) the Swiss Navy.

So years later Mencken revealed that his history, though widely
believed and propagated, contained no actual bits of truth. He reports:
"This article, as I say, was planned as a piece of spoofing to relieve the
strain of war days, and I confess that I regarded it, when it came out,
with considerable satisfaction."

It's perhaps no surprise that the war elevated its stature. We might
note that the height of the James Frey scandal occurred while the u.s.
government perpetuated mistruths leading to an unmeritorious war.
We might note that the Clifford Irving hoax (subject of the film *The
Hoax*, in which he faked the authorized biography of Howard Hughes)
occurred during the height of the conflict in Vietnam. I point these out
to suggest (and I am not the first) that our anger against these authors
became a sort of national sport, an entertainment in which we built
ourselves a safe outlet for our rage that we didn't feel safe directing
against the architects of the lies we were fed by the government and
duly reported by the press, until they got wiser.

Today—this year, this decade, which feels like it's on the edge of slip-
ping into something—we occupy a precarious space, perched between
the age of the authority we've ceded to journalism (because who has
time to check everything or maybe even anything?) and the age of
crowd-sourced, immediate (sometimes mis-) information, which makes
up a good story.

We need to trust our information, but what we really want is entertainment. We don't want to blink. A country's doomed: we are non-
plussed. We keep clicking for something newer. The speed of news

delivery, and the increasing devolution of those tasked to report and verify it as fact, from the salaried to freelance staff, do not jibe well with increased reliability. What does that mean for how we can expect to live our lives? Must we O.K. the fudge, understand the imprecision, understanding that at least we're getting speed and something fun to—in the words of the pre-chewed nineties pop act the Spice Girls—spice up our lives like Doritos Locos Tacos?

Today—April 1—we occupy a particularly precarious space, perched between belief and disbelief, and it's a lovely one. I ask us to hold it and consider it: a moment of wonderment in which the impossible is briefly possible before it disappears and drops us back into our lives this afternoon.

*

Though Mencken admitted that he made it up, no one took much notice. Probably because that's what papers did at that time. Or because *essayist confabulates fake bathtub history* doesn't have much pop or salability. (Or it wasn't a story then; it might be now: *see also* Jonah Lehrer, *see also* Jayson Blair, *see also* Stephen Glass—how we like to hound our boys.) Mencken's bathtub tale is still in fact perpetuated and propagated. The Museum of Hoaxes reports "as recently as February, 2004, the *Washington Post* noted in a travel column, 'Bet you didn't know that . . . Fillmore was the first president to install a bathtub in the White House.' It sheepishly ran a correction a few days later."

(Maybe the ease of cut and paste exacerbates all this. In the time it took to use the keyboard shortcut to drop that bit of text in here, it did occur to me that I might want to check that out, at least on Wikipedia, before reporting it to you again, but that seemed like a lot of work, and besides, I've spent enough time faking Wikipedia entries to not invest all that much trust there either.)

Of course we know Mencken as an essayist. And the essay (thus the essayist) gets by on the authority, such as it is, of the "I." We take it for granted, sure: we have to—we don't get to suspend our disbelief; to engage in an essay is to engage with the "I" in front of us, the simulated self speaking. If we didn't trust its intentions—that at least it's leading us wherever for a reason—then why are we listening to it speak? Of course the "I" in essay doesn't come out and claim that what it is telling us is truth, or absolute: it claims its subjectivity. It is an "I" after all, and it can be mistaken or duped, led astray, confused, inveigled, mis- or disinformed. How well do we know ourselves, we ask: not as well as we would hope. We would not be this way if we did: confused, seemingly blind some days to the primacy of our habits and habituations. Otherwise the world would be a less surprising and dramatic place than it is, with a capacity for such glorious wreckage: we are weak in ways we cannot know, even though we should better gauge our seams and faults and accommodate for them. The essay prizes these, gets squinty trying to see things straight. It's O.K.

In fact Mencken goes out of his way to occasionally foreground the "I" in his essay: "and, for all I know to the contrary, [the first bathtub] may still be in existence and in use," "Moreover, the English bathtub, then as now, was a puny and inconvenient contrivance—little more, in fact, than a glorified dishpan," "This legislation, I suspect, had some class feeling in it, for the Thompson bathtub was plainly too expensive to be owned by any save the wealthy," and so forth. Admitting the "I" to reflect upon the subject—or in the first instance to lie directly to the reader (since Mencken knew well to the contrary)—increases its believability. It dimensionalizes the tale: there is the story, and there is the "I" telling the story, and we occasionally see one or both or the space between them. Harder, oddly, to doubt an "I" that knows it's telling a story.

As such the essay as a form doesn't (mostly: one could make an argument for "The Facts of the Matter" by Anonymous as a legit piece of hoaxery with a righteous point) have much truck with April Fool's: we are all fools to believe what we read or hear on April 1. We are fools to try to pin an "I" too closely to the truth or to project our rage on those who tried too hard to entertain—and failed, it must be said, except as quarry.

Instead we might do better to recognize performance and appreciate it when it's in front of us, and simply say that we are entertained, that we were fooled, and that we can own our falling-for-it and think what that might mean for us.

*

I remember mornings growing up on April 1 when I would switch the sugar with the salt containers on the kitchen table and wait for my brother's howl as he dug into his cereal. That might be a practical joke— anyway, it's practically a joke—but it's not an April Fool. I suppose I might have reminded him that In Life Sometimes the Names on the Containers Do Not Always Correspond with Their Contents, and that this should be celebrated, not condemned, and also that I was bigger than him, which is unfortunately no longer the case, thereby changing the tenor of our relationship. Now he is an investment banker and I am up late writing an essay about a dead man I thought was fat for no good reason.

Still, I believe there was a lesson there for my brother: don't believe the world is as stable as you think. It doesn't take much to tip a life into submission, an economy into recession, a country into upheaval, a career into a downward spiral.

Still, there's not much to be gained by my childhood joke: a wasted bowl of cereal, an irritated sibling, a story to be related years later without much narrative fizz or pop.

Whatever Fool the Authorities choose to perpetrate this year, whether it's the Swiss Spaghetti Harvest, instant color TV, a guide to the small republic of San Serriffe, life found on the moon, the *Economist* theme park, or the *Guardian's* shift to an all-Twitter feed, etc., these hoaxes undercut themselves amusingly: even as you're reading them you're thinking, hmm, really? They're only sort of plausible at best, not really designed to fool us, or not for long.

If Mencken's essay isn't really a joke, and it's not an April Fool, perhaps it was a prank designed to illustrate something that he understood about how news propagates, un-fact-checked, even in the pre-internet age. Though it might come in the voice of a noted humorist and essayist, published in a Newspaper of Note (perhaps not coincidentally

the *Evening Mail,* which also counted among its contributors emi-
nent cartoonist and maker of elaborate machines Rube Goldberg), and
reinforced with some essaytastic goodness, that didn't mean it was
strictly true. I'm not exactly sure it is an essay, actually. Or if it is, it's a
speculative one (à la Robin Hemley; note also Hemley's insistence on
the usefulness of wonder—a rare commodity today).

Or maybe the lesson we might draw is that the *Evening Mail* is no
longer in operation, but the essayist is—as is his fake history of the bathtub. I'm operating the essayist right now, even if he turns out on a Google
search (see, there are uses for these quick excursions) not to be all that
fat (or fat at all: but maybe we can get this misinformation propagating).

That's how we get by, isn't it? By propagating? By trust and a little
optimism, a laptop in the bathtub, the occasional salt in our cereal, and
a bit of wonder after?

RYAN VAN METER

On Endings

All in All, It Was a Really Weird Summer

December 14 is the 348th day of the year, with only 17 days remaining. This notation is written at the top of the page in my diary devoted to December 14; a similar notation is written on the pages devoted to all of the other days. I have been writing in a diary this year because last year my grandmother died. Until she did, she wrote in a diary every day, every year, for forty-three years, which is something like sixteen thousand pages. Very little about these pages is reflective; mostly they are a record of her activities—loads of laundry washed and folded, shifts at the grocery store worked, meals cooked, visitors to the house, letters in the mail. What happened, but not much of what she thought about what happened. The last day in the diary that she wrote about was not the last day she lived, and so when she wrote it, she did not know that *that* page would be the ending of the record she'd been writing for four decades. It was simply the most recent day on which she'd written, and then later, it was the last. The ending of my diary this year will be a record of what activities I do on the year's last day. It will be the last page of the book, but I'm coming to understand that that's different than it being the book's ending.

Grandmothers end just like years end. Countries and movements and religions and languages end, and so do football games, wars, flowers and storms. Even our solar system ends, and a probe we launched in 1977 reached its outer boundary only this year. It is recording its journey on eight-track tape machines, and before it exited our solar

281

system, scientists instructed the probe to erase all of its previously recorded data so that it would not reach the end of its capacity to record. But around the year 2025, the probe's plutonium batteries will end, and while it will continue blazing across interstellar space filling up its eight-track tapes with new findings, when the batteries stop functioning, the probe's ability to transmit those recordings back to Earth will end. Besides diaries, books have endings, like weddings, recipes, and theories. The Bible has an ending. The last word of it is "Amen," the same word I was taught to say as the ending of a prayer when I was being taught to pray, which suggests that even extremely long and exquisitely detailed prayers have endings. We already have a few names for the world's ending though it hasn't happened. Even the movie "The Neverending Story" has an ending. The only thing I can think of that has neither end nor ending is time.

Essays have endings, but I wish they didn't, or I wish they didn't have to have them. Because if an essay is an attempt to understand an experience or idea, if it is a recording of the activity of a mind as it thinks over an experience or idea, can that actually end? Could it ever really be finished? It seems antithetical to impose a fixed point on thinking that could go on given more time or new information, and more than that, it also seems untrue—a big problem for a form defined by its truth. Life goes on after writing an essay, and so does thinking, even about the subjects we've written into essays. So how to square an essay needing to end with thinking that couldn't possibly? The only way an essay really could have a fixed point as its ending is, if as soon as the essay was finished, the essayist went brain dead.

When I write essays, I have trouble with the endings. More than once (three times) an editor of mine has suggested (one demanded) that I remove the entire penultimate paragraph from an essay. This was suggested each time because these entire penultimate paragraphs were superfluous—they stated what I'd already implied or demonstrated elsewhere. I agreed with these suggestions because as soon as they were pointed out to me, I saw how nervous the paragraphs were. I was trying so hard to create that fixed point of my thinking that I started thinking for the reader too, and these paragraphs were me making sure that everyone was O.K. right before I, the essayist, slipped out the door.

There is an episode of *The Simpsons* where Bart is being stalked by a dog. The dog is huge, powerful, and snarling. He sits at one end of a seesaw and stares at Bart, while Bart sits in his classroom, terrified. The dog rings the doorbell, is always behind a blind corner. One day on his way to school, Bart is carrying his textbook, *The Second-Best American Short Stories*, when the dog tries again to attack. For momentary protection, Bart flings the book into the dog's mouth, the dog's teeth shred it, and the last page of a story flies into frame, in close-up. We can read its ending: "All in all, it had been a weird, weird lottery." (Presumably a reference to the last sentence of "The Lottery" by Shirley Jackson, which is actually, "And then they were upon her.") The sentence is a joke because it's so nervous about straightening up before the storyteller closes the door. It's telling the reader to think that the lottery was weird right after the reader has already experienced a really weird lottery. When I think about the endings of essays, I think about the joke sentence on that ripped-out page.

The name of this episode is "The Lastest Gun in the West." (A very old cowboy shows up.) The *lastest.* That's what I appreciate when an essay ends well—that difference between an essay that has a lastest sentence and an essay that has an ending. It's that orchestration I'm becoming skeptical of—the feeling of inevitability forced, of tidiness, of an insight arrived at just in time. At some point, I started to think of that joke sentence as concluding some imaginary essay, and I changed it to the more widely applicable, "All in all, it was a really weird summer." In my teaching and in my writing, "All in all, it was a really weird summer" is the term for the nervous ending—the ending that's a little too *ending.*

If this is an essay—an essay about attempting to understand the endings of essays—this must be the paragraph that's getting nervous because I haven't finished thinking about endings yet, but the essay itself needs to end. So I could pick up an idea again and ask a startling question about it. I could finally reveal the insight for which I've been quietly laying groundwork the whole time. I could return to an image

I referred to earlier in a seemingly offhand way, and show it again, but this time it will encapsulate my primary concern. That probe, for example, hurtling out of our solar system, still recording what it comes upon even though we won't be able to read what it finds for very much longer. I could write something about how the best kind of ending for an essay is one that suggests a mind still thinking even after our moment to see inside that thinking has ceased.

Though another way of ending is to introduce a related but still new direction of development that will resonate somehow. So there is a book called *A Really Weird Summer.* Written by Eloise Jarvis McGraw, published in 1977, it's a novel for young adults about (among other things) a kid who befriends another kid living inside an antique mirror during the summer his parents are splitting up. Its lastest sentence: "And Nels suddenly felt it the best thing in the world to be doing, and the most solidly important—just to be collecting insects for Stevie's zoo."

Bibliography

Page numbers indicate the first reference in each essay.

ANDER MONSON: Here's How You Use the Lion Mints:
   An Introduction to *How We Speak to One Another*
Page 1. Hoagland, Edward. Introduction to *The Best American Essays 1999.*
   Edited by Edward Hoagland. Boston: Houghton Mifflin, 1999.
Page 3. Beattie, Ann. Afterword to *Fare Forward: Letters from David Markson*
   by Laura Sims. Brooklyn: PowerHouse Books, 2014.
Page 4. D'Agata, John. *Halls of Fame.* Minneapolis, MN: Graywolf Press, 2001.

MARCIA ALDRICH: Invisible Engineering: The Fine Art of Revising
   "The Fine Art of Sighing"
Page 11. Cooper, Bernard. "The Fine Art of Sighing." In *Truth Serum: Memoirs.*
   New York: Houghton Mifflin Harcourt, 1997.

KRISTEN RADTKE on Chris Marker's *Sans Soleil*
Page 21. Sans Soleil. Directed by Chris Marker. New York: Criterion Collection,
   1983.

Majestic Ruins: ROBIN HEMLEY on the Work of James Agee
Page 29. Agee, James. *A Death in the Family.* New York: Bantam, 1938.
Page 29. Agee, James. *The Morning Watch.* Boston, Houghton Mifflin, 1951.
Page 29. Irving, John. *The World According to Garp.* New York: Ballantine
   Books, 1990.
Page 30. Cable, George Washington. *The Grandissimes: A Story of Creole Life.*
   New York, Sagamore Press, 1957.
Page 30. Evans, Walker. *Let Us Now Praise Famous Men.* Boston: Houghton
   Mifflin, 1941.

V. V. GANESHANANTHAN on Essays, Assays, and Yiyun Li's "Dear Friend,
   from My Life I Write to You in Your Life"
Page 34. Li, Yiyun. "Dear Friend, from My Life I Write to You in Your Life." *A
   Public Space,* no. 19 (Fall 2013). http://apublicspace.org/magazine/detail
   /dear_friend_from_my_life_i_write_to_you_in_your_life.
Pages 36–37. Li, Yiyun. "From the Horse's Mouth: Yiyun Li." Interview by Mark L.
   Keats. *Iron Horse Review* 20 (April 2015). http://www.ironhorsereview
   .com/single-post/2015/4/20/From-the-Horses-Mouth-With-Yiyun-Li.

ROBERT ATWAN: The Assault on Prose: John Crowe Ransom, New
    Criticism, and the Status of the Essay
Page 40. White, E. B. Foreword to *Essays of E. B. White.* New York: Harper &
    Row, 1977.
Page 41. Ozick, Cynthia. "What Henry James Knew." *New Criterion* 11, no. 5
    (January 1993). http://www.newcriterion.com/articles.cfm/What-Henry
    -James-knew-4669.
Page 41. Stuckey-French, Ned. *The American Essay in the American Century.*
    Columbia, MO: University of Missouri Press, 2011.
Page 42. Ransom, John Crowe. *Topics for Freshman Writing: Twenty Topics for
    Writing with Appropriate Material for Study.* New York: Henry Holt & Co.,
    1935.
Page 43. Brooks, Cleanth, and Robert Penn Warren. *Understanding Poetry.*
    New York: Henry Holt & Co., 1938.
Page 43. Young, Thomas Daniel, and John Hindle. Introduction to *Selected
    Essays of John Crowe Ransom.* Edited by Thomas Daniel Young and John
    Hindle. Baton Rouge, LA: Louisiana State University Press, 1984.
Page 43. Ransom, John Crowe. "Criticism as Pure Speculation." In *Selected
    Essays of John Crowe Ransom.* Edited by Thomas Daniel Young and John
    Hindle. Baton Rouge, LA: Louisiana State University Press, 1984.
Page 43. Mailer, Norman. *Advertisements for Myself.* New York: Putnam, 1959.
Page 43. Mitford, Nancy. "The English Aristocracy." In *Noblesse Oblige:
    An Enquiry into the Identifiable Characteristics of the English Aristocracy.*
    London: Hamish Hamilton Ltd., 1956.
Page 44. Berlin, James A. *Rhetoric and Reality: Writing Instruction in American
    Colleges, 1900–1985.* Carbondale, IL: Southern Illinois University Press,
    1987.

MATT DUBE on Joan Didion, *Repo Man,* and a '76 Malibu
Page 47. Didion, Joan. "Quiet Days in Malibu." In *The White Album.* New York:
    Simon & Schuster, 1979.
Page 48. Repo Man. Directed by Alex Cox. Hollywood: Universal Studios, 1984.
Page 48. Repo Man. Music from the original motion picture soundtrack.
    Universal City, CA: MCA Records, 1984.

AISHA SABATINI SLOAN on Collage, Chris Kraus, and
    Misremembered Didion
Page 53. Didion, Joan. "Why I Write." *New York Times Book Review,*
    December 5, 1976.

Page 54. Didion, Joan. "On Keeping a Notebook." In *Slouching Towards Bethlehem.* New York: Farrar, Straus and Giroux, 1968.

Page 54. C.K., Louis. "Ikea/Piano Lesson." *Louie.* Season 3, episode 7 (August 9, 2012).

Page 55. Kraus, Chris. "Art Collection." In *Video Green.* Boston: MIT Press, 2004.

T CLUTCH FLEISCHMANN: Looking for Samuel Delany

Page 57. Delany, Samuel. *Times Square Red, Times Square Blue.* New York: New York University Press, 1999.

Page 61. Freeman, Elizabeth. *Time Binds: Queer Temporalities, Queer Histories.* Durham, NC: Duke University Press, 2010.

RIGOBERTO GONZÁLEZ: Observations about Writing Memoir in My Twenties, Thirties, and Forties

Page 65. González, Rigoberto. *Crossing Vines.* Norman, OK: University of Oklahoma Press, 2003.

Page 67. González, Rigoberto. *Butterfly Boy: Memories of a Chicano Mariposa.* Madison, WI: University of Wisconsin Press, 2006.

Page 67. González, Rigoberto. *Red-Inked Retablos.* Tucson, AZ: University of Arizona Press, 2013.

Page 70. González, Rigoberto. *Autobiography of My Hungers.* Madison, WI: University of Wisconsin Press, 2013.

KATHERINE E. STANDEFER on the Mysterious Leslie Ryan and the Structure of a Trauma Narrative

Page 73. Ryan, Leslie. "The Other Side of Fire." In *Circle of Women: An Anthology of Contemporary Western Women Writers.* Edited by Kim Barnes and Mary Clearman Blew. New York: Penguin Books, 1994.

JULIE LAUTERBACH-COLBY on Arianne Zwartjes's "This Suturing of Wounds or Words" and Kisha Lewellyn Schlegel's "Cannulated Screw"

Page 78. Zwartjes, Arianne. "The Suturing of Wounds or Words," *Gulf Coast* 241 (Winter/Spring 2012). http://gulfcoastmag.org/journal/241-winter /spring-2012/this-suturing-of-wounds-or-words.

Page 78. Lewellyn Schlegel, Kisha. "Cannulated Screw." *The Drunken Boat* 15 (2012). http://www.drunkenboat.com/db15/kisha-lewellyn-schlegel.

Living within the Ellipses: CÉSAR DÍAZ on Ilan Stavans's *On Borrowed Words: A Memoir of Language*

Page 81. Stavans, Ilan. *On Borrowed Words: A Memoir of Language.* New York: Penguin Books, 2002.

Page 81. Negrete, Jorge. "México Lindo y Querido." Audio recording, 1950. https://www.youtube.com/watch?v=ysSvX21PYBs.

Page 85. C.K., Louis. "Louis C.K.: I'm an Accidental White Person." Interview in *Rolling Stone,* April 11, 2013. http://www.rollingstone.com/music/news /louis-c-k-im-an-accidental-white-person-20130411.

Page 87. Finocchiaro, Peter. "Louis C.K. Talks 'Mexican Past' in *Rolling Stone* Cover Story." *Huffington Post,* April 11, 2013. http://www.huffingtonpost .com/2013/04/11/louis-ck-mexican-rolling-stone_n_3063036.html.

EMILY DEPRANG on Joan Didion, on the Morning After My Twenties

Page 87. Romero, Frances. "Top Ten End-of-the-World Prophecies: Y2K." *Time,* May 20, 2011. http://content.time.com/time/specials/packages /article/0,28804,2072678_2072683_2072599,00.html.

Page 87. Haeck, Tom. "Seattle's Former Police Chief, Mayor Recall Mistakes of WTO Riots." MyNorthwest.com, May 1, 2013. http://mynorthwest.com/11 /2264290/Seattles-former-police-chief-mayor-recall-mistakes-of-WTO-riots.

Page 87. Rosenthal, Andrew. "O'Connor Regrets Bush v. Gore." *New York Times,* April 29, 2013. http://takingnote.blogs.nytimes.com/2013/04/29 /oconnor-regrets-bush-v-gore/?_r=0&mtrref=undefined&gwh=620E81A13 F8939781794C12E6B48A302&gwt=pay&assetType=opinion.

Page 88. Didion, Joan. "On the Morning After the Sixties." In *The White Album.* New York: Simon & Schuster, 1979.

LUCAS MANN on Writing Young

Page 91. Lopate, Phillip. Introduction to *The Art of the Personal Essay.* Edited by Phillip Lopate. New York: Anchor Books, 1995.

Page 93. Sullivan, John Jeremiah. "Upon This Rock." In *Pulphead.* New York: Farrar, Straus and Giroux, 2011.

Page 95. Jamison, Leslie. "Grand Unified Theory of Female Pain." In *The Empathy Exams.* Minneapolis, MN: Graywolf Press, 2014.

DANICA NOVGORODOFF on Losing Yourself

Page 99. Solnit, Rebecca. *A Field Guide to Getting Lost.* New York: Penguin Books, 2006.

E-mail from **BONNIE J. ROUGH**
Page 117. Bakewell, Sarah. *How to Live: Or, A Life of Montaigne in One Question and Twenty Attempts at an Answer.* New York: Other Press, 2010.

ALBERT GOLDBARTH: Leaping
Page 130. Walton, Izaak. *Lives of John Donne, Sir Henry Wotton, Richard Hooker, George Herbert, and Robert Sanderson.* London: Routledge, 1888.
Page 131. Donne, John. "The Flea." In *The Norton Anthology of Poetry.* Edited by Margaret W. Ferguson, Mary Jo Salter, and Jon Stallworthy. New York: W. W. Norton, 1996.

ALISON HAWTHORNE DEMING: Julian Barnes Brings Light to a Thanatophobe's Conundrum
Page 133. Barnes, Julian. *Nothing to Be Frightened Of.* New York: Alfred A. Knopf, 2008.

STEVEN CHURCH on Tom Junod's "The Falling Man"
Page 137. Junod, Tom. "The Falling Man." *Esquire,* September 2003. http://classic.esquire.com/the falling-man.

BETHANY MAILE: We Sought but Couldn't Find: Coming Up Empty in David Shields's "Death Is the Mother of Beauty"
Page 143. Shields, David. "Death Is the Mother of Beauty." In *The Thing about Life Is That One Day You'll Be Dead.* New York: Alfred A. Knopf, 2008.
Page 143. Didion, Joan. "After Life." *New York Times Magazine,* September 25, 2005. http://www.nytimes.com/2005/09/25/magazine/after-life.html?_r=0.

Movie Quotes as Misery: **DAVID LEGAULT** on Claudia Rankine's *Don't Let Me Be Lonely*
Page 148. Rankine, Claudia. *Don't Let Me Be Lonely.* Minneapolis, MN: Graywolf Press, 2004.

JONI TEVIS: A Paperback Cabinet of Wonder: Unlocking the Long Lyric Essay
Page 151. Coover, Robert. "On Reading 300 American Novels." *New York Times Book Review,* March 3, 1984. http://www.nytimes.com/1984/03/18/books /onb-reading-300-american-novels.html?pagewanted=all.

Page 151. LeClair, Tom. *The Art of Excess.* Chicago: University of Illinois Press, 1989.

Page 151. Barthes, Roland. *The Pleasure of the Text.* Paris: Farrar, Straus and Giroux, 1975.

Page 152. Didion, Joan. "The White Album." In *The White Album.* New York: Simon & Schuster, 1979.

Page 153. Carson, Anne. "Just for the Thrill: An Essay on the Difference between Women and Men." In *Plainwater.* New York: Vintage, 1995.

Page 155. Ammons, A. R. *Garbage: A Poem.* New York: W. W. Norton & Co., 2002.

JOHN D'AGATA: The Essays of Ansel Adams: An Allegory
Page 159. Adams, Ansel. *Making a Photograph: An Introduction to Photography.* New York: Studio Publications, 1935.

THOMAS MIRA Y LOPEZ on Donald Hall's "Out the Window"
Page 163. Hall, Donald. "Out the Window." *New Yorker,* January 23, 2012. http://www.newyorker.com/magazine/2012/01/23/out-the-window.

DANIELLE CADENA DEULEN on the Virtues of Drowning: Lidia Yuknavitch's *The Chronology of Water*
Page 169. Yuknavitch, Lidia. *The Chronology of Water,* 1. Portland, OR: Hawthorne Books, 2010.

Page 170. Irigaray, Luce. *This Sex Which Is Not One,* 22–33. Ithaca, NY: Cornell University Press, 1985.

JOHN T. PRICE on Hoagland, Animal Obsession, and the Courage of Simile
Page 175. Hoagland, Edward. "The Courage of Turtles." In *Heart's Desire: Essays from Twenty Years.* New York: Touchstone, 1988.

Page 175. Hoagland, Edward. "What I Think, What I Am." In *The Tugman's Passage.* New York: Random House, 1982.

Page 177. Hoagland, Edward. "The Problem of the Golden Rule." In *Heart's Desire: Essays from Twenty Years.* New York: Touchstone, 1988.

Page 177. Hoagland, Edward. "Hailing the Elusory Mountain Lion." In *Heart's Desire: Essays from Twenty Years.* New York: Touchstone, 1988.

MAYA L. KAPOOR on David Quammen and Writing Trout
Page 183. Quammen, David. "Synecdoche and the Trout." In *Wild Thoughts from Wild Places.* New York: Scribner, 1998.

Page 183. Quammen, David. "So Huge a Bignes." In *The Song of the Dodo.* New York: Touchstone, 1996.

Page 184. Quammen, David. "Places Wilder and Less Traveled: Interview with David Quammen." By Simmons B. Buntin. *Terrain.org: A Journal of the Built + Natural Environments,* February 22, 2008. http://www.terrain.org /2008/interviews/interview-with-david-quammen.

Page 184. Quammen, David. "Eat of This Flesh." In *Wild Thoughts from Wild Places.* New York: Scribner, 1998.

CHELSEA BIONDOLILLO on Long Winters, Short Essays, and a Sky That Stretches Forever

Page 187. Ehrlich, Gretel. *The Solace of Open Spaces.* New York: Penguin Books, 1986.

Page 188. Spragg, Mark. "Wind." In *Where Rivers Change Direction.* New York: Riverhead Books, 2000.

Page 188. Kitchen, Judith. *Short Takes: Brief Encounters with Contemporary Nonfiction.* New York: W. W. Norton & Co., 2005.

Page 189. Ehrlich, Gretel. "The Smooth Skull of Winter." In *The Solace of Open Spaces.* New York: Penguin Books, 1986.

Page 189. Lott, Bret. "Writing in Place." In *Rose Metal Press Field Guide to Writing Flash Nonfiction.* Edited by Tara L. Masih. Brookline, MA: Rose Metal Press, 2009.

Page 190. Woiwode, Larry. "Winter." In *Short Takes: Brief Encounters with Contemporary Nonfiction.* Edited by Judith Kitchen. New York: W. W. Norton & Co., 2005.

Page 192. Cappello, Mary. "Propositions; Provocations: Inventions." In *Bending Genre: Essays on Creative Nonfiction.* Edited by Margot Singer and Nicole Walker. New York: Bloomsbury Publishing, 2013.

MEGAN KIMBLE on Wendell Berry and Why I'm Not Going to Buy a Smartphone

Page 195. Berry, Wendell. "Why I'm Not Going to Buy a Computer." *New England Review & Bread Loaf Quarterly,* 1987.

Page 196. Berry, Wendell. "Feminism, the Body, and the Machine." *CrossCurrents,* Spring 2003. http://www.crosscurrents.org/berryspring 2003.htm.

Page 197. Berry, Wendell. "Economy and Pleasure." In *What Are People For?* Berkeley, CA: Counterpoint Press, 1990.

BRIAN DOYLE: It Is a Shaggy World, Studded with Gardens

Page 200. Stevenson, Robert Louis. "Memoirs of an Islet." In *Memories and Portraits.* London: Chatto & Windus, 1887.

Page 200. Stevenson, Robert Louis. "Pan's Pipes." In *Virginibus Puerisque and Other Papers.* London: C. Kegan Paul & Co., 1881.

Page 200. Stevenson, Robert Louis. "The Plains of Nebraska." In *Across the Plains.* New York: Charles Scribner's Sons, 1883.

Page 201. Stevenson, Robert Louis. "An Island Landfall." In *In the South Seas.* Edited by Sidney Colvin. New York: Charles Scribner's Sons, 1896.

Page 201. Stevenson, Robert Louis. "Winter and New Year." In *Edinburgh: Picturesque Notes.* London: Seeley, Jackson, and Halliday, 1878.

Page 202. Stevenson, Robert Louis. "The Old Pacific Capital." In *Across the Plains.* New York: Charles Scribner's Sons, 1883.

Page 202. Stevenson, Robert Louis. "To Miss Rawlinson." In *The Letters of Robert Louis Stevenson,* vol. 3. Edited by Sidney Colvin. London: Methuen & Co. Ltd., 1899.

Page 203. Stevenson, Robert Louis. "Another in Time of Rain." In *Prayers Written at Vailima.* New York: Charles Scribner's Sons, 1904.

Page 204. Stevenson, Robert Louis. "Requiem." In *Modern British Poetry.* Edited by Louis Untermeyer. New York: Harcourt, Brace, and Howe, 1920.

NICOLE WALKER: Nonfiction Like a Brick

Page 210. Shelley, Percy Bysshe. "A Defense of Poetry." In *Essays, Letters from Abroad, Translations and Fragments.* London: Edward Moxon, 1840.

Page 210. Leach, Amy. "Sail On, My Little Honey Bee." *A Public Space,* no. 7 (2009).

Page 212. Hopkins, Gerard Manley. "The Windhover." In *Poems.* London: Humphrey Milford, 1918.

Page 213. Mitchell, Susan. "Notes Toward a History of Scaffolding." *Provincetown Arts* 6 (1990).

Page 213. Whitman, Walt. "This Is What You Shall Do." In *Leaves of Grass.* Boston, MA: Thayer & Eldridge, 1860.

PAUL LISICKY on the Fugue, Alison Bechdel's *Are You My Mother?*, DFW, and the Resistance to the One Thing

Page 216. Bechdel, Alison. *Are You My Mother?* New York: Houghton Mifflin Harcourt, 2012.

Page 216. Foucault, Michel. "Of Other Spaces." In *Rethinking Architecture: A Reader in Cultural Theory.* Edited by Neil Leach. New York: Routledge, 1997.

Page 218. Hammer, Michael. "What's in a Name: Fugue." Pianonoise. Accessed June 17, 2016. http://www.pianonoise.com/Whats_in_a_name.fugue.htm.

BRIAN OLIU on *The Squared Circle: Life, Death, and Professional Wrestling* by David Shoemaker

Page 219. Shoemaker, David. *The Squared Circle: Life, Death, and Professional Wrestling.* New York: Gotham Books, 2013.

Page 220. Kaneko, W. Todd. [Poetry] & [Professional Wrestling]. *Superstition Review,* November 23, 2013. http://blog.superstitionreview.asu.edu/2013/11/23/guest-blog-post-w-todd-kaneko-poetry-professional-wrestling.

PAM HOUSTON on Rick Reilly's "Need a Fourth?" from *Sports Illustrated,* March 31, 1997

Page 223. Reilly, Rick. "Need a Fourth?" *Sports Illustrated,* March 31, 1997. http://www.si.com/vault/1997/03/31/225168/need-a-fourth-the-public -course-has-become-a-refuge-for-oj-simpson-though-many-golfers-wish -he-would-take-his-game-elsewhere.

DAVE MONDY on Jim Bouton's *Ball Four*

Page 229. Bouton, Jim. *Ball Four.* New York: World Publishing Company, 1970.

Page 236. DeLillo, Don. *Pafko at the Wall.* New York: Harper's, 1992.

Page 239. Berkow, Ira. "Bouton Gives Eulogy for His Daughter." *New York Times,* August 19, 1997. http://www.nytimes.com/1997/08/19/sports/bouton-gives -eulogy-for-his-daughter.html.

PHILLIP LOPATE on a Little-Known Gem by Max Beerbohm

Page 243. Beerbohm, Max. *And Even Now.* London: Heinemann, 1920.

Page 243. Beerbohm, Max. "Quia Imperfectum." In *And Even Now.* London: Heinemann, 1920.

Page 246. Cecil, Lord David. *Max.* New York: Houghton Mifflin, 1965.

Page 247. Woolf, Virginia. "How It Strikes a Contemporary." In *The Common Reader,* vol. 1. London: Hogarth Press, 1925.

AMY BENSON on Eliot Weinberger's "Wrens"

Page 249. Weinberger, Eliot. "Wrens." In *An Elemental Thing.* New York: New Directions Publishing, 2007.

PATRICK MADDEN on Charles Lamb's "New Year's Eve"
Page 253. Lamb, Charles. "New Year's Eve." *The London Magazine,* January 1821.
   http://essays.quotidiana.org/lamb/new_years_eve.
Page 255. Madden, Patrick. "In Which the Madden Family Files to Montevideo
   and Plays the Uruguayan Lottery." *McSweeney's,* September 25, 2012.
   http://www.mcsweeneys.net/articles/in-which-the-madden-family-flies
   -to-montevideo-and-plays-the-uruguayan-lottery.

ELENA PASSARELLO on the *Book of Days*
Page 257. Chambers, Robert. *Book of Days.* Philadelphia: J. B. Lippincott, 1879.
   http://digicoll.library.wisc.edu/BookofDays/0001R003.html.
Page 260. Hillman's Hyperlinked and Searchable Chambers' Book of Days.
   Accessed April 6, 2016. http://www.thebookofdays.com.

ERIN ZWIENER on the False Glint of Fool's Gold and Cliché
Page 264. Schmitt, Richard. "Sometimes a Romantic Notion." *Gettysburg
   Review* 25, no. 3 (2012): 383.

The Present of Our Past: PATRICIA VIGDERMAN on Alexander Stille
Page 268. Stille, Alexander. *The Future of the Past.* New York: Picador, 2003.
Page 270. Frost, Robert. "The Master Speed." In *The Poetry of Robert Frost.*
   Edited by Edward Connery Lathem. New York: Henry Holt and Company,
   1979.

A Fat Man Story: ANDER MONSON on H. L. Mencken's "A Neglected
      Anniversary"
Page 271. Mencken, H. L. "A Neglected Anniversary." *Evening Mail,* December 28,
   1917. http://hoaxes.org/text/display/a_neglected_anniversary_text.
Page 272. Ehling, Mark. "Two Clowns on Tarkovsky." *Essay Daily,*
   February 14, 2013.
Page 273. Satran, Joe. "Doritos Locos Doritos?! PepsiCo Unveils Incredibly
   Meta Taco Bell-Inspired Chips." *Huffington Post,* March 26, 2013.
   http://www.huffingtonpost.com/2013/03/26/doritos-locos-doritos_n
   _2957967.html.
Page 273. Jumbaco commercial. Youtube. Accessed April 10, 2016. https://
   www.youtube.com/watch?v=OZFA87ZF71U&feature=youtu.be.
Page 274. Love, Robert. "Before John Stewart." *Columbia Journalism Review*
   (March/April 2007).

Page 275. Mencken, H. L. "Melancholy Reflections." *Chicago Tribune,* May 23, 1926. http://hoaxes.org/text/display/melancholy_reflections_text.

Page 276. The Museum of Hoaxes. "Mencken's History of the Bathtub." Accessed April 10, 2016. http://hoaxes.org/archive/permalink/the_history _of_the_bathtub.

Page 277. Anonymous. "The Facts of the Matter." *TriQuarterly,* October 22, 2012. http://www.triquarterly.org/craft-essays/facts-matter.

Page 278. Swiss Spaghetti Harvest 1957 video. Youtube. Accessed April 12, 2016. https://www.youtube.com/watch?v=GXmaS1ZzpA8&feature =player_embedded.

Page 278. "San Serriffe." *Guardian,* April 1, 1977. http://www.scribd.com/doc /87368327/San-Serriffe-1977.

Page 278. Herschel, Sir John. "Great Astronomical Discoveries Lately Made." *New York Sun,* August 1835. http://longform.org/posts/great-astronomical -discoveries-lately-made.

Page 278. The Economist. "The Economist Group Expands," *Economist,* April 1, 2009. http://www.economist.com/node/13395767?story_id –13395767.

Page 278. Palof, Rio. "Twitter Switch for *Guardian,* after 188 Years of Ink." *Guardian,* April 1, 2009. http://www.theguardian.com/media/2009/apr /01/guardian-twitter-media-technology.

Page 279. Hemley, Robin. "Study Questions for the Essay at Hand: A Speculative Essay." In *Bending Genre: Essays on Creative Nonfiction.* Edited by Margot Singer and Nicole Walker. New York: Bloomsbury, 2013.

RYAN VAN METER on Endings: All in All, It Was a Really Weird Summer

Page 283. "The Lastest Gun in the West." *The Simpsons.* Season 13, episode 12 (February 24, 2002).

Page 283. Jackson, Shirley. "The Lottery." *New Yorker,* June 26, 1948.

Page 284. McGraw, Eloise Jarvis. *A Really Weird Summer.* New York: Atheneum, 1977.

Contributors

MARCIA ALDRICH is the author of the free memoir *Girl Rearing*, published by W. W. Norton and part of the Barnes and Noble Discover New Writers Series. She has been the editor of *Fourth Genre: Explorations in Nonfiction.* Her book *Companion to an Untold Story* won the AWP Award for Creative Nonfiction. Her essays have appeared in *The Best American Essays.* She is at work on *Haze,* a narrative of marriage and divorce during her college years. Her website is MarciaAldrich.com.

ROBERT ATWAN is the founder and series editor of *The Best American Essays.* The 2016 volume, the thirty-first in the series, is guest-edited by Jonathan Franzen. Atwan has published on a wide variety of subjects, from American advertising, early photography, and political discourse to dreams and divination in the ancient world, Hollywood memoirs, and Shakespearean drama. His criticism, essays, humor, poetry, and fiction have appeared in numerous periodicals nationwide. He lives in New York City. His personal account for *Essay Daily* of how *The Best American Essays* series got started can be found at http://www.essaydaily.org/2015/12/robert-atwan-best-american -essays-some.html.

AMY BENSON is the author of *Seven Years to Zero,* winner of the 2016 Dzanc Books Nonfiction Prize, and *The Sparkling-Eyed Boy,* winner of the 2003 Bakeless Prize in Nonfiction. Recent work has appeared in journals such as *AGNI, BOMB, Boston Review, Gettysburg Review,* and *New England Review.* She teaches creative writing at Rhodes College in Memphis and is the co-founder of the First Person Plural Harlem Reading Series.

CHELSEA BIONDOLILLO is the author of the prose chapbooks *Ologies* and *#Lovesong.* Her essays are collected in *The Best American Science and Nature Essays 2016* and *Waveform: Twenty-First-Century Essays by Women* and have appeared in *Orion, Passages North, River Teeth, Hayden's Ferry Review,* and others. She has a dual MFA in creative writing and environmental studies from the University of Wyoming and keeps a journal at RoamingCowgirl.com.

KEN CHEN is the 2009 recipient of the Yale Series of Younger Poets Award, the oldest annual literary award in the United States, for his debut poetry collection *Juvenilia.* A recipient of fellowships from the National Endowment for the Arts, the New York Foundation for the Arts, and the Bread Loaf Writers' conference, Ken is the executive director of the Asian American Writers' Workshop and one of the founders of CultureStrike, a national artist movement on immigration.

STEVEN CHURCH is the author of *The Guinness Book of Me: A Memoir of Record*, *Theoretical Killings: Essays and Accidents*, *The Day After the Day After: My Atomic Angst*, and a collection of essays, *Ultrasonic*. A fifth book of nonfiction, *One with the Tiger: On Savagery and Intimacy* was released by Soft Skull Press in November 2016. His work has been published in *Creative Nonfiction*, *River Teeth*, *Fourth Genre*, *Brevity*, *AGNI*, the *Rumpus*, *Salon .com*, *Terrain.org: A Journal of the Built + Natural Environments*, and others. He is a founding editor and nonfiction editor for the *Normal School* and teaches in the MFA program at Fresno State.

MEEHAN CRIST is writer-in-residence in biological sciences at Columbia University. Previously, she was editor-at-large at *Nautilus* and reviews editor at the *Believer*, and her work has appeared in publications such as the *New York Times*, *Los Angeles Times*, *Tin House*, *Lapham's Quarterly*, *New Republic*, the *Believer*, *Nautilus*, *Scientific American*, and *Science*. Awards include the 2015 Rona Jaffe Foundation Writer's Award and the Olive B. O'Connor Fellowship, as well as fellowships from MacDowell, the Blue Mountain Center, Ucross, and Yaddo.

JOHN D'AGATA is the author of *About a Mountain*, *Halls of Fame*, and *The Lifespan of a Fact* and the editor of the three-volume series, *A New History of the Essay*. He directs the nonfiction writing program at the University of Iowa.

ALISON HAWTHORNE DEMING is the author, most recently, of *Zoologies: On Animals and the Human Spirit* and a book of poems, *Stairway to Heaven*. She is Agnese Nelms Haury Chair of Environment and Social Justice at the University of Arizona and a 2015 Guggenheim fellow.

EMILY DEPRANG is a writer and investigative journalist in Austin. Her work has appeared in several outlets, including the *Atlantic*, *Marie Claire*, and *VICE*, and has been honored by the American Society of Magazine

Editors, the Society of Professional Journalists, Media Consortium, and the Quattrone Center for the Fair Administration of Justice, among others. She is working on a novel about radiation.

DANIELLE CADENA DEULEN is the author of three books: *Lovely Asunder,* which won the Miller Williams Arkansas Poetry Prize and the Utah Book Award; *The Riots,* which won the AWP Prize in Creative Nonfiction and the GLCA New Writers Award; and *Our Emotions Get Carried Away Beyond Us,* which won the Barrow Street Book Contest in poetry. She has been the recipient of a Jay C. and Ruth Halls Poetry Fellowship from the University of Wisconsin–Madison and an Ohio Arts Council Individual Excellence Award. She lives in Salem, Oregon, where she teaches creative writing at Willamette University.

CÉSAR DÍAZ is a writer living in Austin, Texas. He teaches creative non-fiction at St. Edward's University. His essays and other think pieces have been published in *Guernica* and *Essay Daily.* He is also writing a memoir about his experiences as a migrant farmworker.

BRIAN DOYLE is the editor of *Portland Magazine* at the University of Portland. He is the author of many books of essays, "procms," and fiction, most recently the novels *Martin Marten* and *Chicago.*

MATT DUBE's family finally got a VCR on January 28, 1986, the day the Challenger shuttle exploded. It was the first major purchase after his father left, and actually, they leased it from Rent-A-Center's downtown Worcester Store. In that massive media showroom, disaster occupied every screen, in every degree of fidelity. If it was too big, find a smaller TV. If it was too loud, find a TV whose captions replaced sound: there were no words on the screen that the image didn't communicate more clearly. It's luck his brother didn't choose to record that instead of *Repo Man.*

T CLUTCH FLEISCHMANN is the author of *Syzygy, Beauty* (Sarabande), the curator of the digital chapbook *Body Logic* for Essay Press, and a nonfiction editor at *DIAGRAM.* Clutch is currently an emerging-writer-in-residence at Columbia College in Chicago and can be reached at tee.fleischmann@gmail.com.

V. V. GANESHANANTHAN teaches fiction and nonfiction writing at the University of Minnesota. Her debut novel, *Love Marriage* (Random House), was long-listed for the Orange Prize and named one of Washington Post Book World's Best of 2008. The recipient of fellowships from the National Endowment for the Arts and the Radcliffe Institute of Advanced Study at Harvard, she is at work on a second novel, excerpts of which have appeared in *Granta, Ploughshares,* and *The Best American Nonrequired Reading 2014.*

ALBERT GOLDBARTH has been publishing notable books of poetry for over four decades, two of which have received the National Book Critics Circle Award, and has published five collections of essays, most recently *The Adventures of Form and Content,* published by Graywolf Press in January 2017. He lives in Wichita, Kansas, completely offline: his fingers have never touched a computer/tablet/laptop keyboard.

RIGOBERTO GONZÁLEZ is the author of fifteen books of poetry and prose and the editor of *Camino del Sol: Fifteen Years of Latina and Latino Writing.* He is the recipient of Guggenheim and NEA fellowships and the winner of the American Book Award, the Poetry Center Book Award, the Shelley Memorial Award of the Poetry Society of America, and a grant from the New York Foundation for the Arts. He is a contributing editor for *Poets & Writers* magazine and is a professor of English at Rutgers–Newark, the State University of New Jersey.

PETER GRANDBOIS is the author of seven previous books, including most recently, *The Girl on the Swing* (Wordcraft of Oregon 2015). His work has previously appeared in such journals as the *Kenyon Review, Gettysburg Review, North Dakota Quarterly, Denver Quarterly,* and *DIAGRAM,* among many others, and has been short-listed for both *The Best American Essays* and the Pushcart Prize. His plays have been performed in St. Louis, Columbus, Los Angeles, and New York. He is a senior editor at *Boulevard* magazine and teaches at Denison University in Ohio.

ROBIN HEMLEY is the author of eleven books of nonfiction and fiction and the winner of a Guggenheim Fellowship and many other awards for his prose. From 2004–13 he was the director of the nonfiction writing program at the University of Iowa, and he is the founder of the biennial conference

NonfictioNOW. A contributing editor of the *Iowa Review,* he currently directs the writing program and is writer-in-residence at Yale-NUS in Singapore and is a visiting professor at RMIT University in Melbourne, Australia.

PAM HOUSTON is the author of five books of fiction and nonfiction including *Contents May Have Shifted, Waltzing the Cat,* and *Cowboys Are My Weakness.* Her work has been widely anthologized, appearing, among other places, in *The Best American Short Stories,* the O. Henry Prize anthology series, and *The Best American Short Stories of the Century.* She teaches in many different venues around the country and the world, is the director of the literary nonprofit Writing By Writers, and lives in Colorado near the headwaters of the Rio Grande.

MAYA L. KAPOOR's work has appeared in or is forthcoming from *Terrain .org, ISLE, The Sonoran Desert: A Literary Field Guide,* and *Edible Baja.* Prior to completing an MFA in creative nonfiction from the University of Arizona, she received a master's degree in biology from Arizona State University. She currently lives in Tucson, where she writes about ecology, the environment, and underappreciated desert species.

MEGAN KIMBLE is the editor of *Edible Baja Arizona,* a local food magazine serving Tucson and the borderlands. She is the author of *Unprocessed: My City-Dwelling Year of Reclaiming Real Food.* Her work has been anthologized in *Best Food Writing 2015* and *Coming of Age at the End of Nature.*

JULIE LAUTERBACH-COLBY lives in Tucson, Arizona, where she serves as deputy director for the Arts Foundation for Tucson and Southern Arizona. A graduate of the University of Arizona MFA program in nonfiction, her work has appeared in *CutBank, DIAGRAM, Lost Magazine,* and *Small Po[r]tions,* among others.

DAVID LEGAULT's first collection of essays, *One Million Maniacs,* will be published by Outpost 19 in June of 2017. His other recent work appears in *Passages North,* the *Sonora Review,* and *Continue? The Boss Fight Books Anthology of Video Game Writing.* He lives and writes from Prague in the Czech Republic. More information and writing can be found at www.david legault.com

PAUL LISICKY is the author of five books: *The Narrow Door*, a *New York Times* Editor's Choice; *Unbuilt Projects; The Burning House; Famous Builder;* and *Lawnboy*. His work has appeared in *Tin House, Conjunctions, Fence, Ploughshares,* the *Iowa Review,* the *Offing,* and other magazines and anthologies. A 2016 Guggenheim fellow, he teaches in the MFA program at Rutgers University–Camden and at the Juniper Summer Writing Institute. He divides his time between New York, Provincetown, and Philadelphia.

PHILLIP LOPATE's most recent books are *Portrait Inside My Head* (the fourth collection of his personal essays) and *To Show and to Tell: The Craft of Literary Nonfiction.* He directs and teaches in the graduate nonfiction program at Columbia University.

PATRICK MADDEN, author of *Sublime Physick* (University of Nebraska Press 2016) and *Quotidiana* (University of Nebraska Press 2010), teaches creative nonfiction at Brigham Young University. His essays have appeared in the *Iowa Review, Portland Magazine, Fourth Genre, Hotel Amerika,* and other journals, as well as in *The Best Creative Nonfiction* and *The Best American Spiritual Writing* anthologies. He coedited *After Montaigne: Contemporary Essayists Cover the Essays* (Georgia 2015) and cotranslated Eduardo Milán's *Selected Poems* (Shearsman 2012). He maintains an anthology of classical essays and essay resources at http://quotidiana.org.

BETHANY MAILE received an MFA in creative nonfiction from the University of Arizona. Her essays have appeared in some places, including the *Normal School, Prairie Schooner,* and *River Teeth.* She lives in Alaska with her husband and baby and teaches creative writing at the University of Alaska.

LUCAS MANN is the author of *Lord Fear: A Memoir* and *Class A: Baseball in the Middle of Everywhere.* His essays have appeared in the *Kenyon Review, TriQuarterly, Guernica, BuzzFeed, Slate,* and elsewhere. He earned his MFA in nonfiction from the University of Iowa, where he was the Provost's Visiting Writer in Nonfiction, and is currently an assistant professor of English at the University of Massachusetts, Dartmouth.

THOMAS MIRA Y LOPEZ's essays appear in *Alaska Quarterly Review,* the *Georgia Review,* the *Normal School,* and *Seneca Review,* among others. He holds an MFA in nonfiction from the University of Arizona and is an editor for *Territory,* a literary project about maps and other strange objects. He's at work on his first book, an essay collection on resting places.

DAVE MONDY has been lauded for work in many genres: food writing (Best Food Writing 2014), travel writing (four National Solas Awards), sports writing (2014 Iowa Review Awards), memoir (*Cincinnati Review, Iowa Review,* NPR), and live storytelling (national tours of solo theatrical shows); he's recently served as Randolph College writer-in-residence and the New York Mills artist-in-residence. In addition to literary magazines, you can find his writing at prominent online sites (like *Slate*), and he's also penned work for many public radio programs (like *A Prairie Home Companion*). He's currently working on a book about the stories and real people behind famous sports photos.

DANICA NOVGORODOFF is an artist, writer, and horse wrangler from Kentucky who currently lives in Brooklyn, New York. Her graphic novels include *The Undertaking of Lily Chen* (First Second Books 2014), *Refresh, Refresh* (First Second Books 2009), *Slow Storm* (First Second Books 2008), and *A Late Freeze.* Her art and writing has been published in *The Best American Comics, Esquire, Slate, Orion, Seneca Review, Ecotone Journal,* and many others. She is a 2015 fellow in literature from the New York Foundation for the Arts.

BRIAN OLIU is originally from New Jersey and currently teaches at the University of Alabama. He is the author of three full-length collections, *So You Know It's Me* (Tiny Hardcore Press 2011), a series of Craigslist missed connections, *Leave Luck to Heaven* (Uncanny Valley Press 2014), an ode to eight-bit video games; and *Enter Your Initials for Record Keeping* (Cobalt Press 2015), essays on NBA Jam. He is also the author of *i/o* (Civil Coping Mechanisms 2015), a memoir in the form of a computer virus. His works-in-progress deal with professional wrestling and long-distance running (not at once).

ELENA PASSARELLO is the author of the essay collections *Let Me Clear My Throat* and *Animals Strike Curious Poses,* both with Sarabande Books. The winner of the 2015 Whiting Award in nonfiction, she teaches in the MFA program at Oregon State University and is a-Twitter as @elenavox.

JOHN T. PRICE is the author of three nature memoirs—*Daddy Long Legs: The Natural Education of a Father* (Shambhala 2013), *Man Killed by Pheasant and Other Kinships* (Da Capo 2008), and *Not Just Any Land: A Personal and Literary Journey into the American Grasslands* (University of Nebraska Press 2004)—and the editor of *The Tallgrass Prairie Reader* (University of Iowa Press 2014). A recipient of an NEA fellowship and other recognitions, he teaches at the University of Nebraska at Omaha, where he directs the English Department's creative nonfiction writing program.

KRISTEN RADTKE is the author of the graphic memoir *Imagine Wanting Only This* (Pantheon 2017). She is the managing editor of Sarabande Books and the film and video editor of *TriQuarterly* magazine. She holds an MFA from the University of Iowa's nonfiction writing program and lives in New York.

BONNIE J. ROUGH is the author of *The Girls, Alone: Six Days in Estonia*, selected by Amazon editors as one of the Best Kindle Singles of 2015, and the memoir *Carrier: Untangling the Danger in My DNA* (Counterpoint 2010), and she is the winner of a Minnesota Book Award. Her essays have appeared in dozens of publications, including the *New York Times, Iowa Review, Florida Review, Brevity*, and *Brain, Child*. Recent anthologies featuring her work include *I'll Tell You Mine: Thirty Years of Essays from the Iowa Nonfiction Writing Program* (University of Chicago Press 2015) and *Because You Asked: A Book of Answers on the Art and Craft of the Writing Life* (Lost Horse Press 2015).

AISHA SABATINI SLOAN is the author of the essay collection *The Fluency of Light* (University of Iowa Press 2013). Her nonfiction has appeared in journals such as *Callaloo, Ninth Letter, Guernica, Southern Review, Michigan Quarterly Review, Sierra Nevada Review,* the *Offing*, and *Ecotone*. A contributing editor for *Guernica: A Magazine of Art and Politics* and a staff writer for *Autostraddle*, her essays have been named notable by *The Best American Essays* and *The Best American Nonrequired Reading* anthologies and nominated for a Pushcart Prize. Her most recent book of essays, *Dreaming of Ramadi in Detroit*, won the 1913 Open Prose Book contest judged by Maggie Nelson and will be published in 2017.

KATHERINE E. STANDEFER won the 2015 Iowa Review Award in Nonfiction. Her recent work appears in *The Best American Essays 2016* (edited by

Jonathan Franzen), the *Iowa Review, Fourth Genre, Colorado Review, Indiana Review, CutBank, Terrain.org: A Journal of the Built + Natural Environments,* and the *High Country News,* and she has been nominated for a Pushcart Prize. She writes about the body, consent, and medical technology from Tucson, where she earned her MFA in creative nonfiction from the University of Arizona. She teaches intimate classes that help people write their experiences of sexuality, illness, and trauma and lectures at the University of Arizona's College of Medicine in a narrative medicine pilot. Follow her @girlmakesfire.

JONI TEVIS is the author of two books of essays, *The Wet Collection: A Field Guide to Iridescence and Memory* and *The World Is On Fire: Scrap, Treasure, and Songs of Apocalypse,* both published by Milkweed Editions. Her essays have appeared in *Orion, Oxford American, Poets & Writers,* the Pushcart Prize anthology, and elsewhere. She serves as the Bennette E. Geer Professor of Literature at Furman University in Greenville, South Carolina.

RYAN VAN METER is the author of the essay collection *If You Knew Then What I Know Now,* published by Sarabande Books. His work has appeared in journals and magazines and has been selected for anthologies, including *The Best American Essays* and the *Touchstone Anthology of Contemporary Creative Nonfiction.* He lives in California, where he teaches at the University of San Francisco.

PATRICIA VIGDERMAN is the author of *The Memory Palace of Isabella Stewart Gardner* and *Possibility: Essays against Despair,* both from Sarabande Books. Her new book, *The Real Life of the Parthenon,* is forthcoming from Ohio State University Press. Her writing has appeared in the *Boston Review, Georgia Review, Harvard Review, Iowa Review, Kenyon Review,* the *Nation, New York Times, Raritan Quarterly, Seneca Review, Southwest Review,* and other places. She lives in Cambridge, Massachusetts, and Gambier, Ohio, where she teaches at Kenyon College.

NICOLE WALKER is the author of *Egg* from Bloomsbury, *Canning Peaches for the Apocalypse* from Atticus Press, *Micrograms* from New Michigan Press, and *Quench Your Thirst with Salt,* which won the Zone 3 Award for Creative Nonfiction. She is the author of a collection of poems, *This Noisy Egg* from Barrow Street Press, and is a coeditor, with Margot Singer, of *Bending Genre: Essays on Creative Nonfiction* from Bloomsbury and, with Rebecca Campbell,

"7 Artists, 7 Rings: An Artist's Game of Telephone" for the *Huffington Post*. A recipient of a fellowship from the National Endowment for the Arts, she is a nonfiction editor at *DIAGRAM* and an associate professor at Northern Arizona University in Flagstaff, Arizona, where it rains like the Pacific Northwest, but only in July.

ERIN ZWIENER is at work on a memoir about mules, the Continental Divide National Scenic Trail, and the legacy of women in the American West. Her essays have previously appeared in the *Butter* and the blog *VIDA: Women in Literary Arts*. Erin is also the author of the children's picture book *Little Red Riding Boots* and the forthcoming *Snow White and the Seven Burros*. She was the 2015 Pattie Layser Writer-in-Residence at the Murie Center in Grand Teton National Park.

LITERATURE
is not the same thing as
PUBLISHING

Coffee House Press began as a small letterpress operation in 1972 and has grown into an internationally renowned nonprofit publisher of literary fiction, essay, poetry, and other work that doesn't fit neatly into genre categories.

Coffee House is both a publisher and an arts organization. Through our *Books in Action* program and publications, we've become interdisciplinary collaborators and incubators for new work and audience experiences. Our vision for the future is one where a publisher is a catalyst and connector.

Funder Acknowledgments

Coffee House Press is an internationally renowned independent book publisher and arts nonprofit based in Minneapolis, MN; through its literary publications and *Books in Action* program, Coffee House acts as a catalyst and connector—between authors and readers, ideas and resources, creativity and community, inspiration and action.

Coffee House Press books are made possible through the generous support of grants and donations from corporations, state and federal grant programs, family foundations, and the many individuals who believe in the transformational power of literature. This activity is made possible by the voters of Minnesota through a Minnesota State Arts Board Operating Support grant, thanks to the legislative appropriation from the arts and cultural heritage fund. Coffee House also receives major operating support from the Amazon Literary Partnership, the Bush Foundation, the Jerome Foundation, The McKnight Foundation, Target Foundation, and the National Endowment for the Arts (NEA). To find out more about how NEA grants impact individuals and communities, visit www.arts.gov.

Coffee House Press receives additional support from the Elmer L. & Eleanor J. Andersen Foundation; the David & Mary Anderson Family Foundation; the Buuck Family Foundation; the Carolyn Foundation; the Dorsey & Whitney Foundation; Dorsey & Whitney LLP; the Knight Foundation; the Rehael Fund of the Minneapolis Foundation; the Matching Grant Program Fund of the Minneapolis Foundation; the Schwab Charitable Fund; Schwegman, Lundberg & Woessner, P.A.; the Scott Family Foundation; the US Bank Foundation; VSA Minnesota for the Metropolitan Regional Arts Council; the Archie D. & Bertha H. Walker Foundation; and the Woessner Freeman Family Foundation in honor of Allan Kornblum.

The Publisher's Circle of Coffee House Press

Publisher's Circle members make significant contributions to Coffee House Press's annual giving campaign. Understanding that a strong financial base is necessary for the press to meet the challenges and opportunities that arise each year, this group plays a crucial part in the success of Coffee House's mission.

Recent Publisher's Circle members include many anonymous donors, Mr. & Mrs. Rand L. Alexander, Suzanne Allen, Patricia A. Beithon, Bill Berkson & Connie Lewallen, the E. Thomas Binger & Rebecca Rand Fund of the Minneapolis Foundation, Robert & Gail Buuck, Claire Casey, Louise Copeland, Jane Dalrymple-Hollo, Ruth Stricker Dayton, Jennifer Kwon Dobbs & Stefan Liess, Mary Ebert & Paul Stembler, Chris Fischbach & Katie Dublinski, Kaywin Feldman & Jim Lutz, Sally French, Jocelyn Hale & Glenn Miller, the Rehael Fund-Roger Hale/Nor Hall of the Minneapolis Foundation, Randy Hartten & Ron Lotz, Jeffrey Hom, Carl & Heidi Horsch, Amy L. Hubbard & Geoffrey J. Kehoe Fund, Kenneth Kahn & Susan Dicker, Stephen & Isabel Keating, Kenneth Koch Literary Estate, Jennifer Komar & Enrique Olivarez, Allan & Cinda Kornblum, Leslie Larson Maheras, Lenfestey Family Foundation, Sarah Lutman & Rob Rudolph, the Carol & Aaron Mack Charitable Fund of the Minneapolis Foundation, George & Olga Mack, Joshua Mack, Gillian McCain, Mary & Malcolm McDermid, Sjur Midness & Briar Andresen, Maureen Millea Smith & Daniel Smith, Peter Nelson & Jennifer Swenson, Marc Porter & James Hennessy, Jeffrey Scherer, Jeffrey Sugerman & Sarah Schultz, Nan G. & Stephen C. Swid, Patricia Tilton, Stu Wilson & Melissa Barker, Warren D. Woessner & Iris C. Freeman, Margaret Wurtele, Joanne Von Blon, and Wayne P. Zink.

For more information about the Publisher's Circle and other ways to support Coffee House Press books, authors, and activities, please visit www.coffeehousepress.org/support or contact us at info@coffeehousepress.org.

How We Speak to One Another was designed by
Bookmobile Design & Digital Publisher Services.
Text is set in Warnock Pro.